RING
THEORY

RING THEORY

MEDITATIONS ON
35 YEARS IN BOXING

William Dettloff

WINDING ROAD STORIES

NEW YORK   LOS ANGELES

Jacket design by Michael Kronenberg
Photo by Holly Stein/Getty Images Sport courtesy of Ringside Seat Magazine
Jacket Copyright 2026 by Winding Road Stories
Interior book design by A Raven Design
ISBN#: 978-1-960724-56-4 (pbk)
ISBN#: 978-1-960724-57-1 (ebook)

Published by Winding Road Stories
www.windingroadstories.com

CONTENTS

For Kayla, Angelina and Billy Boy

INTRODUCTION

Some years ago, my friend and colleague Eric Raskin and I were recording an episode of our boxing-themed podcast when Eric innocently and quite casually referred to boxing as "entertainment." I received it like a jolt of electricity. Boxing as *entertainment*? How could something as serious as boxing be mere entertainment?

There really is nothing to be gained from just entertainment. One learns nothing from it. There is no personal growth one should hope to undergo from being entertained, no improvement to the spirit or mind, or to understanding. Entertainment is frivolous, unserious, something bored humans engage to pass the time. *Sitcoms* are entertainment. *Wheel of Fortune* and *The Real Housewives of Beverly Hills* are, ostensibly, entertainment. *Marvel* films, pop music and yes, other sports, are mere entertainment.

Boxing? *Serious* shit. Life and death. Like war, or hurricanes, or disease.

And not just because of the danger and the damage boxing does to humans, all well documented, some immediately and some over the long term. After all, American football scrambles brains and breaks bones almost as much as boxing does, but for all its mayhem and violence, there is almost an artificiality to it, the uniforms and equipment, the sound over and over of hard plastic colliding with hard plastic. The players may as well be robots for all we are able to observe of their humanity, until one of them topples head over heels and we witness an ankle dangling loosely from a leg, flopping this way and that. They cart him off and the robots resume launching themselves at one another.

Besides that, football is a team sport and in all team sports one can get lost in a crowd, hide out when something goes wrong or is about to. As has often been observed, there is no place to hide in a prize ring, and no "timeouts," save for those necessitated by an injury serious enough to require examination by a ringside doctor. That separates prizefighting from the other individual sports, such as tennis, or fencing, or, if you can stand it, pickleball.

It's been said enough times and by better writers than I that boxing is the perfect metaphor for life and that alone qualifies it as something beyond sheer entertainment, but it is the utter nakedness and vulnerability with which it is practiced that elevates it further. Everything you want and must see about a fighter is right there in front of you. Again, I am not the first to observe there is no place to hide in the prize ring, literally or figuratively. The outside of a man and the inside are visible to all.

The journalist and broadcaster Larry Merchant once called heavyweight champion Joe Frazier a "truth machine," meaning that whatever the truth was about a man, what kind of heart and spirit he had, Frazier, who was preternaturally tough and aggressive, would expose it in the ring. But he could have been talking about prizefighting in general as well. For all these reasons and more, boxing was always more to me than mere entertainment, more than anything, really, and the stories herein can only be a reflection of that.

These stories represent a lifelong obsession with the game and with the fighters and with their stories, and their fights, and the stories *of* their fights. I've been inordinately lucky to have spoken with and written about the giants and heroes and villains -- from Willie Pep to Canelo Alvarez, from Jake LaMotta to Floyd Mayweather, from Lennox Lewis to Bob Foster to Emmanuel Steward to Evander

Holyfield, from Oscar de La Hoya to Roberto Duran to Miguel Cotto and a hell of a lot of guys in between. Included too are some scribbles from my own times in the ring, a tiny speck compared to the presence left by most, but revealing and precious to me in their own ways and perhaps to you, the reader, too.

And imagine my surprise after all these years to discover that Eric was right, that despite its myriad irresistible vulgarities and truth-revealing properties and all the rest, that boxing is indeed entertainment – it's so much more than that too, but entertainment it is, and my inability to see value in other art forms – some film, television, and music, was the result of my lifelong immersion in prizefighting to the exclusion of everything else. Certainly, these other things have merit too, known by those who have studied them, like I boxing, and to the masses too, if they care to look. Boxing is in league with them.

In the end, all I can hope for is that the pages that follow provide a reasoned look into what I found over 35 years covering the sport—everything that makes it special in good ways and bad, that makes its participants as human and as frail and as strong as the rest of us, and if these stories fail in that endeavor, then I should hope you find them to be, if nothing else, entertaining.

THE CHAMPIONS

THE BROTHERS KLITSCHKO

A CONTINUING EDUCATION

ORIGINALLY PUBLISHED AT *HBO.COM* ON DECEMBER 1, 2003

To see them outside the ring, you wouldn't guess that they are prizefighters. Neither Vitali Klitschko nor his younger brother Wladimir has a flattened nose, or cauliflower ears. Their eyebrows aren't crisscrossed with scar tissue, and their speech isn't thick yet with the residue of too many punches. If you didn't know any better and spoke with them in their business suits, about world events or the weather or other things unrelated to sport, you might think them investment bankers or art distributors or physicians (indeed, both have doctorate degrees in sports science). You wouldn't picture them dealing in the business of broken teeth and scarred knuckles and concussions. But they do.

The Brothers Klitschko, born in the Ukraine, living in Germany, and making their livings primarily now in these United States, are heavyweight prizefighters in flux. Both were undefeated, or may as well have been, and cautiously touted not very long ago. Both suffered defeats at the very top levels of the sport and now are doing what fighters do: making their way back, or at the very least trying, which is mostly all that a fighter who has lost wants to do -- even very bright, multi-lingual, personable fighters like the Klitschkos.

Of the two, it is Wladimir, 27, who, right now at least, appears to have further to go, as his fall was steeper. Better looking than his older brother and with a celebrated amateur background—he won the gold medal in the super-heavyweight division at the 1996 Olympic Games in Georgia—he generally was acknowledged by the American fight press as the more talented of the two, even as Vitali garnered more attention early on. It was an accurate assessment: he is fairly fluid for a man who stands 6'6" and weighs in the 240s and can put together combinations that would make some middleweights envious. Aesthetically, he is the male ideal, a characteristic not lost on the female fans who attend his fights in surprisingly high numbers.

There was a time when a fighter as big as Wladimir is was inevitably oafish and lacking balance, regardless of his schooling. But Wlad, 41-2 (38), is mechanically sound, even if a little too upright, but that's not unforgivable when you can hit the way he can. Punch for punch, he hits harder than does Vitali, and out of the gate, he won 24 in a row, 22 by knockout, before American journeyman Ross Puritty outlasted him and stopped him in the 11th round in December 1998.

The loss, which was seen by few American press or fans, unfairly resulted in Wladimir being labeled a quitter. No matter; impressive follow-up wins over Chris Byrd, Monte Barrett, Derrick Jefferson, Charles Shufford, Frans Botha, and highly-rated Jameel McCline restored his luster before, in a major upset, hard-hitting South African Corrie Sanders overwhelmed him in two rounds last March. A one-round stoppage of one Fabio Eduardo Moli in August put him back on the right path. If he is to make more gains in an increasingly wide-open heavyweight division, he must impress against American veteran Danell Nicholson, whom he is scheduled to face on December 20 in Germany.

If Wladimir has won on power and style, in that order, then Vitali, 32-2 (31) has won with power and awkwardness. He lacks his brother's fluidity and physical symmetry and, despite the knockout record, the consistent one-punch power. But his physical strength and deceptively fast hands produce the same effect. His herky-jerky awkwardness, which in the fight game is a weapon, may have something to do with his past involvement in kickboxing, which frequently produces odd gaits in boxers. Still, he pulls the trigger quickly on a sneaky right hand and knows how to use his height and strength, which are considerable—he stands 6'8", weighs around 245. Unlike Wladimir, who is polished and more dispassionate in the ring, there are times when Vitali looks no more educated than your average Golden Glove novice. But he knows what he's doing. And he makes it work.

Like Wladimir, Vitali took off on turning pro, beating the same level of fighters on which all heavyweight prospects feed while on the way up. After winning 27 straight (all by kayo), he submitted to the combined effects of Chris Byrd's elusiveness and an injured rotator cuff and elected to sit on his stool after the ninth round. The fight media and much of the American fight public dismissed him at that moment as a quitter—much in the way they dismissed Wladimir—and at the time it seemed appropriate; Vitali was ahead on the cards and could see the finish line just a few rounds away. And in terms of his ability to hurt a big, strapping opponent like Vitali, Byrd is next to harmless.

Vitali, 32, had his shoulder repaired and, over the next two years, stopped well-known American heavyweights Orlin Norris, Vaughn Bean, Larry Donald, and Puritty, his brother's one-time conqueror. But it wasn't until his wild slugfest with heavyweight champion Lennox Lewis that Vitali's capitulation against Byrd was forgiven. He hurt Lewis several times early with right hands, fought him on even terms when Lewis stepped up his intensity, and was leading on all cards when a hideous gash around his left eye caused the fight to be stopped in the sixth round. On December 6, he faces the dangerous Kirk Johnson on HBO in a compelling match between top contenders. If Vitali wins, there is no one between him and a rematch with Lewis, unless Lewis chooses retirement.

Having arrived at virtually the same place, albeit with a different set of tools as well as their own distinct flaws, the Brothers Klitschko haven't snuck up on anyone, despite their easy intelligence, polished manners, and affable personalities. They're heavyweight fighters. Watch them do what they do, and you can't mistake them for anything else.

FORREST-MAYORGA

BEAUTY AND THE BEAST

ORIGINALLY PUBLISHED AT *HBO.COM* ON JANUARY 16, 2003

WORLD WELTERWEIGHT CHAMPION Vernon Forrest is a fine fighter, a good, sound stand-up boxer-puncher. Fundamentally, you won't find many better. He does everything by the book: he jabs before throwing the right, he hooks after bringing the right all the way back, or clinches if he's in too close, he moves his head after punching and his chin is forever tucked.

Forrest is always on-balance, his punches straight and true. If you go to his body, expect an uppercut for your troubles. It's all very efficient and correct; he doesn't so much fight as operate. He is occasionally dull in the ring, though that's often the price one pays for good schooling. He says the right things. He lives clean. He is fit and disciplined and polite -- a trainer's dream. It's almost an insult to call him a fighter.

After flattening Andrew "Six Heads" Lewis last March, Ricardo Mayorga, who challenges Forrest for the title on January 25, showed up at the postfight press conference smoking a cigarette. A few minutes in, someone handed him a beer. He smoked and drank throughout the conference, inhaling deeply, gesturing and speaking passionately and emotionally, with neither inhibition nor fear.

"I was waiting for Mayorga back in his locker room after he beat Six Heads, and one of the first things he did was reach for a cigarette, which caused a stir among Don King's PR people," a member of the press said. "They didn't want their newly minted champ seen by a member of the media smoking a cigarette right after five grueling rounds in the ring. But someone said, `What the hell, there's no sense in hiding who Mayorga is.'"

There is no hiding who Mayorga is. Watch him fight. He does not jab to get close to his opponent or to set up power punches; he wades in, very frequently with his chin exposed. His heavy punches are not short and precise, but looping usually, and telegraphed. He often is off-balance and when he misses a blow, he stumbles. He headbutts -- often. He seems not to care much for defense or for feinting or smart body punching or for any of the scholarly stuff on which Forrest so prides himself.

Mayorga fights angry, and with a passable modicum of technique, he tries to hit his opponent as hard as he can as many times as he can. That's his strategy. It is one built on passion and fearlessness. His trainers will tell you he is a difficult case. He'll disappear from training camp to party and he sneaks smokes and beers when they aren't looking. He is the anti-Forrest. Where Forrest is cool, Mayorga is reckless. Where Forrest is patient, Mayorga is unrestrained. His nickname is "El Matador," and he has it tattooed across his neck. It's really a misnomer, though. He is far closer to the beast than the artist.

Common sense tells you it should be easy for Forrest. He was traveling around the planet fighting the world's best international amateurs when Mayorga was begging for pennies in the streets of Managua, Nicaragua. When Forrest was coming up through the welterweight ranks, slowly, patiently, until he got so good that apparently no one wanted to fight him, Mayorga was brawling with club fighters in San Jose, Costa Rica, where most of his fights have taken place.

While Forrest has twice put it to Shane Mosley, one of the best in the world, the biggest name on Mayorga's record is Lewis, who was in the fight until Mayorga blasted him with a series of clubbing right hands in the fifth round in Reading, Pennsylvania. That was the rematch.

The first time they met, Mayorga ran in punching with his head as much as with his fists and the resultant cut forced a technical draw. His match with Diosbelys Hurtado, a top junior welterweight and the only other well-known fighter on his record, yielded a similar result. For all that, it is an intriguing matchup, made so by Mayorga's passion for the street fight, by his contempt for convention. He is all fighter.

You've got to make Forrest the favorite going in. What happens in the ring doesn't happen by accident. It happens mostly because one guy is better at all the right things than the other guy is, all the fundamentals they teach in the gym. But sometimes fundamentals go out the window. Then it's just a fight. If Mayorga can make it a fight, he's halfway home.

MIGUEL COTTO AT 30

HOW MUCH DOES HE HAVE LEFT?

ORIGINALLY PUBLISHED IN *THE RING*, JUNE 2011

FROM THE WAY IT ENDED, you'd have thought Miguel Cotto had an easy night of it. His left hook caught Ricardo Mayorga with his chin up in no-man's land, where it often is, bless his heart, and landed hard enough not only to drop Mayorga, but apparently to break his left hand from the looks of it (it turned out to be a dislocated thumb). Mayorga got up, considered the seriousness of the situation, and told referee Robert Byrd he'd had enough fun for the evening, thank you very much.

Just like that, it was over, and, when Cotto raised his hands, it was over a head dotted with bright red welts and scrapes, but there were none of the deep, jagged cuts we've often seen on him after 12 rounds of hard labor. No bulbous swelling, no rivulets of blood disappearing into a landscape of tattoos below. There was no bucket of bright red water in his corner, no plasma-filled sponge. So if you saw just the end, you'd have thought Cotto had an easy night, maybe one like he had against Yuri Foreman or Michael Jennings. A little longer, but still.

But it wasn't an easy night—not like it should have been. Yes, the judges all had Cotto ahead 107-102 when it ended, and he didn't look like he'd been pushed face-first into the business end of a wood chipper. But he had been in a fight. And if you are the kind who worries about prizefighters and what their lives will be like after they finally quit and you saw Antonio Margarito smiling to the crowd and know Bob Arum wants to make Margarito-Cotto II, then you are worried a little about Cotto.

Not because Margarito might beat him, although anything can happen in a fight, but because Cotto is 30 years old now, and it's not an Archie Moore 30. At 30, Moore was still in diapers in terms of what he would get done in prize rings and how much he had left. Cotto looks like what he is: a world-class athlete who very probably won't be one for very much longer no matter how many tattoos he gets, how many more big left hooks he has in him, or how long 40-somethings like Bernard Hopkins and Glen Johnson keep looking good.

The better fighters today are just hitting their stride at 30. Look at the ages of some of Cotto's contemporaries. Manny Pacquiao is 32. Floyd Mayweather is 34, same as Wladimir Klitschko and Steve Cunningham. Sergio Martinez is 36 and has never looked as good as he does now. Lucian Bute is 31.

Still, more than once against Mayorga, Cotto looked like an old fighter. If you want, you can blame it on genetics or style or 10 hard years in the ring. Or, if you're one of those who attributes all things everywhere to the brilliant wonder that is Pacquiao, you can say Pacquiao put 10 years on Cotto when he brutalized him over 12 bloody, brain-stem loosening rounds in November 2009. Others might be inclined to grant Pacquiao a more sensible, say, 30 percent or so of the credit for Cotto's seemingly premature aging and split the balance among the wars Cotto waged with Zab Judah, Joshua Clottey, Margarito, and, to a lesser degree, Shane Mosley. Whatever the case and whatever the number, Cotto is not what he used to be.

How else to explain the wild, awkward right hands Mayorga 29-8-1 (23), was able to land frequently enough to keep things interesting and with particular effect in the fourth, seventh, and 11th rounds?

How else to explain the absence of the smooth technical skills the 20-something Cotto once used to outbox and break down all manner of Mayorga-like tough guys such as Muhammad Abdullaev, Randall Bailey, and Kelson Pinto? How else to explain the anxious look that came over Cotto's face at the end of the seventh when three Mayorga right hands landed on the side of his shaved dome and put just a bit of a wobble on him?

"He hit me with some hard punches, but I always stayed on my feet," Cotto said afterward. He didn't offer how hard it was to do that or how close he was to losing that battle to stay upright. "We just stayed with the game plan we practiced [in training camp] in Miami."

It's true that Cotto, 36-2 (29), landed the better punches all night and that his jabs and right hands were the difference. Also, on the occasions when he stepped to the side and dug left hooks into Mayorga's flank, he looked just like he did against, say, Carlos Quintana or Paulie Malignaggi. You got the sense that Cotto, from Caguas, Puerto Rico, was in charge for most of the fight, but that it could all change with one Mayorga right hand. And that if Mayorga, of Managua, Nicaragua, had just a modicum of appreciable technical skill, Cotto would have been there for the taking. That's how it felt watching. Just 30 years old? Really?

Emanuel Steward, who started training Cotto after the loss to Pacquiao, offered his own reasons for the occasional difficulties Mayorga presented his charge, and they had nothing to do with the wear on Cotto's tires.

"I was very satisfied with Cotto's performance," Steward said at the postfight press conference. "Mayorga was much, much tougher and better conditioned than I expected. He takes a good punch and has a very strong constitution. It's very difficult to get away from his punches sometimes because he runs at you from so many angles. But Miguel operated behind that jab and never did get into the mind games."

Steward said he hadn't seen Mayorga in such good condition since his fights with Vernon Forrest eight years earlier. Mayorga thought so too, as evidenced by his continual need to lift his shirt and show off his abdominal muscles whenever Cotto or a camera came within 30 feet of him in the days leading up to the fight.

Mayorga was indeed in shape, but it looked to us like the typical performance from the man who has become boxing's crazy uncle – the guy who shows up every other Christmas, acts like he's out of his gourd, entertains us with his vulgarity and then, on cue, disappears until next time. He's now provided entertaining, though not overly compelling, losing performances against Felix Trinidad (KO by 8), Oscar De La Hoya (KO by 6), and Mosley (KO by 12), and, if you want, you can throw in the win over the entirely dilapidated Fernando Vargas (W12).

As always, it was Mayorga's bravado and emotion that kept him in the fight, kept the fight entertaining and also proved his biggest liability. The crowd of 7,247 at the MGM Grand in Las Vegas went wild whenever he taunted Cotto, which he did quite frequently, and the dynamic offered a stark look into their respective psyches: Mayorga the reckless hot-head, Cotto the cool stoic. Mayorga's Sonny Corleone to Cotto's Michael. And you'll see him again. Despite his comments immediately afterward that it was time for him to leave boxing and get a job, the Spanish-language news agency EFE said he told Don King to get him three more fights—two easy ones, "and then I'll return against someone tough."

Cotto should follow the same plan. Over the course of his decade-long career, he's faced a larger number of high-quality fighters than anyone else in the game with the possible exception of Pacquiao. And it's been that way from the start. Someday soon, people in the fight business will begin to evaluate his worthiness for Hall of Fame induction, and they would do well to remember that, from all appearances, he has fought everyone around his weight who was willing to face him. He is on a long list of those avoided by Floyd Mayweather, but that was never of his doing. You get the sense he would have fought Mayweather at any time over the last 10 years if given the chance.

The smart money says Cotto and Margarito will meet in June in the rematch that will have Arum's publicity guys working overtime to come up with synonyms for "revenge." It will be a blockbuster you can be sure and is evidence of the continuing good fortune our friends at Top Rank are able to manufacture. There is a soap opera-like quality to Arum's large and high-quality stable and the deals he makes among and for them, with stories ripe for exploitation and sale to the masses.

Certainly, Margarito has been a boon to him. Every good story needs a villain, and, despite his broad smile and polite manners, Margarito plays the role perfectly – if not for his universally panned Parkinson's-stricken impression of Freddie Roach, then certainly for the loaded hand wraps he attempted to use against Mosley. Particularly against Cotto's dignified stoicism, Margarito is seen as the worst of all cheaters – worse even than steroid offenders – and even boxing fans, a famously forgiving lot, will be hard pressed to root for him. But then, all rooting is not created equal. You root for a man every time you buy a ticket or a pay-per-view to watch him. Maybe you're rooting for him to get his ass kicked. Doesn't matter to him. You're putting money in his pocket. So there.

Steward talked about the rematch at the post-fight press conference. "In the first fight, I thought Antonio Margarito made Miguel Cotto fight too fast and run away too fast when he threw his punches, so he never did get the full maximum power of his punches. Because before he could finish a combination, Margarito would have him running away. Margarito will always be a tough fight style-wise for Miguel. But Miguel has to punch with authority and fight a much more intelligent fight and maybe force Margarito to back up."

Margarito is viewed generally as being even further past it than Cotto, based almost entirely on his own horrendous performance against Pacquiao. But Pacquiao does that to guys – guys in their prime, guys past their prime, guys who haven't reached their prime yet. So you can't hold that against him. There is a danger for the Mexican in a rematch with Cotto. It is that if he loses, it will serve as "proof" that his wraps were loaded when he beat Cotto in their first fight. But honestly, most already assume that to be the case, whether or not it's true.

The fighter with the most to lose is Cotto. Today, he is able to point to the mere suspicion that Margarito's wraps were loaded in the first fight and he is more or less forgiven for the loss. If he wins the rematch, he has "proved" that the first match was illegitimate. But what if he loses it? He has nowhere to go and little time to get there. He has paid a price for his fearlessness, one that few of us are willing to pay. He is old before his time in a business in which even the young and strong are often lost to the cause. The clock ticks for all of us, but faster for him. One hopes he knows what time it is.

Epilogue: Cotto went 5-5 over the next six years against top competition and even won a middleweight world title. He retired in 2017 after losing to Sadam Ali on points in New York.

A LOOK BACK AT ROY JONES

WHAT WAS ... WHAT COULD HAVE BEEN ... WHAT SHOULD HAVE BEEN

ORIGINALLY PUBLISHED IN *THE RING*, MARCH 2006

BASED on the comments he made in the days following his fairly dismal performance against Antonio Tarver in their rubber match, it seems clear that Roy Jones doesn't know yet that his days as a top prizefighter are over. Of course, that comes as no great surprise to anyone who's ever fallen for a fighter and then watched him age, become human and then impotent in the ring, and finally delusional. Fighters never know it. Try sometime to convince someone of something they don't want to know. It's a hard road. And it takes a while.

Jones's denial of the obvious is ironic. For one who spent much of his career denying in action and deed that he was, indeed, a fighter— he'd rather we thought of him as an entertainer /performer/businessman—he now insists he is a fighter, and always has been. Critics might observe that over his long career, this last-gasp denial of one of nature's sad truths is one of the more fighter-*ly* things he's done.

Nevertheless, Jones is indeed done. Believe it. If he wasn't after Tarver stretched him in their rematch, if he wasn't after Glen Johnson pancaked him after that, then surely he is now, after fighting mostly just to last the distance against a surprisingly ineffectual Tarver. He can say he'll beat anyone but Tarver. Maybe he even believes it. But he can't. Not anymore. It's over.

That being the case, the rest of us are now free to rank and judge him appropriately, when nothing else can be done to change anything. It is only when a fighter is done that his career and accomplishments can be viewed in the proper context and weighed against the careers and accomplishments of the fighters who came before him and did business at or around his weight.

And Jones is rather a special case: Because of the sheer enormity of his talent, he was placed by many alongside some of the sport's great figures. This engendered a backlash from those who saw in Jones something less than what is, or should be, required to gain entrance to the pantheon.

Going by the numbers, Jones's greatness seems irrefutable: alphabet titles in four weight divisions, 17 title defenses overall, a four-year reign as the light heavyweight world champion, wins over two near-certain Hall of Famers in Bernard Hopkins and James Toney, and roughly a six-or seven-year tenure as one of the two or three best prizefighters in the business. By any standard against which you care to measure, and in any profession, those kinds of accomplishments equal uncommon success. They equal, let's face it, *greatness*. There's no way around that.

There's this, too: It could have been *five* weight divisions. Jones, 49-4 (38), could have decided at any point during his light heavyweight reign that he'd like to snatch a title at cruiserweight as well. And he would have. Who was there to oppose him? Vassiliy Jirov? Arthur Williams? Carlos Gomez? He'd have been a heavy favorite over any of them.

This means that at just around the midpoint of his reign at light heavyweight, Jones would have been favored to beat the middleweight champion – Hopkins, whom he'd already beaten – any of the super middleweight titlists, and any of the cruiserweight titlists. (You'll recall that there was a lot of talk about a rematch with Hopkins and also a match with Joe Calzaghe. Jones dropping down in weight to fight either of them was not implausible.)

Try to name another fighter in your lifetime who would be favored to simultaneously beat belt-holders in three divisions outside his own. And then Jones won an alphabet title at heavyweight. You cannot dispute it: Jones's unique talents put him at a very high level, over a long period of time. That must count for something.

"In order to rate someone with any degree of objectivity, you must ask how he did in his time. The rest is fun and grist for the mill, but it's opinion," said HBO's Larry Merchant. Jones fought virtually the entirety of his championship tenure with Merchant and the rest of the HBO broadcast crew at ringside. "In his time, Roy Jones was one of the best fighters. The fact that he won titles from middleweight to heavyweight is pretty good. No one had done anything like it for a century or so, but there is a different standard today because there are so many titles. The heavyweight he beat was not regarded as the heavyweight champion, but he still beat him. If he had spent his career at middleweight, there would be more certainty of his place."

Merchant's last point is especially well taken. Not only because middleweight is where Jones did his best and most inspired work, but because, as Showtime analyst and respected historian Steve Farhood points out, "Fighters who jump divisions often get cheated because they don't stay put long enough for proper evaluation at a single weight. Jones is going to fare better in an overall career assessment than at one weight. He was a light heavyweight for about nine years, which is a long time, but he suffered all four of his career losses at 175. While wins over Virgil Hill, Reggie Johnson, and Antonio Tarver are nice, they pale in comparison to the three biggest wins of his career, versus Bernard Hopkins, James Toney, and John Ruiz, none of which came at light heavyweight."

Jones's record of multiple titles and division-hopping is, counterintuitively, emblematic in the eyes of many of precisely why he doesn't compare to the greats at, say, light heavyweight, which is where he fought most of his title fights. All the titles and belts, and, by association, all the defenses, are reduced in value when the game is watered down to the degree that it is by so many so-called champions and superfluous weight classes. All the adornments make a guy like Jones look better than he really is when you put him next to the great fighters from earlier eras.

Historian and Hall of Fame promoter J Russell Peltz told *The Ring* he would have trouble placing Jones in the top 10 or 12 among the all-time great light heavyweights, ranking him not just below Archie Moore, Harold Johnson, Bob Foster, and Ezzard Charles, but also Maxie Rosenbloom, Joey Maxim and Eddie Mustafa Muhammad.

"It's hard to compare Jones's win over Ruiz to, say, Mickey Walker's draw with Jack Sharkey," said Peltz. "Sorry, but I cannot buy it. And don't give me that argument about heavyweights being bigger today. Bigger does not necessarily mean better. Don't forget, (Jack) Dempsey was 187 when he blitzed the 245-pound (Jess) Willard and opened boxing's Golden Age."

Farhood places Jones at about the same spot historically that Peltz does. "Jones certainly doesn't crack my all-time top five at light heavyweight, which is Ezzard Charles, Archie Moore, Bob Foster, Gene Tunney and Tommy Loughran," he said. "Top 10? Maybe, though I wouldn't rank him ahead of Michel Spinks."

There is also the question, as there always has been, of the quality of the opposition Jones has faced, particularly at light heavyweight. Jones's 175-pound division is regarded as one of the weakest of the last hundred years. But this may be a case of a higher standard being applied to Jones. The light heavyweight division Jones dominated was probably no worse off than was the middleweight class over which Hopkins reigned, and Hopkins is considered by many a top-10 all-time middleweight, and was viewed as such even before his wins over Felix Trinidad and Oscar De La Hoya.

"I've always believed that those who criticize the quality of Jones's opposition were unfair," said Farhood. "With a bad hand he beat Hopkins, who went on to be number one pound-for-pound. He dominated against Toney, who was, at worst, number two pound-for-pound at the time. And at heavyweight, he beat Ruiz for fun, something a handful of top-10 heavyweights have failed to do.

Ultimately, and at the end, Jones was somewhat of a disappointment. But his prime was awesome."

Even if you don't penalize Jones for the guys he fought, you could penalize him for those he did not, particularly at super middleweight. Jones could have fought Nigel Benn or Gerald McClellan. He could have faced Steve Collins or Chris Eubank. He chose not to. Eric Lucas, Vinny Pazienza, and Bryant Brannon were easier. Later on, Rick Frazier was easier than, say, Michael Nunn, who, like Tarver, was a tall, rangy southpaw.

And, of course, there was Dariusz Michalczewski, whom Jones repeatedly refused to face because doing so would have involved going to Europe. You could make the argument, as Jones did, that as the champion, he wasn't required to go to a challenger's home country. He didn't think it was a smart move. It turned off many fans: If you're the real champion, you fight the second-best guy in the division. That's what real champions do.

"Harold Johnson went to Berlin to defend his world title against Gustav Scholz in June 1962, before 40,000 in a Berlin soccer stadium," said Peltz. "Scholz was one of the greatest German fighters ever, maybe the best ever, but certainly no worse than number two behind (Max) Schmeling. He had lost something like one or two fights out of 65 or 70 when he challenged Harold. Both the judges and the voting referee were from Europe.

"Harold won a 15-round decision," Peltz said. "But would Roy go to Germany to fight Michalczewski? No! Sure, Harold went for the money, which Roy had here. And that makes Roy a great businessman, not a great fighter."

Peltz isn't alone in his thinking that what Jones possessed in natural talent and business acumen, he lacked in the kind of fighting courage we insist our great ones possess. Particularly at 175, it was clear that Jones was not interested in taking risks in the ring. Much of it was attributed to his attachment to McClellan, who suffered debilitating, life-altering injuries in his knockout loss to Benn. But what did that matter from the perspective of the fan? Or the media? Be a fighter or don't be a fighter. It appeared on many nights that

Jones was content to fight with one foot in the ring and the other one out. And he wanted to get paid well to do it. That didn't win him many fans among the hardcore.

"The resentment that was built up against Jones came when he moved to light heavyweight and often dominated opponents and was satisfied to coast to victories," said Merchant. "There was a general feeling that he never pushed himself to be as dominant as we expect great champions to be, and he often left fans with a feeling of anticlimax. It was his basically cautious nature that led to a lot of these anticlimactic fights.

"As a middleweight, he was so dazzling and so hungry and ambitious to make his reputation that the caution could be overlooked because he was doing things that were breathtaking," Merchant said. "He created a high standard and that led to expectations, and when he fought bigger guys, he became more cautious. That led some people to believe that he didn't live up to the standard he created."

It is the height of irony that when Jones finally did display the real heart and grit of a prizefighter, it was too late and it did him in. He didn't have to take the rematch with Tarver after having squeaked by him in their first match. If he had retired afterward, who would have blamed him? He'd done everything he wanted to do.

But when there was some residual question as to his superiority, he did what we expect courageous fighters to do: He gave Tarver a rematch. And he paid for it. He paid for it against Johnson, too. Those two fights, and the final, limping, mostly half-hearted and rather sad challenge of Tarver in the rubber match, told us a little more about Jones than we wanted to know. And it wasn't good.

"Everybody has his or her own criteria for what makes an all-time great," said Farhood. "One of my requisites is the ability to overcome adversity. With the arguable exception of Tarver I, where he won the last couple rounds, during which fight did Jones tough it out? His skills were unparalleled, and as long as he had physical advantages, he dominated. But toward the end, and against Tarver and Johnson, he failed miserably in competing when that wasn't the case. Even Pernell

Whitaker, who won for most of his career in similar fashion to Jones, showed something when he came back to stop Diosbelys Hurtado. Jones has no such fight to point to. The first Montell Griffin fight might have provided him one, but the unfortunate ending ruined his chances."

Indeed, two straight knockout losses – to guys who aren't known as big punchers – and then a sad, stumbling decision defeat is not the end many predicted for Jones, even when we know it has to end that way. But it has ended, and we are left with the impression that he was a magnificent physical specimen, brilliantly talented, and gifted well beyond what should be considered fair. Gyms all over the world are full of fighters who won't approach accomplishing one-tenth of what he did. We all should be so successful. And shame on him for not doing more.

Epilogue: Jones fought 23 more times after the final Tarver fight, going 17-6 with three of the losses by knockout. He retired for good in 2023 after losing an eight-round decision to a fighter making his pro debut.

BEAUTY & THE BEAST

THE TWO SIDES OF OSCAR DE LA HOYA

ORIGINALLY PUBLISHED IN *KO*, MARCH 2003

YOU KNEW Fernando Vargas was in trouble when he tried to convince everyone he would beat Oscar De La Hoya because De La Hoya was too rich to be hungry anymore. He trotted out the well-used line about it being hard to get out of bed to run when you're wearing silk pajamas. Many times, that logic makes sense. After all, you can trace Riddick Bowe's decline almost directly back to when he'd made enough money to build a kitchen in his bedroom. And really, why would anyone who has as much money as De La Hoya has want to go to hell and back just to win a prizefight? What sense would it make? When the fight was on the line and either guy could win it, who would pull it out of his gut? Vargas, all angry still and with a chip on his shoulder the size of all of Big Bear, or De La Hoya, who lives the life of a rock star?

It would be De La Hoya, we know now, and not solely because he's the better fighter, but because he is a walking, breathing, punching contradiction. De La Hoya appears one thing and is something else altogether – out of the ring even more so than in, and maybe not even deliberately, but rather by his nature, he is the master of the feint: get

23

you thinking one thing and do another; have you looking this way and give it to you there; he can't be this way because he's that. But he is. Silk pajamas indeed.

Most of the time, we like our fighters straightforward, literally and figuratively. Most of them happily satisfy this need of ours. It's one of the reasons for our ongoing fascination with Mike Tyson; we know what we're getting with him: brutality. Malevolence. In the ring and out. He doesn't surprise us. He can tell us all he wants about the literature he's reading or how he wants to be the world's greatest father. We know he can't change, even if he wants to. And really, we don't want him to. There's just one side of Tyson. Maybe it's different shades depending on the mood he's in, but overall, everything makes sense. Everything fits. There are no incongruous parts. He is what he is.

De La Hoya is what he is too, but have fun trying to figure out what the hell that is, as he is anything but straightforward. He is a pretty boy with killer instincts, completely capable of stealing your girlfriend and kicking your ass at the same time. He is a prizefighter who gets giddy at the prospect of punching the daylights out of other prizefighters, but shrinks from the slightest hint of uncomfortable confrontation outside the ring. He is a multimillionaire who deals in his own blood and sweat and bruises and anger when clearly he doesn't need to and could succeed probably at this point just as well at less dangerous pursuits. He routinely is thoroughly rehearsed and politically correct, and then, on occasion, brutally blunt. He is the fight game's boldest dichotomy.

Fighters as good as De La Hoya shouldn't look the way he looks. It's against the rules. You should be able to spot a fighter a mile away. He should have a flattened or curved nose and lumpy, cauliflower ears. He should be thick-limbed or especially ropy and sinewy. And hirsute. He should have big, bony fists and would it kill him to have a little scar tissue around the eyes or a tooth or two missing? But that's not De La Hoya. While not exactly swarthy, he's got that classically handsome thing going that evidently evokes something in women that is wholly unknown to the rest of us. Throughout his career, many have mistaken that quality, along with his distaste for thuggish colloquialism, as a sign that he's soft – indeed, Vargas clung to this rhetoric during the prefight buildup – or at the very least, not the killer we like our fighters to be. It's simply wrong.

"Oscar definitely has a mean streak," said HBO's Jim Lampley. "You saw how happy he was when Rafael Ruelas went down in their meeting, and you saw the happy dance he did when Julio Cesar Chavez's face exploded in blood in their first fight. There's something in the experience that gets to him. The mean streak is there. Oscar was having fun once he realized in round seven or eight of the Vargas fight that he had Vargas (beaten) mentally."

Indeed, De La Hoya did a modified, celebratory Ali shuffle in the middle of the ring when Vargas collapsed under the left hook. In the ring, during the post-fight interview, he was downright giddy in the way that only a real fighter would be after concussing a man.

In this regard, De La Hoya is not unlike past fighters of similar reputation and accomplishment who, at first, had trouble convincing the masses that, despite their impish smiles and romantic charms, they were stone killers in the ring. Muhammad Ali was one. Ray Leonard was another.

"I think every great fighter has a mean streak in him that doesn't show itself in real life," Lampley said. "I thought Sugar Ray Leonard was the nicest guy in the world. Then I saw him hit Donny Lalonde in the Adam's apple because the opening was there and he could and because he knew that if it landed, it essentially would end the fight."

The part of De La Hoya that more resembles Jack Dempsey than Gene Tunney is at severe odds with his civilian persona, especially when it comes to business dealings. He's made a career-long habit of having subordinates deliver bad news to managers, trainers, and other business partners rather than do it himself. It's gotten him a lot of negative press, as it's not a manly or mature thing to do. Gil Clancy, Jesus Rivero, and Emanuel Steward all got news of their releases second-hand. Clancy, who served in an "advisor" role to lead trainer Robert Alcazar, got the news from Bob Arum.

"It was on account of money," Clancy told *KO*. "Arum called me up and told me that their next fight they were fighting in New York (against Derrell Coley) and that since I live in New York and wouldn't have to travel to Big Bear, they were only going to pay me so much. I told them there was no way I would do it for that amount. Arum said, 'Okay, let me call them back and see what they want to do.' I don't know if he ever called them or not, but the next day he called me, said they weren't willing to pay and that was it."

Clancy said that usually it's the fighter who tells his trainer his services aren't needed any longer. He never heard from De La Hoya, just as Rivero hadn't, just as Steward hadn't. Still—another contradiction coming—Clancy said De La Hoya never gave him a bit of trouble in training and was always receptive to what Clancy tried to impart.

"Here's the kind of guy Oscar is to train," Clancy said. "He was in camp sparring, and I'm watching him, and I counted during a round the number of times he threw a right hand without coming back with the hook. It was 17 times. So the round ended, and he came back to the corner and I told him, 'Oscar, look, after the right hand you have to come back with the hook.' He said, 'Okay,' and I counted again the next round how many times he threw the right hand without coming back with the hook. The number was zero."

Though perhaps there should be, Clancy said he sees no evidence of embarrassment or awkwardness when he runs into De La Hoya at boxing functions. "I've seen Oscar quite a few times since then, and it's like nothing happened," he said.

That De La Hoya can be so vicious in the ring while at the same time avoiding the awkward unpleasantness associated with conflict that can't be resolved with a left hook may be nothing more than simple ego-driven laziness. You know, the state of mind that says, "It's not something I absolutely have to deal with, and if there's something unpleasant I can avoid doing, why do it?" It's not unlike hiring a person to scrub your toilets once you've made your second or third million. Sure, it would be nice if you did it yourself, and it might make you a better, more grounded person, but, well, you just don't feel like it, and damn it, you've earned the right and enough money not to feel like it. So screw it.

De La Hoya's reluctance to be the bad guy may have another genesis: "I don't hold Oscar too much to task for not being able to do that (fire people)," Lampley said. "In his mother's world, he got approval and love and the nice things in life, and firing someone wasn't something you did to people." It's been documented in many places, including in Tim Kawakami's book, *Golden Boy*, that as a child, De La Hoya was exceedingly close to his mother and that he was fairly shattered when she died of breast cancer when he was a teen. Every account of the woman judges her a gentle, diplomatic soul, and in the view of many, the De La Hoya that one often sees outside the ring is a reflection of her.

(In 2023, De La Hoya revealed in an HBO documentary that his mother often beat him and that he frequently pictured his mother's face on an opponent as a way to get emotionally fired up.)

There has to be a flipside, of course, to account for the terror that De La Hoya becomes in the ring, for the duality that the fighter presents. That would be Joel, Oscar's father, who most see as the driving force, albeit a bitter one, behind much of De La Hoya's success. Lampley says he came to understand the relationship during De La Hoya's second fight with Chavez, when De La Hoya stood with Chavez in the center of the ring in the eighth round and traded blows for the last minute, so that both of them were covered in blood by the end.

"Oscar walked back to his corner at the end of the round and had such a look of vengeance on his face, and I realized he was looking at his father, who was seated right behind me," said Lampley. "The look said, 'Did you see that? Did you see what I just did?' Later, at the postfight party, Joel came up to me before Oscar got there and said, 'Do you believe how stupid that was? That was disgusting. That was the most disgusting thing I've ever seen.' It became clear to me then that nothing Oscar could ever do would please him."

The battles De La Hoya must fight with himself – the mother's influence versus the father's—surely must account for his occasionally bizarre conduct in the media. It's been that 98 percent of the time, when he talks with the media, it is in measured tones meant to deflect controversy, speculation, and criticism. He often is a writer's nightmare, droning on with the most banal platitudes. But on two occasions he went completely the other way: Six years ago, when he was quoted by a West Coast newspaper saying black fighters couldn't take it to the body like Hispanic fighters could, and then, of course, the infamous remark that punctuated his temporary divorce from Bob Arum: "I beat the biggest Jew ever to come out of Harvard."

Many of us were tired of trying to keep up with De La Hoya's multiple layers, and when he all but abandoned the game and started recording pop albums, it looked certain that his career was ending—abruptly or gradually, but either way ending. He lost controversially to Felix Trinidad, fair and square to Shane Mosley, and then we didn't hear anything for a long time. Talk surfaced now and again about his hand injury, and we heard he was getting married, then he wasn't, then he was, and if you asked us, it looked like the end. And now here he is at the top again with the victory over Vargas, and he seems more motivated than ever.

"It looks very much like Oscar is refocused now, and I'm very happy about it," Steward told *KO*, who, despite the circumstances of his release from Camp Golden Boy (they were similar to Clancy's), says he remains very close to the fighter. "It's all part of growing up. Since he's been five years old, it's been boxing, boxing, boxing, boxing, boxing, and when you get older, sometimes you have to drift away from it for a while. And that kind of rekindles your interest. Now he's married and he's very happy living in Puerto Rico and spending time here, too. He's settled down. It's that stage of growing up that we all go through."

Steward hopes this is a side of De La Hoya we see more of in the future.

"The Vargas fight was the first very impressive fight Oscar's had in a few years. He was better than he was against Arturo Gatti and Javier Castillejo. I'd like to see more impressive victories consecutively, not just one."

It may in the end be that it is De La Hoya's multiple sides that have made him one of the wealthiest prizefighters ever. For all the enmity many hardcore Hispanic fans hold toward him, De La Hoya remains the biggest draw in boxing outside perhaps two or three heavyweights. Everyone else he dwarfs. It's not an accident. It's not necessarily wholly deliberate, either. It's who he is. We still haven't figured out quite who that is, but we're trying. As Lampley said, "Oscar is the most obvious and the most interesting psychological case study in the sport because he's the spoiled kid who will never get any satisfaction from all that he's accomplished."

Put another way, silk pajamas aren't everything.

BERNARD HOPKINS

WE'LL NEVER SEE THE LIKES OF HIM AGAIN

ORIGINALLY PUBLISHED IN *THE RING*, JANUARY 2009

YOU NEVER WOULD HAVE BELIEVED we were only 65 miles from the town where Bernard Hopkins was born. It's only about an hour from Atlantic City to Philadelphia, more if you get off the Expressway and take in all the wonderful back-road scenery, which consists principally of miles and miles of low-rent garages, convenience stores, saloons, bungalows, and other assorted dingy hideouts and alleyways.

It sounded like every one of the 11,332 souls in Boardwalk Hall booed, lustily and with great vigor, when the Hall's giant overheard screen cut to a scene of Hopkins warming up prior to his monumental 12-round win over Kelly Pavlik on October 18. Conversely, the building shook with cheers when the cameras cut to Pavlik, looking confident and stoic alongside his trainer, Jack Loew.

The difference was even more pronounced during the ring walks. The deep, spine-rumbling base that is the result of thousands of simultaneous, diaphragm-driven "boos!" swept over the Hall like a dark, enveloping wave, easily drowning out cheers for Hopkins, if there were any. It was impossible to tell. Pavlik, meanwhile, was received like a returning war hero, his legions of young Ohio ruffians eager to watch him administer a serious beat-down, Youngstown-style.

Were we really just an hour from Philly?

Any fighter who's gone on the road knows what it's like to be booed heartily and with great joy. That's sport. That's the way this roadshow works. That's the business. But to be booed so passionately and commandingly an hour from where you played ball in the park and ran in the streets and went to school and dated and became a man? It's not supposed to work that way, and your average fighter put in that sad position could be forgiven for going into the ring a little demoralized, if not already defeated.

But then, Bernard Hopkins is not your average prizefighter, 43 years old or otherwise. He's not your average anything. There's nothing average about him. Chances are very good that he is shrewder than you are, tougher than you are, braver than you are, and much, much wealthier. We already know he's a better fighter than you are. We know that he's more disciplined than you are, and harder-headed, yes, and more famous, in better shape (far, far better shape) and will be in a Hall of Fame someday (probably several).

You will not.

Maybe you can throw a baseball farther, or cook a better eggplant parmigiana. Big deal. On the whole, he is much further away from average than you or anyone you personally know. We are, all of us, in the same boat.

What's worse, when you leave your job someday, or if it leaves you, you will be replaced and shortly thereafter forgotten entirely. Some other mostly anonymous (and, yes, *average*) drone will fill your cubicle and things will continue on as if you never existed. There will just be a new guy. There will always be a new guy, for all of us.

But there will never be another Bernard Hopkins. Not even someone like him. Not in our lifetime, anyway. Maybe when our grandkids are grown. Maybe then. Of course, Hopkins is not shy about telling you this himself.

"You're going to miss me when I'm gone," he told the assembled and mostly crow-eating press after overcoming 4-1 odds and trouncing Pavlik over 12 wholly one-sided rounds. He needn't have repeated it; he'd made it very clear in the whipping he gave Pavlik that we will indeed miss him when he's gone, but you could forgive him for repeating himself, as we seem to keep forgetting.

There are many, Loew among them, who will ascribe to Pavlik's impotence the contest having been fought at a catchweight of 170 pounds. After it was over, Loew partook of the curious and decades-old practice of proclaiming, "No excuses," and at the same time offering what else but an excuse.

"You can't take anything away from Bernard; he fought a great fight tonight. It just wasn't our night—no excuses," he said, and followed up with, "I don't think 170 pounds is our weight class, but no excuses. We took a shot at a legend, that's what we wanted to do. We took our shot."

Loew spoke at the press conference while his fighter went to the hospital to get stitches that we must presume from his absence required emergency application. He talked about Pavlik not having anything on his punches, having no hand speed, no ability to bend his legs.

In short, he had nothing, which, aside from implications that he was poisoned, sounds suspiciously like the excuses offered by Antonio Tarver when he, like Pavlik, was favored to beat Hopkins and was promptly administered the beating of his life. It is a remarkable coincidence of nature that a fighter often loses everything he has on the very same night he happens to be in the ring with an opponent who is stronger, tougher, and better than he is.

Whatever the case, from appearances it looked as though the two could have fought at any weight between 120 and 280 pounds and Hopkins would have won. He set the tone when, at the opening bell, he went to Pavlik and backed him up with hooks and body punches. It surprised not just the crowd, but surely Pavlik as well.

"They anticipated me backing up, grabbing, holding and running, so I wanted to come out fast, pushing Kelly back," said Hopkins, 49-5 (32) with 1 no-contest. "Kelly Pavlik cannot fight, I feel, backing up, successfully. Not comfortably; he comes forward."

It is very close to the observation Pavlik, 34-1 (30), once made in happier times, about his kayo of Edison Miranda, which now seems so long ago. But Hopkins had no intention of standing right in Pavlik's punching range all night; he's no dummy. Displaying the versatility, smarts, and gumption that mark him as the game's premier technician, he varied his attack throughout, some of the time standing with Pavlik, others using the ring, but never languishing and always punching in combination, especially on the rare occasion when Pavlik landed a telling blow.

It is a testament to Pavlik's youth and earnestness that he lasted the full route, so comprehensive was the thrashing he received. It was so one-sided that the judges all were in relatively close agreement as to the margin of victory, a rare occurrence indeed these days. They tuned in scores of 119-106 (Alan Rubenstein), 118-108 (Steve Weisfeld), and 117-109 (Barbara Perez). *The Ring* saw it 119-106.

Indeed, the only drama came primarily at about the fight's midway point, when everyone, not least of all Pavlik, started to watch for signs that Hopkins was slowing down, as he had so precipitously over the second half of his loss to Joe Calzaghe last April. Along with Pavlik, we waited. It didn't happen and so it is no coincidence that around this same time that the Hopkins contingent, so overwhelmed by the Pavlik armies earlier and maybe a little afraid to believe fully that the old man could do it and therefore reluctant to raise their voices, began to stand up.

They saluted every Hopkins combination, of which there were many, with raucous cheers. "It's okay, we can believe," you could almost hear them thinking. Every member of a ringside section to the right of press row stood and crisscrossed their forearms in front of their faces, as Hopkins had when he entered the ring adorned, for the first time in a long time, with the old "Executioner" garb.

Now it was the Pavlik crowd that was cowed, and down the stretch, when it was clear that the upset would happen, the chants of "B-Hop! B-Hop!" rolled around the arena, echoed off the stands and through the souls and hearts of everyone who knew the full length of the dark concrete earth that stretches from the boardwalk to North Philly.

There would be no late fade. Hopkins appeared as fresh in the final round as he had in the first and tried for and almost got the knockout he wanted.

"Normally, when I know I got the lead, I just go ahead and try to win the fight," he said. "I've done well with my purses, but I just wanted to fight like a poor man. I wanted to go and finish it. Body shots broke him down earlier to set him up later. I wanted to step on the gas pedal and be out of character. And that was to fight hard the last two or three rounds. Yes, I held a couple times, but I'm 43 years old – I'm supposed to hold."

Strategic holding or not, there could be nothing to detract from the win over Pavlik, a 26-year-old buck and the world middleweight champion, with whom the fight world was rapidly falling in love. It is a historic win matched only in its genre by George Foreman's stoppage of Michael Moorer to reclaim the world heavyweight title in 1994. But there is a difference between the two events.

"What George did is the greatest single accomplishment of any fighter beyond the age of 40 and from our way of thinking maybe the greatest accomplishment of any athlete beyond the age of 40," said HBO's Jim Lampley. "To win the legitimate heavyweight championship of the world at age 45, I don't think you can match it with too many other things.

"But what Bernard did is the greatest performance from the beginning to the end of the fight, of any fighter over the age of 40. To put together 12 rounds like that – you couldn't conceive it."

It was a remarkable win, better even, Hopkins said afterward, than his career-defining upset stoppage of Felix Trinidad in 2001 at Madison Square Garden. It was hard not to recall that fight, when, before the decision was announced in Atlantic City, Hopkins stood by the ropes and glared at the ringside press who had doubted him, just as he had after stopping Trinidad. And for a moment, this man who survives – no, who thrives - on the doubts of others, almost became emotional. Right there on the ring apron.

"I'm human," he said. "I fought back emotion because where I'm from, and what I had to overcome from my own doing, in the penitentiary, you have to control your emotions or you're considered weak. And when you're a lamb around a bunch of wolves, you're finished. But I'm human."

To change the subject, he returned to the theme that has sustained him.

"I'm tired of proving myself to the same naysayers. That motivates me. Do I have to kill somebody? I'm the most underrated fighter when it comes to defense, when it comes to offense, when it comes to my heart ... and every time they say Bernard is old, yes I am. And they say Bernard is finished. They ain't saying that now."

One of the doubters was Freddie Roach, who made a stir by advising Hopkins to retire after the loss to Calzaghe, for which Roach trained him, and then expressing worry over Hopkins having headed to the wrong corner four times during that match. His assessment of Hopkins' win over Pavlik was blunt.

"It was unexpected, but I was happy for him. He fought the fight of his life," Roach told *The Ring*. Asked what the difference was between the Hopkins who beat Pavlik and the one he trained for the close loss to Calzaghe, Roach replied, "I'm not sure. He has a thyroid problem and Mackie (Shillstone) tried to control it with diet for the Calzaghe fight. I've talked to doctors, and that's pretty hard to control with (just) diet.

"He looked like a whole different person in there, so I was thinking he must have taken care of that problem. I wasn't in camp with him this time, so it's hard to say from the outside, but he came in in shape and proved everybody wrong – or, at least me."

Hopkins told *The Ring* that tests run before the Calzaghe fight indicated he might have a thyroid problem, but he refused to blame his performance on it. He said during the post-fight press conference in Atlantic City that activity, and nothing else, was the difference. "This old car is hard to keep starting up," he said, so he wants to fight again in less than a year.

It doesn't matter what happens from here on. Hopkins has

established himself among the great figures in the dirty little history of the prize ring, comparable to any fighter you can name in any era. He is one of them, in league with Sam Langford and Archie Moore, Joe Louis, and Ray Robinson. More than anything, he is a 43-year-old prizefighter from Philadelphia, doing things in the ring that only great ones have done.

"I wanted to let you know you have someone special amongst you and you all aren't going to realize it until I'm gone," he said. "It's always like that, in the history of the sport."

We realize it, Bernard. We do.

DINAMITA BLOWS
AWAY KATSIDIS

JUAN MANUEL MARQUEZ NOT
THE BORING ONE ANYMORE

ORIGINALLY PUBLISHED IN *THE RING*, MARCH 2011

IF HUMANS ARE STILL FOLLOWING boxing 70 or 80 years from now, and we all should hope for their sake that they are, they will look back at the 1990s and a little after as a golden age of Mexican featherweight-*ish* prizefighters. This is not an original thought. We've known for as long as Marco Antonio Barrera, Erik Morales, and Juan Manuel Marquez have been splitting eyebrows and flattening noses that, as a set, they are as good as anything this business has produced, in any era. They have been three uncommonly and singularly committed, skilled, and tenacious Mexican warriors all doing business at the same time, at or around the same weight, and largely against one another.

Future historians will note that of the three, it was Barrera who broke out first, his left hook and body attack evocative of a miniature Julio Cesar Chavez, all pressure and steely arrogance. Then came Morales, not more than a year later, hollow-eyed, long-armed and emaciated, a 125-pound Tommy Hearns. They eventually would make wonderful, terrible, bloody music together.

Trailing behind them was Marquez. More cerebral than the other two, more deliberate, not nearly as exciting, and maybe a tad unsure of himself. He was the technician, content to jab and counter where Barrera and Morales charged in, fists flying. He was the dull one.

The determined historian will note that by the halfway point of the following decade, Barrera and Morales were more or less finished, each done in to some degree or another by a whirlwind Filipino, who, certainly by coincidence he will think, had the same name as a Filipino Congressman. "Must be an uncle or cousin," he will conclude before moving on.

Then he will see this: Marquez fought at the highest level in the sport well into his later 30s and was still one of the best in the world when the other two had already lost most of what had made them special. And he was no longer the dull one.

It must be with some bemusement that Barrera and Morales watch Marquez at work these days, at 37 years old, beating back strong, young pressure fighters like he did Juan Diaz in 2009's Fight of the Year. Then, in his most recent bout, on November 27 at the MGM Grand in Las Vegas, Marquez battered 30-year-old Australian buzzsaw Michael Katsidis into such a state of bloody helplessness that referee Kenny Bayless had to rescue Katsidis at the 2:14 mark of the ninth round.

If Barrera and Morales had ever been friendly with one another, one could imagine them back in the old days celebrating their manliness over a few *Tecates* or *Coronas*, their chests puffed out, sniggering over younger Marquez's reluctance to engage.

There is little for them to feel superior about now, and not only because Marquez outpointed Barrera straight up in 2007. "Dinamita" is the world lightweight champion and the fourth best prizefighter on the planet, pound for pound. Neither of those designations seems in danger for the foreseeable future. Indeed, if Marquez has his way, his resume will only be enhanced down the road. And yes, a 37-year-old fighter can have a "down-the-road." At least this one can. But more on that later.

Barrera, a year younger than Marquez, was surprisingly spry

against third-tier Adailton De Jesus in a June 2010 decision win but hasn't been considered an elite fighter since twice scraping by Rocky Juarez in 2006. He is all but retired. Morales, the youngest of the three at a mere 34, lost four straight—including a humiliating blowout against the Congressman in the rubber match—and retired for three years. Early in 2010, he launched a comeback that, as of this writing, has seen him win over modest competition.

It is a testament to Marquez's reputation that he went into the Katsidis fight a considerable betting favorite. If it were any other 37-year-old with 58 fights and 17 hard years in the business, you could be forgiven for hoping for a good physician at ringside and maybe a defibrillator. The list of very good fighters with so much behind them is short and grows shorter by the year. But Marquez is not just a fighter. He is an athlete of perhaps the most extraordinary type, an old athlete in a young athlete's body, and his stoppage of Katsidis served as proof, as if you needed any more, that we are watching in this fighter something remarkable. Not just world-class ability. Not just exceptional longevity. Both together.

"With all the good Mexican fighters I've been associated with down through the years, he's lasted longer than any of them," Hall of Fame promoter Don Chargin told *The Ring*. "Usually, with the Mexican fighters, the ones from Mexico start very, very young and by their mid-20s, that's it, they're usually on their way out, or when they get close to that 30 mark. This guy's amazing."

That Marquez, 52-5-1 (38), was floored in the third round by a thunderous hook from Katsidis but, by the round's end, was nonetheless peppering his challenger with typical efficiency, underlines what resides at the core of this man, who was once thought of as a safety-first dullard. He is a fighter through and through. Marquez has effectively reinvented himself, to use a modern and mostly reprehensibly overused phrase that in this case happens to fit.

Barrera did the same thing, if in reverse, when he discovered after losing to Junior Jones in 1996 that he could not left-hook his way to victory over everyone. He became a classical boxer and broke opponents down piece by piece with one of the best jabs in the game. To those of us who marveled at the beautiful and deadly savagery he displayed against Kennedy McKinney and others, this could have been seen as a kind of insult, but it added years to Barrera's career, good years, and millions to his bank account. And against the right guy, he could still get in there and crank hooks to the body. The jab gave him options. It made him a new fighter.

Marquez's abandonment of his safety-first style has done similar things for him. The hardcore still adore him for his craft, combination punching, footwork, head movement, and precision. But he lays his head in there more now, so even a lesser-skilled banger like Katsidis 27-4 (22) can find it without trying too hard. Now the masses can love him, too. Katsidis landed dozens of hooks square on Marquez's head and jaw, and if it weren't so damned exciting, you might wonder if Marquez made the right decision to fight more and box less.

Chargin related a story about Bobby Chacon, the wonderful featherweight and lightweight titleholder from the 1970s and '80s, who, like Marquez, started off more boxer than puncher and today lingers in dire straits in California, debilitated with dementia and other unpleasantness related to his willingness to take punches.

"He was such a good boxer when he was very young and coming up that you could absolutely not hit him," Chargin said. Then came a night, Chargin recalled, when Chacon went into a fight out of shape, and as a result, stood and punched with his opponent and eventually knocked him out. "Afterward, he told me, 'Wow, I love hearing that crowd cheering for me.' And from then on, even in shape, he'd go in flat-footed and trade punches, and that's why the poor guy is like he is today."

We should hope, of course, that the same tragedy does not befall Marquez. But examined from another angle, it is hard to imagine that he would be scoring the paydays he is today if he were still jabbing and countering his way to efficient wins rather than fighting, if not with the abandon of Morales, then the calculated ferocity of, say, prime Ray Leonard. Provided he is saving some of that money, Marquez will at least be well cared for should all these hard nights add up to harder ones later on.

Of the three—Barrera, Morales, and Marquez—only Morales stayed true to his original style, which is to say he still sees taking punches not only as a necessary part of the game but perhaps even an enjoyable one. So long as he is able to get close enough to land his own, he seems perfectly happy to take a few: *Go ahead and hit me so I can hit you better.* This may explain why he seemed to lose his taste for both the game and for the firefights when he did. Morales was just 31 when he took the full count while wide awake in his second loss to Pacquiao and retired after losing to the ordinary David Diaz is his next fight. The hard fights – and they're all hard when you don't move your head – wear on you. We will see how long into his comeback his rediscovered love for the battle lasts. Except for the truly deranged, it doesn't last forever.

It may be that Marquez's seemingly unquenchable desire for hard contact and victory is what fuels his exuberance. As trainer Ronnie Shields told *The Ring*, "The guy is just determined to be the best. Normally, when you get to be a certain age and you get these young kids putting pressure on you like these young guys are doing to him, they say, 'I'll give it up.' But this guy, he wants to be the best fighter in the world." Shields has been in the corner opposite Marquez at least three times – twice with Juan Diaz and once with Rocky Juarez, whom Marquez tortured over 12 rounds in 2007 – and he remains perplexed by the man.

"Before the Juarez fight, I studied Marquez over and over and over, especially the Chris John fight, and I figured he was really going to take it to Rocky," Shields said. "And he did the opposite. He ended up outboxing Rocky." Shields got another chance with Diaz and fared no better.

"We figured Marquez was going to have to box Juan, but at some point, he would have to stand and fight. At that point, we thought Juan would wear him down and make him say, 'I can't continue like this. I can't take this pressure.' Juan did everything we asked him to, but this guy wasn't going nowhere. I couldn't say that to Juan, but in my mind I'm thinking: Juan's doing everything we asked him to, but no matter what he did, this guy was still there."

It is this immense stubbornness that Marquez hopes will get him a third fight with Pacquiao. Marquez advocated for such a meeting following the win over Katsidis, reminding everyone that in his mind – and in the minds of many others – he has two wins over the Congressman. Shields hopes too that he gets another shot.

"I understand why he wants the Pacquiao fight. He has the style to beat him," Shields said. "I was at the first fight and I saw him get knocked down three times in the first round. I was sitting next to a friend of mine, Jesse James Leija, and I told Jesse, 'Look man, Marquez is going to win this fight.' Jesse said, 'He just got knocked down three times!' I said: 'You know what? Look at him. He's not hurt. He's gonna come back and win this fight. And truthfully, I thought he pulled it out.

"It's the way this guy adapts to your style. He does it right away. I thought the second fight was really close, but I thought he won that fight, too. That's just a style Pacquiao can't handle."

Beating Pacquiao officially certainly would give Marquez the edge over Barrera in terms of their competing legacies. Barrera was a magnificent fighter at his best but could do nothing with Pacquiao, particularly in their first meeting. Their second was closer, but that seemed more Pacquiao's choice than anything.

Morales, of course, outpointed a strangely sluggish Pacquiao in their first meeting for reasons no one has been able to explain beyond Pacquiao not being permitted to wear his preferred brand of glove (this from Freddie Roach). Whatever. The knockout wins Pacquiao scored in their subsequent meetings cleared up any confusion involving the identity of the superior fighter.

Marquez hopes he gets the same chance that Morales did, and so do we. He has come quite a long way to get where he is, and the trip has not been easy. The worthwhile ones never are, but it is nice if at the end one gets the sense there is nothing left to see.

. . .

Epilogue: Marquez got two more chances against Pacquiao. He lost a majority decision in November 2011 in Las Vegas, and in their final meeting, knocked Pacquiao out in the sixth round in December 2012, also in Las Vegas.

THE UNRAVELING OF ANTHONY JOSHUA

ORIGINALLY PUBLISHED IN *RINGSIDE SEAT*, SUMMER 2022

"We are what we pretend to be, so we must be careful what we pretend to be."

— KURT VONNEGUT IN THE INTRODUCTION TO HIS
NOVEL *MOTHER NIGHT.*

OLEKSANDR USYK IS a Rubik's Cube of a heavyweight, so he might have beaten any version of Anthony Joshua during their recent heavyweight title fight in Saudi Arabia, of all places. Usyk's speed and darting style will be anathema to most of the giants lumbering around the heavyweight division these days, but I can't help wondering how things might have gone if Joshua hadn't suffered a late-career identity crisis brought on by who knows what - insecurity, boredom, an overzealous trainer.

Whatever the cause, Joshua's rise through the professional ranks following an amateur career topped off with an Olympic gold medal produced highlights that suggested the rise of a great heavyweight puncher, which remains the rarest and most valuable commodity in all of sport.

And then one day, we tuned in and saw him boxing and moving. Jabbing. Counterpunching. Holding inside. "Fighting off the back foot," they call it in England. In Joshua's case, I call it throwing away your strengths. Watching him box his way to wins over Carlos Takem, Joseph Parker, and especially Andy Ruiz in their rematch, was like watching a Porsche 911 racing a field of Hyundai SUVs and never taking it out of first gear.

Then came the first fight with Usyk. That Joshua did as well as he did while trying to outbox a smaller, faster, technically superior boxer speaks to his talent and resolve, but it was a strategy doomed from the start.

Most pinpoint Joshua's transition to a kind of boxer-puncher to his memorable brawl with Wladimir Klitschko, another one-time slugger who successfully, more or less, compensated for numerous frailties by adopting a jab-and-clutch style that extended his career and earning ability but bored American fans to tears. Joshua himself said, after rising from the canvas to stop Klitschko, that he never wanted to go through that type of fight again.

Fighters say all kinds of things. The truth is he made it harder than it had to be by boxing Klitschko from the outside. Every time he stepped forward and threw punches, Klitschko crumpled.

Joshua promised a return to his old ways for the rematch with Usyk, and hiring Robert Garcia seemed a good move in that direction, but it was too late. As in the first fight, he hesitated. He looked for openings instead of creating them. He stood outside and waited for Usyk to punch. On the occasions when he gritted his teeth and dug into Usyk's body, you got a glimpse of what he used to be, when he fought with a swagger and a certainty that all great punchers possess. And then it was gone again.

Very few big men are able to tinker with their style to the degree that Joshua has and succeed. Lennox Lewis did. When he knew he could blow out an opponent - Andrew Golota, Frans Botha—he did so with a suddenness that must have looked to his opponent like the end of the world. When faced with a sturdier man - Evander Holyfield, David Tua—he was content to jab and win on points.

Of course, Tyson Fury, whose presence hung over Usyk-Joshua I like cheap cologne at a strip club, boxed the bejesus out of Deontay Wilder in their first fight, then used his, *ahem*, girth, to wear down and club Wilder into unconsciousness in their subsequent fights. A mega-money unification match with Usyk awaits.

And Wilder, for all his flaws—which include not knowing some of the basic fundamentals of boxing taught to amateurs in even the whitest American neighborhoods—knows precisely what his identity is as a prizefighter and that all of his success is predicated on landing his right hand. It is just the kind of singlemindedness that great punchers are born with and that Joshua evinced before he decided to pretend he was something he was not—or maybe when he realized he'd been pretending all along.

SAUL ALVAREZ LOOKS LIKE OPIE

BUT THIS FRECKLE-FACED, REDHEADED MEXICAN CAN FIGHT!

ORIGINALLY PUBLISHED IN *THE RING*, AUGUST 2010

To LOOK AT HIM, you wouldn't think Saul Alvarez was anything special as far as prizefighters go. For starters, there's the red hair and freckles. We associate them with the Irish or the Scottish, and it's been a long time indeed since those countries distinguished themselves as mass producers of high-quality prizefighters, though natives of both remain earnest, and, with the right encouragement, tenacious and charmingly easy to provoke.

Alvarez's body doesn't strike one as very fighter-like, either. Neither musclebound nor sinewy or elongated, it gives the impression of being most useful perhaps on a soccer field or volleyball court, where its stocky athleticism would whisk Alvarez from corner to corner in gleeful pursuit of a victory that does not demand quite so much from its participants as does boxing.

"I'm different from the other boxers. My personality and appearance are different, but I still love boxing," Alvarez told *The Ring* with the help of Golden Boy Promotions publicist Ramiro Gonzalez, who interpreted. (Alvarez speaks no English.) "Good or bad, I know a lot of people say, 'Look! Look at this guy with the red hair.' But it doesn't matter to me, I just love boxing."

Red hair or no, Alvarez, just 19 years old, is all fighter, as he demonstrated to 1.4 million boxing consumers, give or take, when he stopped the competent Jose Cotto underneath Floyd Mayweather's win over Shane Mosley on May 1 at the MGM Grand in Las Vegas.

It was not merely the win over Cotto that established Alvarez's boxing bona fides to an American audience mostly seeing him for the first time. After all, Cotto, 32, for all his pedigree and shiny 31-1-1 (23) record, was by most estimates at least a couple weight classes over his head at junior middleweight and had come up short in two fights against better opponents—at lightweight, no less—a draw against Prawet Singwancha in 2007 and a decision loss a year earlier against Juan Diaz. And the last three guys he faced before meeting Alvarez had 46 (!) losses between them.

Still, in the first round, a left hook sent Alvarez reeling into the ropes. Cotto, of Cuagas, Puerto Rico, pounded him there, and a less levelheaded referee than Tony Weeks might have stopped it. Alvarez, 32-0-1 (24), slips punches the way trailer parks slip tornadoes – that's part of his charm – and Cotto unloaded. A good 30 seconds later, Alvarez was still there, and in the next round he spun Cotto around and dropped him with a heavy right.

Alvarez, 150, eventually wore down Cotto, 149, with straight, heavy punches. In the ninth, a series of thudding rights convinced both Weeks and Cotto that enough was enough, and Weeks called it at the 2:51 mark. Alvarez led on the judges' cards by three scores of 78-73.

For Alvarez fans, there are a couple of ways to look at that nearly disastrous first round. The good news: He almost got his head handed to him by a much smaller guy, but he survived and eventually won. The bad news: He survived and eventually won, but he almost got his head handed to him by a much smaller guy.

As any educated fighter—or one who has been well coached by his promoter—will tell you, surviving a round like Alvarez did is a learning experience. It's hard to know yet whether he is educated or just well coached, but the kid says the right things. He even concedes, more or less, that the pressure of fighting on a very big card – the second biggest non-heavyweight pay-per-view ever, as it turned out – got to him.

"(The fight) was a very important situation, a different atmosphere," Alvarez said. "It was a very big card, a big show. The good thing was I learned in that first round that I knew how to control the situation. I knew how to control the panic. I knew how to handle those punches and show the public and the media that I have a good chin. That was the best thing that could have happened to me because in that first round, I learned a lot."

Alvarez was born and raised in Juanacatlan, Jalisco, Mexico. Juanacatlan is named, more or less, for its history of producing tasty onions, which may or may not explain the fighter's red hair. Jalisco is one of Mexico's more economically and culturally developed states, which means that if you're looking for a storyline that involves a fighter's desperate quest to rescue a loving and long-suffering family from a life of dusty Mexican squalor, you won't find it here. This is not the story of The Brothers Marquez. It is closer to that of Marco Antonio Barrera.

"We were a middle-class family," Alvarez said. "I got into boxing naturally because I wanted to help my family and myself, but also because I love boxing. We are not a rich family, but whatever we need, we have it."

Alvarez started learning to box at 11 years old after a fight with another boy in the street. As one of five brothers, all of whom have fought professionally, he had choices; a boy with five brothers has many back-ups and bodyguards. (Interestingly, he and his brothers hold the world record for most siblings fighting on one card. At least two of these brothers had never fought before and probably won't ever again, but you take world records where you can get them.)

Alvarez said it was attending the pro debut of his older brother, Rigoberto, that hooked him. He turned pro at 15 with no appreciable amateur experience, yet never felt like a boy fighting men. It was too much fun.

"I really love boxing and always had a desire to start in the boxing business," he said. "And I was so hungry. I wanted to start, so that's why I did it when I was 15 years old. I didn't want to wait anymore."

It didn't take his fans long to appreciate his two-fisted style or his red hair and freckles. "El Canelo" (Spanish for cinnamon) quickly built a following that has made him one of Mexico's brightest young stars. How bright? Last January, Oscar De La Hoya went to Mexico to sign Alvarez to a contract and afterward called it, "a historic day for Golden Boy." He then told the press that Alvarez had the potential to be the next Julio Cesar Chavez. Heady praise indeed. But in terms of his appeal to the masses, the numbers don't lie. Neither does the buzz he created with the win over Cotto, even if it was touch-and-go early on.

"He definitely has chemical appeal," said HBO's Jim Lampley, who called Alvarez's fight against Cotto. "I based that on the fact that in the week following our showing him on pay-per-view, I got a lot of comments from fans, especially my friends here in Southern California who are Chicano fans. They loved what they saw. Just the physical look of the kid, the poise that he showed getting past the rough spot in the first round."

Lampley's friends weren't the only ones interested. Fighting almost exclusively in Mexico, Alvarez has attracted huge crowds for a prospect, on occasion selling out 15,000-seat arenas. His televised fights reportedly draw a 15 share, an extraordinary reach. He appears to be on his way to supplanting Julio Cesar Chavez Jr., a Mexican juggernaut for Bob Arum's Top Rank.

Chavez has been headlining his own pay-per-view show for several years, though he's never faced a top fighter or even one as threatening as Cotto. That Chavez will have faced John Duddy in a showdown of sorts by the time you read this is a reflection of the care with which he's been moved (if one can say he's been moved at all, as it implies a heading in some direction). Alvarez has received no such accommodations and doesn't care for comparisons to Chavez.

"It's not who's better, me or him. I don't want to be compared; it matters what the fans say and what the media says. I will be the number-one boxer in Mexico.

"I always offer good fights and the people like it. They like how I fight. I'm the only one in Mexico that can get that attention right now. The only one. People crave fights and people are seeing that I am getting better and better and better. Each fight I have, I try to have the people like it."

Like any exciting fighter, Alvarez has some flaws, some of them serious. He is primarily a right-hand puncher who mixes in a competent body attack. His defense is fairly porous. He's not especially quick on his feet, and that Cotto was able to so perilously shake him, even if the kid did ride it out, raises questions about his chin. Finally, there is an obvious lack of hand speed. That was evident perhaps to a greater degree than during any other fight in his points win over Larry Mosley in California in 2008. Many thought Mosley, a smart, quick boxer, outboxed Alvarez before eventually succumbing to Alvarez's greater youth and exuberance. Still, he remains an outstanding prospect.

"This kid has a tremendous wish about him, as there would be about any Mexican prospect at this point," Lampley said. "I really like him. He has maturity. But I don't think he has the kind of speed that it takes to succeed at or near the top of the welterweight division.

"He's a quality fighter who will be able to fight quality opponents and look for upward mobility, but won't be able to do it at 147 or to the level that Mexicans would like," he said. "He reminds me of Fernando Vargas, specifically because Vargas had everything but the great quickness. At the end of the day, he wasn't as quick as Oscar De La Hoya or Felix Trinidad and it cost him."

It's unfortunate for Alvarez, then, that the top fighters at or around 147 are speed merchants – Mayweather, Manny Pacquiao, Mosley, Andre Berto. Those at 140 today and likely to move up sooner or later or no less flashy: Tim Bradley, Devon Alexander, Lamont Peterson. Alvarez might be better off trying to make his mark at 154, where *The Ring* currently ranks him 10th.

Alvarez said he wants to win world titles in the welterweight, junior middleweight, and middleweight divisions and be "remembered in boxing forever." We don't know if he'll do all that. He may have to settle for proving there's no guarantee that a guy with red hair and freckles can't fight. You can't count on anything anymore.

Epilogue: Alvarez went on to win world championships at 154, 160 and 168 pounds, become boxing's biggest box office draw, one of the 10 best fighters on the planet and a certain first-ballot Hall of Famer. At this writing, his record is 63-2-2 (39).

READY FOR MANFREDY

NO GIMMES FOR PRETTY BOY FLOYD!

ORIGINALLY PUBLISHED IN *KO*, FEBRUARY 1999

THE PHONE RANG three times before a drowsy-sounding Floyd Mayweather Jr. picked it up. The guy on the other end apologized for waking him, but the new WBC super lightweight champion insisted it was no big deal. He wasn't really sleeping, just getting the rest that had been eluding him since his title-winning victory over Genaro Hernandez four days before.

"Rest is real important to a fighter," he said, a refrain he had no doubt heard countless times over the years. That's why he was at a hotel, where he couldn't be reached by the legions of friends, fans, and well-wishers who had been calling him around-the-clock at home, to spout congratulations, give verbal pats on the back, and, of course, advice.

"People were calling all night," he yawned. "Yesterday, we got 120 calls." It wasn't that he minded, of course, and that's a good thing. Because Mayweather's phone will be ringing for some time to come.

It's not every day, after all, that we see a prodigy with the power, skills, and hand speed of young Mr. Mayweather. It's not every day that a 21-year-old prospect with 17 fights has the cojones to gun for

53

an established, respected champion like Hernandez, and then make one of the craftiest fighters of the day surrender without ever having threatened to take over. And it's not every day that a brand-new champion has the conviction to christen the title belt by taking on one of the division's best fighters, as Mayweather did when he agreed to make his first defense against "El Diablo" himself, Angel Manfredy. Think the kid has a little confidence?

"I put myself right up there with the best fighters in the world," he said, clearly awake now and warming to the conversation. "I'm up there with Roy Jones and Oscar De La Hoya. When Oscar fought Hernandez, he had more fights and more years (as a pro) than I did. I'm right up there with those guys. I told people I was going to win the title, and I did."

All right, so he's cocky—aren't all the great ones? But there is more to Mayweather than his brazen self-assurance. His boasts are backed up not only by his obvious talent, but by his willingness— make that his eagerness—to face the toughest guys in his weight class. He could have, for example, gone after Roberto Garcia's IBF belt rather than Hernandez's WBC title. At least on paper, Garcia looked the much easier opponent. But that was never an option.

"To be the best, you got to fight the best," Mayweather said, and yes, we've heard dozens of fighters say that before and then watched them go out and sign to fight some god-awful mandatory from Croatia or Namibia. And everyone knows it smells rotten and the laughing rings on, all the way to the bank. But Mayweather starts to make a believer out of you when he says things like, "I want to fight the best now so that 50 years from now people will look back at Floyd Mayweather and say, 'That Floyd Mayweather fought everybody—he was a heck of a fighter.'"

He sounds like a fighter from another era when he says he isn't interested in moving up in weight right away, that "winning the title was my main goal, and my goal now is to hold on to the title and to stay undefeated." He says that eventually he'd like to win some more titles, "maybe in a bigger weight class," and when you think of his wide shoulders and back and the way he threw Hernandez around, you wonder how long he'll be able to make 130.

Before the Hernandez fight, there were those in the business who thought—some out loud, but most to themselves—that Floyd Mayweather Sr., who began guiding his son's fortunes after serving a stint in the slammer, was rushing his progeny. Indeed, if you were so inclined, you wouldn't have had much trouble finding someone to agree with you that the elder Floyd reminded one a little of Joe Frazier, who most people thought recklessly pushed his son Marvis into fights against Larry Holmes and Mike Tyson before the kid was ready. But Papa Mayweather stood his ground.

"People say I'm moving him too fast, but if he wasn't ready for Hernandez, I'd be the first one to tell him," Mayweather Sr. said in the weeks leading up to the bout. "I chose this fight. I call the shots. I told Floyd to whip his ass."

Rumor had it that Mayweather's promoter, Bob Arum, opposed the fight on the grounds that the kid wasn't ready yet. Not so if you believe Floyd Jr.

"Bob said, 'Tell me when you're ready.' I said, I'm ready.' He said 'Are you sure?' I said, 'Yes, I'm sure. And I'll win.'"

In retrospect, we should have expected the title shot to come as early as it did and we should have expected the virtuoso performance we received. History tells us two things about the fighting Mayweathers: one, they're early bloomers, and two, they're not a patient bunch. Uncle Roger, a two-time former champion, won the WBA junior lightweight title in his 15th pro fight. Floyd Sr. was duking it out with Sugar Ray Leonard after only 16 pro starts, and five fights later squared off with future champ Marlon Starling. Only Uncle Jeff, who works the corner with the elder Floyd, showed some restraint; he didn't take on a ranked contender until he faced Todd Foster in his 26th bout.

Even so, there was reason to believe Mayweather was in over his head. This wasn't one of the game's ever-growing fleets of nondescript novice champions he was going after. This wasn't a Mayfield or a Woodhall or a

Cherifi. This was Genaro Hernandez, who hadn't lost at 130 pounds. *Ever.* His only defeat, a stoppage against De La Hoya in '95, was justifiable for so many reasons we've lost count (for the record, the two major ones involved the fight being at lightweight and Hernandez's nose being busted by Shane Mosley in sparring). Hernandez's off-the-canvas win over Azumah Nelson in '97 took care of most of the stigma left over from his capitulation to De La Hoya, and, at 32, he appeared as stalwart as ever in recent defenses against Carlos Hernandez and Carlos Gerena.

But there is no holding off brilliance. Mayweather, 18-0 (14), warmed up over the first two rounds by ramming his jab into the center of Hernandez' face. He looked as patient and slick and as strong against "Chicanito" as he did against guys whose records barely broke .500. And before the first round was over, you knew this was going to be either a very long night for Hernandez, or, if he wasn't careful, a very short one. It turned out to be something in between.

Hernandez, 38-2 (17), tried everything. In the second, he attacked Mayweather, at one point even wrestling him to the mat. In the third, he took to using the ring and trying to keep the kid on the outside with the jab. In the fourth and fifth, he tried countering off the ropes, but by that time the message had already arrived, and he knew he wasn't fast enough, strong enough, or good enough to hold the kid off. No matter what he tried, Mayweather was in his face, banging him with jabs, leading with left hooks to the body (against Genaro Hernandez!), lumping up his face.

After a while, it wasn't worth it anymore, at least not to Hernandez. And after one final, desperate, futile attempt in the eighth to get something going, he said to hell with it and sat there on his stool while his brother/trainer, Rudy, told referee Jay Nady to stop it. "I wasn't going to take a beating," Hernandez said afterward, his right eye purple and swollen from Mayweather's hooks.

Don't let Hernandez's mastery of the art of graceful surrender make you think any less of what Mayweather accomplished, for, if nothing else, the manner in which the bout ended put "Pretty Boy Floyd" on a damned short list of the men who have made Hernandez quit. Ask the kid about that, though, about how he made Hernandez roll over and hand him the belt, and the brash young stud whose camp treated Hernandez like a sparring partner before the fight puts the kid gloves on.

"I wouldn't say he surrendered. He was a real good champion and he fought hard. He's awesome," said Mayweather. "He was very slick and snuck in some good shots. When he started moving around, I had to be careful and just jab my way in. I didn't want to take any chances and get myself hurt."

Get himself hurt? He stood a greater chance of injury climbing down out of the ring and into the throng of celebrants when everything was over. Nearly 200 friends and family made the trek from Mayweather's hometown of Grand Rapids, Michigan, to Las Vegas, and most stood by, almost as emotionally charged as he was, as Mayweather fell to the canvas and cried real tears at the fight's conclusion.

"Those were tears of joy, man," he said. "I was giving praise to God for fulfilling my dream. I couldn't believe it. It was what I was waiting for all of my life. Some of the people around me were crying, too, because they know how hard I work and how hard we've all worked."

Fight fans may be crying tears of joy soon, too. As we went to press, Arum was putting the finishing touches on a deal to match Mayweather with Manfredy on HBO, December 19. It's an opportunity for which Mayweather can barely wait. "I'm looking forward to fighting Manfredy. He's an exciting guy, an action-packed fighter. I really like his outfit. He looks like a motorcycle guy, with all the tattoos. He's got the potential to be a world champion."

Ask the new champ who he'd like if the Manfredy fight doesn't come through, and the kid shows that he's been doing his homework. "There are other guys out there: Jesus Chavez, Robert Garcia, Derrick Gainer, and there's always 'The Prince.'"

Doesn't sound like he'll be taking the easy road, does it?

Mayweather and Manfredy are both on a growing list of young studs who many believe will lead the sport into the new millennium. The new regime is busting with bona fide superstars in De La Hoya and Hamed, and potential stars in Shane Mosley, Michael Grant, and

Mayweather's 1996 Olympic teammates, Fernando Vargas and David Reid. The progress of Vargas and Reid is of particular interest to Mayweather, who said that he wishes the two were in different weight classes because, "I like them both a lot and they're so good I really don't want to see them fight each other." The kid may turn out to be better than all of them. If you want a second opinion, just ask him.

"I'm trying to be a winner. I love winning. I haven't even been a pro for two full years. I've had 18 pro fights and I'm only 21 years old. I'm the type of fighter everyone's looking for. I'll bet you never saw hands moving as fast as mine were against Hernandez, have you?"

When someone suggests that Roy Jones may be a tad quicker with his punches, young Mayweather drifts into a dissertation about how Jones has to cock his punches and that because he's a bigger fighter, his hand speed isn't what it seems.

"We'll let everyone rate me after they see more of my fights. "Call me after the Manfredy fight, and you know what I'm going to tell you, right? The same thing I told everyone who said I wouldn't beat Hernandez. I'm going to say, 'I told you so.'" Something tells us the phone will be busy.

THE CHARACTERS

HAS THE WIZARD OF KRONK
LOST HIS MAGIC WAND?

EMANUEL STEWARD ON A COLD STREAK

ORIGINALLY PUBLISHED IN *THE RING*, OCTOBER 2001

THE BEST CAN'T AFFORD missteps the way the rest of us can. They can't have a bad night or a bad week or a streak of crummy luck. The rest of us? No problem. We can make mistakes, screw up, drag a dark cloud behind us for a while. Nobody really cares – if they notice at all. Mediocrity has its rewards. Even if we're engaged in a high-profile profession, if we're not the best there is at what we do, who cares if we have an off night or an unlucky streak? It's expected. We're flawed. We screw up. We move on.

You don't get the same slack if you're the best. Expectations are higher. It's your own fault; you set them there whether you intended to or not. So if you're not on your game once in a while or if you suffer a bad break or an unfortunate streak, get ready for us mediocre types – who outnumber you a trillion to one – to pounce on you and let you know we've noticed. Your misfortune is big news – not because we dislike you, but because it makes us feel better to know that sometimes even the best don't have it all their way.

Remember when Michael Jordan would have one of his rare bad nights and score just 11 or 12 points? It was big news. Same thing happens today when Tiger Woods finishes six strokes behind the leader, or when Ken Griffey Jr. makes an error. We're all over it. It happens in the fight game, too, of course. Wait until Shane Mosley or Roy Jones loses two rounds in a row, or Don King drops a court case or misses out on the prospect he's trying to sign to an exclusive 30-year contract. It'll be big news. That's what happens when you're the best at what you do. You're expected to win – flawlessly, easily, impressively – every time out. When you don't, we're there.

For the last 15 years or so, Emanuel Steward has been among the very best and most successful at what he does, which is training prizefighters. Whether it's been as a hired gun or as the guy who took kids from the Detroit streets to world championships, we associate him with excellence. How could we not? He helped Evander Holyfield win the heavyweight title back from Riddick Bowe. He tied a red band around his head and showed Julio Cesar Chavez how to beat Frankie Randall (more or less). He took Oliver McCall, an ordinary heavyweight pug if there ever was one, and showed him how to knock Lennox Lewis flat and become champ of the world. Then he turned Lewis from a big, clumsy oaf of a heavyweight into a pretty good champion. Oscar De La Hoya never looked better than he did when he was with Steward, regardless of what Floyd Mayweather Sr. says.

That's just a smattering of what Steward accomplished as a freelancer. What about all those good Kronk fighters he nursed to championships almost from the womb? Tommy Hearns, Hilmer Kenty, Jimmy Paul, Steve McCrory, Duane Thomas, Milt McCrory, Michael Moorer. Solid guys, good fighters all. Champions. And Steward took them further probably than anyone else would or could have taken them. So we have come, rightly, to associate him with excellence. Everyone has. He has given us every reason to.

Even the best lose some, though. Steward lost when Naseem Hamed and Lewis, his two big guns, dropped big fights within a couple weeks of one another. Marco Antonio Barrera and Hasim Rahman scored unlikely wins, and suddenly there was Steward without a champion, without a star, without his guy's arm in the air at the end. For any other trainer, it's another day at the office. Win some, lose some. For Steward, altogether different. Foreign. But don't think it's unsettling.

"Yes, April was a bad month," Steward told *The Ring*, and chuckled. "But in big fights, I had a good run for about 15 years, so it's not that bad."

About Lewis's loss, Steward said there was nothing that could have been done. "He just got caught with one of the best right hands I've ever seen a heavyweight throw," he said. But Hamed's loss to Barrera was preventable in Steward's educated eyes, and that it occurred regardless was the straw that ended his relationship with Hamed.

"From the start of camp, it was all wrong. When it was time to start camp, Naz found this place in Palm Springs he wanted to train at. Now, I had been saying all along that Barrera was a very dangerous opponent, and I even told Hamed and his brother, 'Look, I really mean this. It's not hype.' Lennox was training for Rahman and normally would have trained in the Poconos (in PA) at our regular camp, but he knew what a dangerous fight this was for Hamed and agreed to train in Nevada, thinking Hamed was going to end up there too.

"But Naz kept telling me about this place in Palm Springs, so I went down there and checked it out, and I didn't like it," Steward said. "The atmosphere was all wrong. So I told him I was going over to Nevada to train with Lennox and he should come. He said he didn't want to, that he had this beautiful place in Palm Springs. I told him you're right, it's beautiful, but it's got nothing to do with winning fights. He said he wasn't going to change. He would just train there."

Steward went out to Hamed's Palm Springs camp a couple times to gauge his progress. He didn't come back happy. "The whole theme of the camp was to just not face reality. They had him sparring with guys who weren't nearly good enough to get him ready for Barrera. I told them about it, and they just ignored it."

Steward says he had arranged to have a tape of Barrera's win over Jesus Salud in December sent to co-trainer Oscar Suarez so Hamed could study it and see the Barrera he would be facing. Instead, according to Steward, Hamed's handlers insisted on reviewing tapes of Barrera's losses to Junior Jones, and at first denied even having received tape of the Salud fight.

"They didn't want to tell him anything he didn't want to hear," Steward said. "I would rather tell a fighter things he doesn't want to hear and have him win than tell him things he wants to hear and have him lose. At the end, I became just a figurehead. I had no control, no influence. I've been in this business too long and have too much experience and knowledge to let it go to waste like that. So it was better for everyone that I moved on. I still think Naz is one of the most talented fighters I've worked with and I still really like him. He's one of my favorites. But you must be able to hear things that are negative if they will help you win a fight."

The Lewis loss? An entirely different story and not, according to Steward, the one you keep reading about.

"Lewis was in shape," he said. "He did everything he was supposed to do and just a couple days before the fight was running five miles, boxing well in the gym. The altitude had nothing to do with it."

Steward denies rumors that contender Lamon Brewster dropped Lewis in the gym—"Lennox was kicking his ass every day"—or that Lewis was tired after the first round against Rahman, despite how it appeared to viewers. "I talked to him between rounds. He wasn't out of breath."

So what happened?

"It's like when a really experienced pool player is playing a bunch of kids who don't know what they're doing. The experienced guy relaxes, he doesn't concentrate as hard, and he plays around a little. Pretty soon, he's playing at their level, not the way he would against another guy who is at his level. Lennox got caught because he was just playing with the guy. End of story."

Whatever the case, don't think for a moment that his streak of poor luck has Steward fretting. If anything, it has invigorated him. The situation with Hamed in particular was the impetus to make him examine where he was in his career and what fulfills him professionally. Change is imminent.

"My career as a hired gun looks like it's coming to an end. I've had great success, but I like having control, and, as a trainer, you just don't have much, especially with these so-called superstars."

The answer, for Steward, at least, is to return home to stay, to Detroit, to Kronk, to manage and train guys from the ground up, like he did in the old days.

"The only way to really do it right is for me to manage and train together, just like I used to." He said he's working with investors to come up with a couple million dollars they'll use to sign young prospects. He recently signed promising Detroit welterweight Octavio Lara and featherweight prospect Rey Beltran. He looks forward to getting back into the managing end of the business.

"I've been in boxing for 48 years, and I've been very successful. I've built a lot of relationships with a lot of people all over the world. I've acquired a lot of knowledge and it's too much to waste by just training guys. At this point, I'd rather just take my time and develop my own fighters.

"When I work with these other managers now, they're intimidated and uncomfortable around me now because they remember me as a manager. Plus, I do everything for my fighters in terms of making all the arrangements, meeting with officials. I know all the presidents of the ruling bodies and the commissions and all the politics that go on. I handle all of that stuff, and that's not the job of the trainer."

Steward will continue to work with Lewis, whom he calls a true professional.

"Lennox looks for the hardest sparring partners he can find. He works hard all the time in the gym, and we work really well together as a team. He's a professional. When you tell him to go out and run at six in the morning, you can bet he'll be out there at six."

Lewis will be the only fighter Steward trains but doesn't manage. His heart is in management, and he is most proud not of what he's made happen in a gym or corner, but at the negotiating table, over lunches, on the phone, in elevators and conference rooms. His favorite example of his management skills involves former heavyweight champion Michael Moorer.

"When Michael was an amateur, we trained him for a while and I took a liking to him. John Davimos and I signed him to a managerial contract, and everyone told me he was nothing special. Everyone told me I was crazy. I turned him pro in March of 1988. In December, he was the new (WBO) light heavyweight champion. That was managing ability. Not just training, but managing.

"I did that with a lot of fighters. In 1987, Tommy Hearns told me he wanted to fight for the light heavyweight title, so I met with Jose Suliaman and convinced him to let Tommy fight Dennis Andries for the title even though Tommy weighed about 154 pounds. He agreed, and the day after Tommy beat him, Andries asked me to manage and train him. I got him a few fights, got Tommy a shot at the middleweight title, then I had Andries against Tony Willis for the vacant WBC light heavyweight title. Those are my managerial skills, which I take more pride in than my training skills."

Though he hasn't been doing it for nearly as long as he's been managing and training fighters, Steward is getting praise for his work as an analyst on HBO. He replaced Roy Jones on the network's *Boxing After Dark* telecasts and also works *TVKO* cards. He said it's been an education, even for a guy who's been in the game for almost 50 years.

"I didn't realize at first how much work I'd have to put into it," he said. "A week or two before a show, they send me a book with all kinds of records and clips and a box full of tapes. My job is to deal with the real pertinent, detailed stuff, so I really have to study those tapes. Plus I have a lot of contacts in the game, so I can call guys in the Poconos, at Gleason's Gym in New York, in Las Vegas, or wherever else I can get inside information on these guys."

Oftentimes, Steward says, the hardest part is remembering his role and that he's on camera. His instincts as a fight guy, rather than a talking head, take over.

"A lot of the time, I'll get engrossed in a fight from a manager's or trainer's perspective, so I don't say anything. I just sit there and watch the fight. So Jim Lampley has to pull me into the conversation."

Other times, Steward will drift off in his mind to this or that fight or to a matchup or something. Then the camera will be on him, and he'll forget a fighter's name or some other detail.

"I've learned I have to put all of that stuff out of my mind. They pay me to get right to the point, and I don't want to wing it. I want to do it right."

It shows, and even if he screws up on camera occasionally, or puts one of his guys in over his head, or, heaven forbid, fails to manage some kid to a world title by his 12th fight, we'll forgive him. Even the best have off days once in a while.

Epilogue: Steward died in 2012 after undergoing surgery for diverticulitis. He was 68 years old.

TOUGH GUY AT THE MIKE

ESPN'S SCOTT LEDOUX IS
STILL A FIGHTER AT HEART

ORIGINALLY PUBLISHED IN *KO*, FEBRUARY 2004

IF YOU'RE old enough to remember Scott LeDoux when he was a middle-of-the-road heavyweight contender in the 1970s, you remember the kind of fighter he was. He wasn't very talented. He wasn't a big puncher and he didn't move very well, or much at all, for that matter. He was a plodder and when he got good work done, it was because of his ruggedness and clubbing punching and a big, thick jaw. He outlasted some guys. He was deliberate and stubborn. He had zero flash. He wasn't pretty, but he had a decent run in a tough business, getting every bit out of what he had, which wasn't that much. But whatever he had, he gave you, and he didn't play. He gave you an honest fight each time out. He was what he was: Rough, determined, unrefined.

Listen to LeDoux now, some 25 years later, as the color man on ESPN2's *Tuesday Night Fights* series and you recognize the same characteristics: the honesty, the roughhouse persona, the lack of pretense. He broadcasts the way he fought: with heart, single-mindedness and not a little tough-guy bluster. He's straight up.

Whatever he has, he gives it to you in his way and he doesn't play around. If he offends you or one of the guys up in the ring or in the booth or a judge at ringside, it's okay because it's who he is. You can call it part of his appeal. The truth is he's still a fighter first, inside. He's a fighter putting on a suit and doing a good impression of being a broadcaster – but he's still a fighter. You never could mistake him for anything else.

"It's the way I've always been," LeDoux, 54, told *KO*. Away from the microphone, he sounds a lot like fellow Minnesotan and former governor and wrestler Jesse Ventura, toned down a bit. They share an acutely opinionated, tough-guy air. "I've been involved with boxing for 30 years with the amateur fights in Minnesota. I'm always in fighter mode. I still work out all the time. I've always been a student of the game. I know how to fight."

If he were alive today, Howard Cosell wouldn't care for LeDoux as a color man— and not just because LeDoux kicked Cosell's hairpiece loose after dropping a dubious decision to Johnny Boudreaux in Don King's corrupt heavyweight tourney in 1977. Cosell would almost certainly view Ledoux's success as the unfortunate and continued dumbing down of the broadcast industry. It's true LeDoux doesn't have a gift for analogy or the literary sense of HBO's Larry Merchant. Nor does he share the terminal likability of Showtime's Al Bernstein, nor the flair for melodrama that Teddy Atlas flaunts every week.

He does, as Cosell might say, tell it like it is, and does so with obvious conviction. There's no missing LeDoux's point, whether or not you agree with it. "Not everyone's going to like me or my commentary," he says without a hint of regret. "That's all right."

It may be that LeDoux can get away with things other color men can't because he's been in there and knows things the rest of the world cannot. Therefore, he gets the benefit of the doubt.

"As a former fighter, you see certain things," he says. "You can see if the guy's still in the fight by his facial expression and you can see if he's not really there anymore, too. And I can point that out. It's fun. This summer, I've had so many people come up to me and tell me they enjoy my broadcasting because, 'You teach me stuff.' I love to hear that because that means I'm doing my job. To analyze the fight and tell people why a guy is getting hit with the right hand and what he can do to not get hit by the right hand."

There is also, of course, the humor with which LeDoux devotees are familiar. He has an obvious affection for one-liners, and he'll throw one or two out there during nearly every broadcast. Some are better than others, but no one said he is Henny Youngman. Still, you don't hear anyone else in the business accuse Butterbean of fighting guys named "Willie Gettup." LeDoux says it was his humor that was at least partly responsible for him landing the ESPN gig, which began with occasional fill-in assignments and has since become a regular job throughout the summers on TNF.

"I do a lot of charity events and celebrity golf outings," he said. "I was in Montana at an event, and the host was Roger Twibell (ABC Sports commentator and one-time anchor of ESPN's *SportsCenter*). He introduced a bunch of different athletes and each one spoke. As all these athletes were at the podium, I jotted notes about each guy and when I got up, I roasted all of them. I brought down the house with one-liners. It was funny. Later, Twibell asked if I had done any TV. I said no, so he said, 'Give me your business card.' Later, I got a call from ESPN. They gave me an audition."

In one of his first assignments, LeDoux called color during a Stevie Johnston fight in 2000. "Toward the end of the fight, the CompuBox guys said Johnston had thrown, I don't know, a thousand punches. I said I'd thrown a thousand punches too, when I was fighting. 'But it took me 10 years.' They liked what I did."

Over the next two years, LeDoux provided color commentary for ESPN's amateur boxing broadcasts, which air generally during off-peak hours and bring a small audience compared to the *Friday* and *Tuesday Night Fights* series. It gave him time to learn how to translate for viewers what he knew from being in the ring.

"He learned how to be a professional broadcaster," said Bill Graff, coordinating producer at ESPN. Graff was instrumental in bringing LeDoux to ESPN. "Early on, he had all the insight and knowledge, but didn't know how to get it across to the audience. He was a little timid when it came to being himself on the air. We worked with him and brought that out, and now he's able to be himself on the air, which is the funny, honest guy you see and hear."

It's the same blunt honesty that propelled LeDoux in the ring that serves him at ringside. "Scott is a very interesting man," Graff said. "He's glib and very funny. But he's also brutally honest. That's what pushed it over the top for me. At one point, I asked him, "Scott, if a fight is a dog, are you going to be able to say it to the audience? And he said, 'Yeah, of course I will—these fighters are getting paid to do a job, and if they're not doing it, I'm going to say so.' He brings a real insider's perspective."

Indeed, it is difficult to get more "inside" than LeDoux does, considering he frequently spars with ranked heavyweights in an effort to give viewers the most personal analysis any fight broadcaster could give. Over the last couple of years he's gone rounds with Lennox Lewis, Mike Tyson, Michael Grant, Joe Mesi and, most recently, the near-300-pound Tye Fields. Talk about getting perspective.

"Very few announcers who are former fighters get into the ring and work," LeDoux says. "Sparring with guys was my idea. I still go to the gym to work out. I spar all the time. So I thought it would be a great angle. After I boxed with Michael Grant (before Grant's disastrous challenge of Lewis), I came back and said, 'This kid's gonna get killed. It's gonna be a short night. Michael's a wonderful kid, but every time I jabbed, he brought down the right hand to block it. I feinted with the jab, he brought his right down, and I hit him with the left hook. I knew if I, at 50 years old, could hit him, it would be a lot easier for Lennox Lewis."

His analysis after sparring Lewis prior to Lewis' successful title defense against David Tua was also on target. "I came back and said, 'This is going to be a long, boring night for us.' I was shocked at how well Lewis moved. His jab was punishing; I couldn't get past it. He never let me get close. It was impressive. He hit me with a right to the body and my ribs hurt for about five weeks."

One guy LeDoux hasn't boxed but would like to is Butterbean, his accomplice in an on-air feud that began during a *TNF* telecast two years ago following one of the Bean's typically gaudy kayo wins.

"Butterbean is such a joke," LeDoux said. "The fat slob. I don't usually talk like that, but he's just a joke. He fought a kid from Minnesota, and I told the kid, 'If you lay down, don't even think about coming back to Minnesota.' For the first few rounds, he was moving around and boxing, and in the fourth, he stuck his chin out there to get hit and got knocked out. After the fight, Butterbean leaned over the ropes and asked me, 'Hey LeDoux, how come my nose is straight and yours is crooked?' I said, 'Because I fought eight world champions and you fought 50 bums.' I kept bad-mouthing him, right on the air, hoping we could make a fight, but it didn't happen."

LeDoux was a freshman and football player at the University of Minnesota Duluth when he started boxing. A fellow student, a basketball player, had just started boxing and had a fight coming up. He needed someone to spar with. LeDoux had never boxed before, but agreed to work with him in the gym. The basketball player pelted LeDoux with jabs, but LeDoux kept going back to the gym and four months later had his first fight.

"The thing I always like about boxing is you reap what you sow," he said. "If you work really hard and persevere, you'll be okay. If you don't, you'll be in trouble."

You would think a guy so in love with the game and with such a willingness to ball up his fists would have a hard time leaving the ring. But after getting stopped in three rounds in 1983 by Frank Bruno, LeDoux retired with a career record of 33-13-4 (22) and never looked back.

"I don't miss it at all. I never have. I'm blessed. I never had the burning desire to come back that so many guys have. I'm involved with so many charitable foundations, like the Make-a-Wish Foundation, which I've been involved with for 20 years, The American Cancer Society, the Fellowship of Christian Athletes. For years, I averaged 120 charity appearances per year. That's one every three days. That satisfied my ego. Fighters come back because of their egos. They have to have the attention and the spotlight on them. Working with all these charitable organizations took care of that for me."

There is one fighter (besides Butterbean) who could lure LeDoux into a comeback: George Foreman. Big George buried LeDoux in three rounds in '76. LeDoux says he is the hardest puncher he ever faced.

"He hit me with a jab and I said, 'I don't want to feel the right.' He caught me with a right hand in the third and I had to get 12 stitches."

Still, LeDoux gives the impression of being incensed at Foreman's professed intention to come out of retirement at age 55.

"I wanted to fight Foreman. I said, 'You won't be the best 55-year-old around, because I am.' I'll fight him for the 55-year-old fighter title. If he wants to fight at 55 years old, let him fight me. If he can beat me, then he should go and fight the young guys."

It's not just the seniors' tour that LeDoux is passionate about. He laments the diminished state of amateur boxing in America, which he blames on dubious scoring principles, one of which mandates that a power punch warrants no more points than a jab. He addresses it in typical macho fashion. "I said to the head of Olympic boxing, 'Let me hit you with a jab, and then let me hit you with a right hand. Then, after you wake up, you can tell me they're the same thing.'"

The intensity makes one wonder how LeDoux makes it through his day without belting people, but he does – all the more surprising since he is around people all the time in what he calls "the fire protection field" as a salesman. He's also sold real estate and disability insurance and is working on becoming a mortgage broker. "A jack of many trades, a master at none," he says. It remains clear where is heart is.

"This job is a dream," he said of the ESPN gig. "It's been a life's goal of mine to have a job that I love so much that it wasn't going to 'work.' I've got that now and I love it. People come up to me all the time and are so nice. That's the best part of this."

Nevertheless, one gets the sense that if given the choice of being young again and fighting, or being older and describing it from ringside, LeDoux would choose the former, and you can't blame him for that. Any real fighter would do the same.

Epilogue: LeDoux died from ALS, also known as Lou Gehrig's Disease, in August 2011. He was 62.

HAIL AUGUSTUS!

BOXING'S JOURNEYMAN KING

ORIGINALLY PUBLISHED IN *THE RING*, JULY 2006

YOU GET the sense it would be easier for everyone involved if Emanuel Augustus couldn't fight as well as he does. If he couldn't, we wouldn't know him much outside his name appearing like ellipses on so many records. We wouldn't care about him. If we thought of him at all, it would be the way we do about the dozens or maybe hundreds of other guys out there whose only purpose inside the ring is to bulk up the records of guys who can fight. That's the job. We see the name and forget it just as quickly. You can't care about everybody.

Come to think of it, it probably would be easier for Augustus, too, if he weren't quite as good in the ring as he is. There would be no expectations, none of the maddening chase that tortures and wears down anyone who is engaged in something worthwhile or otherwise struggling toward something. If he couldn't fight, he could just surrender to mediocrity, accept it like so many of us do.

Acquiescing has its downside, of course, like anything else, especially for prizefighters, who, let's face it, don't usually have a lot of career options outside the gym. But at least then the man could relax a little. Kick back. Party without the nagging worry of the drug test that will come with the next fight. Because who cares if a guy who isn't expected to win comes up dirty? What difference does it make?

Augustus's great curse, and ours too, it turns out, is that he *can* fight—not so well that he will likely ever be champion, or even so well that he will crack the top 12 of the junior welterweight division—but well enough so that we want to watch him try. Well enough so that he'll always win more than he loses. Well enough so that he'll occasionally bump off an undefeated prospect. And well enough to keep him in the business and keep us caring about him.

Evidence of this curse was apparent during Augustus's 10th-round knockout of the not nearly as bedeviled Jaime Rangel on ESPN2's *Friday Night Fights* in Connecticut in February. After a somewhat languid start that seemed caused to some degree by Rangel's southpaw stance and quick overhand lefts, Augustus, 32-25-6 (17), found his rhythm in the fifth round. After that, he sliced Rangel up with piercing right-hand leads and uppercuts and gradually took over entirely on the way to flooring Rangel twice, prompting referee Dick Flaherty to stop it at 2:27 of the 10th. It was, given Augustus's history, a somewhat more urgent performance than we've come to expect from him. There was a reason for that.

"I played around in boxing long enough and now I have a reason to buckle down and do better," Augustus told *The Ring*. "I got a promoter to fight for now. Now it's the way it's supposed to be. Before, it didn't matter whether I won or lost. Now it does."

Augustus is referring to Lou DiBella, who promotes him now and has won his confidence. "Lou works for the benefit of the fighters. I'm not saying anything bad about promoters I've had in the past, but this is the way it's supposed to be now. It's how it was always supposed to be."

Augustus's up-and-down ring exploits are by now well known to the fight community and are not altogether uncommon. About every generation has a fighter or two like Augustus: talented journeymen who came from nothing and had no direction or good management early and got into a hole record-wise at the start. They take fights on short notice because they need the money and there's no one around to tell them not to, and they take fights in other guys' hometowns for the same reasons. They can fight all right, but it takes more than that, a lot more, to win the boxing lottery, and by the time guys like Augustus realize how it all works, it's too late.

On two occasions, Augustus lost four straight, and during one particularly bad stretch, dropped five of six. He then went 9-0-1 in his next 10. He's lost to Jesus Chavez and Ivan Robinson, Pete Taliaferro and Diosbelyis Hurtado. Leonard Dorin ran roughshod over him and so did Antonio Diaz. Omar Weis outpointed him, as did Olympians Kelson Pinto and David Diaz. He's lost decisions in Puerto Rico, Denmark, Germany, and Nashville, but you'd have to be naïve, at least, to think all those defeats were legitimate in the sense that the right guy got his hand raised at the end.

Ironically, Augustus got the break of his life when he was clearly robbed in a July 2004 points loss to Courtney Burton, which happened to be televised on ESPN2's *Friday Night Fights*. The fan uproar, supported and instigated in the main by broadcasters Teddy Atlas and Joe Tessitore, led to judging and scoring changes in Michigan. But the loss remains on Augustus's ledger, as all of them will.

Officially they are losses, and when we are dust, they still will be losses, so you can argue them all you want. Augustus accepts the business of the sport and how the losses affect his prospects and refuses to rationalize them away.

"The fighter's still got to win the fight. No one's at fault but me. I can always argue that a fight was taken away by the judges, but if you knock them out, they can't take it from you."

Still, the bitterness over so many of those losses, legitimate or otherwise, informs his recent dedication. "When I first started, it was all about having fun in the ring. I used to make up punches based on video games. I had a style that I called 'Crazy Legs' that I tried out in the gym and then in a couple fights. But I never took it too seriously. I never really said, 'I want to be a champion,' but I do now. I really do. And I can't be pushed out of boxing. I won't be. I feel like there are people who want to push me out of boxing. The fighters can't beat me so they get the referees and judges to do it for them."

Augustus's stubbornness can be traced to a past that is the type that breeds toughness. For reasons he is either unsure of or loath to detail, his parents relinquished custody of him to the state when he was around two years old. He grew up "in the system" and spent his childhood and adolescence largely at The Harmony Center, a group home in Baton Rouge, Louisiana. One of the administrators there also ran The Sports Academy, a recreational facility at which Augustus was introduced to boxing, though he'd been informally, one might say, studying the rudiments for a long while already. "I fought all the time and the majority of guys I fought were bigger than me," he said.

Augustus left the system at 17 years old and did two short stints at Baton Rouge City jail for charges related to resisting arrest, battery of a police officer, and the like. But even by then, he'd realized he had to do something with his life.

"I knew that I wasn't really good at anything I could make money at and I'd always have low-rate jobs. I knew I wasn't good at school and wasn't going back. So you do what you're good at. It's a cliché but it's true. I knew I was good at boxing, so I decided to do that." He went to the 16th Street BREC Gym in Baton Rouge, and with the help of good people things started to come together, just a little.

"A great guy named Frank James got me a job, a place to live, I got my GED, and a woman named Alberta Williams, who had a daughter and three sons, took me in and made me part of family. I don't know where I'd be now if it weren't for her and other people in my life who helped me when I needed it." With that stability, he committed himself to boxing and had about 25 amateur fights before turning pro in 1994.

Augusts is philosophical about his childhood and parents. "For the most part, I'm just glad I got a chance to know my mother and father. Whatever it is, it is. I'm grown now, so I don't hold grudges. My state of mind is I'd rather have than not have. A lot of people don't know their mother or father. So I'm lucky. Once I got out of the group home, I had a lot more contact with my brother. He comes to my fights and cheers me on."

For all the losses, there has been much to cheer. Augustus gave Floyd Mayweather what Mayweather later called the toughest fight of his career to that point when they met in Detroit in October 2000. Augustus was a big underdog when he trounced the heavily hyped and very talented Alex Trujillo in April '04. Same thing when he stepped in on two days' notice and stopped Carlos Vilches in '02. His war with Micky Ward in '01 was the springboard to Ward's trilogy with Arturo Gatti and *The Ring's* Fight of the Year. At Augustus's fight with Rangel, Ward could be seen screaming instructions to Augustus from ringside.

"We threw something like 2,000 punches that night," Ward said of his fight with Augustus. "He's as crafty as they come. He knows the ring real well. When he's on, he can give anyone at 140 pounds a hard time. He's a real throwback fighter, like Freddie Pendleton. He had all those losses on his record early in his career, but when he started doing things right, he was unbeatable. I can't say enough about him."

Augustus may have another defeat on his record by the time you read this, and not all of his defeats have been the result of hometown decisions and other shabby treatment. Often, he's fought just hard enough to keep from losing, but a fighter is rarely the best judge of how things are going score-wise. His style, as much as anything else, may be contributing to those close points losses.

"There is some inconsistency in the ring as far as offense goes," Atlas said. "He's a talented kid, he knows how to fight, and he's got a fighter's mentality. But he's not consistent. In spots, he'll be very productive. Then you won't see anything for a while. He goes defensive and doesn't do anything. When he takes time off like that, he gives you opportunities to steal moments and to steal rounds and fights. His spottiness allows a fight to be close, allows the judges to give it to the other guy."

Atlas associates most things involving human performance with self-discipline, and Augustus's lapses are fair game. "He's had a couple drug tests come back bad. I don't hold it against him, it's out there, it's a fact," said Atlas. "I like him a lot, but I think that speaks to a lack of self-discipline in certain areas. And if you show a lack of discipline outside the ring, you're going to show it inside the ring too. It works that way in any profession. Show me a trial lawyer who's undisciplined and inconsistent outside the courtroom and I'll show you one who's the same way inside the courtroom. It's the same way in boxing, same way in everything."

Augustus acknowledges he's made mistakes along these lines. After the Rangel fight, he told writer Robert Mladinich, "People act like I'm supposed to be a role model, but nobody's ever given me anything. I don't understand where I'm at, so how do I act? I know I'm not supposed to smoke weed, but I have no sponsors, no one investing money in me. Still, I promise I won't make that mistake again."

Mistakes haven't hurt his standing with ESPN2, which has televised several of his fights with more planned. "I'm sure we'll have him back on our air soon because we like him," said Atlas. "He makes good fights and is entertaining. The fans like him, too. There's a certain comfort level they have knowing that they're going to see a good fight when he's on. Also, he's a high enough caliber talent that he can be in there with almost anybody and be in a good fight."

Augustus has never turned down a big fight and, at 31, knows he won't be around too much longer and that every fight counts. "My chances (for a big fight) are very high," he said. "I just got to keep doing what the hell I'm doing and not get caught. As soon as I get knocked out or cut, it's over. I know that. I have too many losses. I can't waste anymore. I've got to make it in boxing before my time is up.

"My record will always haunt me, but I don't want it all to be for nothing. I'm the living image of what it means to get knocked down and get back up. When it's over, it's over, but until then, I have to do it right. I have to win these fights."

It's hard not to hope he succeeds.

Epilogue: After losing five straight fights, Augustus retired in 2011. In October 2014, he was hospitalized and placed on life support after being accidentally shot in the back of the neck. He fully recovered and, as of 2016, was living contentedly in Baton Rouge.

THE REMAKING OF A
HEAVYWEIGHT PROSPECT

FOR SHANNON BRIGGS, IT'S
JUST LIKE STARTING OVER

ORIGINALLY PUBLISHED IN *KO*, OCTOBER 1997

THE RIGHT CROSS landed and poor Melton Bowen was asleep before he hit the canvas. For Shannon Briggs, it was just like old times.

Looking at him, one could mistake Briggs for nothing else but the future heavyweight champion of the world. He is large and menacing and sculpted the way we like our heavyweight champions to look. In action, his hands are fast and lethal. He fights the way we like our heavyweight champions to fight.

Briggs may as well have been formed from our collective psyche, the personification of all that we desire our heavyweight champions to be. In addition to having *The Look*, he possesses what casting agent types call "star quality," with his laid-back attitude, easy smile, and good looks.

It is largely for these reasons that in a time when hyperbole is the norm, when fight managers hire marketing consultants and promoters engage entire ad agencies, Briggs stood for a time as the most celebrated East Coast heavyweight prospect since word leaked from the Catskills that crazy, old Cus D'Amato had found himself a stubby heavyweight named Tyson who might make some noise.

In the earliest days of his pro career, the New York press, known to be a cynical lot predisposed to viewing most things with a skeptical eye, embraced Briggs's charm, his intelligence, and his charisma. As an added bonus, he looked to have some genuine fighting ability, at least as far as the amateurs were concerned. He won two New York Golden Gloves championships and a national title with only 32 fights to his credit. All this after starting the sport late, at 19.

When manager Marc Robert brought in highly respected Teddy Atlas to train him, it all seemed a done deal. All that was left to do was the actual fighting, and Atlas would take care of that.

With the publicity machine humming along at full throttle, word spread fairly quickly that we should keep a watchful eye on Briggs, that the kid with the orange dreadlocks could rock. He did nothing to discourage that perception early on, tearing through the usual heavyweight slop like Sherman through the South. Shortly, though, there were dissenters who started wondering, quietly at first and then louder as time went on, when Briggs would step up and face live competition. Later came disturbing rumors from the gym that young Briggs often had a tough go of it in sparring, that fighters nobody had heard of were roughing him up. For reasons many suspected were becoming clear, Roberts continued to mostly match Briggs against opponents with losing records.

Eventually, the level of competition got better, but not by much. It didn't matter. To his credit, Briggs overwhelmed veteran trial horses Marion Wilson, Will Hinton, and Sherman Griffin in successive fights, honing *The Look* until it appeared unmistakable. By the time HBO came to court Briggs and showcase him in its "Night of the Young Heavyweights" card last year, the Brooklyn native sported a glossy 25-0 record with 15 of 20 knockouts coming in the first round.

By the measure of many, Briggs was exposed that night by Darrell Wilson, who accepted Briggs's early thunder, then came back to knock him out in the third. It wasn't so much that he lost that turned off many to Briggs – Wilson was undefeated too, after all, though he didn't have Briggs' star quality – but rather the impression that Briggs left. Because when a fighter gets attention the way that Briggs has, the assumption will always be that he doesn't possess the intrinsic doggedness that the best fighters always carry into the ring. The toughest fighters we can think of – Joe Frazier, Marvin Hagler, Azumah Nelson – earned their stripes the hard way, almost in anonymity, at least early on, and definitely without the fanfare that accompanied Briggs's rise.

Going into the Wilson fight, then, the opinion that lay in the hearts of the critics was that when Briggs's number finally came up, and surely it would, as soon as he met someone who punched back, he would lose – and not by a little. He would not prove himself in defeat, nor distinguish himself in a positive way, fighting his heart out but losing to a fighter who was better that night, the way Ali lost his first fight with Frazier, for example, or even the way Lou Savarese did against George Foreman. No – he would flop. He'd be knocked cold, or he'd just flat-out quit. And that's pretty much the way it happened.

For as soon as it became apparent that Briggs' customary first-round blitz was not going to end matters, his countenance changed. He hesitated and looked tight. He backed off, and when Wilson started landing, Briggs got the look that a fighter gets when his mind fills with doubt, when he realizes he probably can't win, not on this night, not against this opponent. One could see his resolve and his confidence wane every time Wilson landed a clean blow. When he was cut and hurt by a hard left hook near the ropes, he did the only thing he could: He went down hard and stayed there.

Future heavyweight champions don't get blown out that way. Or do they? "Hey, they said Joe Louis was a bum when he got knocked out by Max Schmeling," Briggs says now with a laugh. Wilson is no Schmeling, but the point is valid.

Perhaps as a result of getting burned too many times, those who follow this game are often too quick to write off a boxer after he's had a bad night or two (ask Junior Jones). The truth is that prizefighters far better than Briggs will ever be have gotten themselves knocked out and still turned out to be champions. Jersey Joe Walcott was stopped in his 10th pro fight, Henry Armstrong in his pro debut, of all things. Foreman, Evander Holyfield, and Mike Tyson all have "KO by" designations on their records.

The fans may never be quite able to reconcile such a bomb against a fighter like Wilson, who soon after was summarily flattened by David Tua, but as far as Briggs is concerned, it is history and an event for which to be thankful.

"It was a blessing in disguise. I've matured from it," Briggs said. "It was a growing part of my life and got me to where I am now." It also served to teach him the lesson that all young, successful fighters learn sooner or later.

"It showed me who my friends are, because a lot of the guys that were around when I was undefeated were gone or treated me differently after the loss."

It also gave Roberts the opportunity to practice some damage control. After the fight, he announced that Briggs suffers from asthma (cold-induced asthma to be specific), which he says he has the medical reports to prove, and "which explains why Shannon couldn't breathe in the Wilson fight." This came as rather a surprise to Atlas, who trained Briggs for four years. He left after the loss to Wilson.

"I'm surprised that they chose asthma, I wasn't surprised that there was some kind of excuse," Atlas told *KO*. Atlas is a demanding trainer known mostly of late for his stirring, between-rounds pleas to IBF heavyweight champion Michael Moorer (with whom he is no longer associated), and is candid about the reasons that led him to split with Briggs, even as he stood to make big money with him. Those who know Atlas know he will never be satisfied to be one of those trainers who throws a towel around his neck, tells the fighter when to duck and then calls it a day. He appears to be as concerned with loyalty and integrity as he is with remembering to jab, or moving away from a puncher's right. With him, it's largely about commitment.

"I felt at the end that I was sincerely trying to make him a pro, and I thought he was on the same page, but he wasn't. He was conning me," Atlas said. "He disappointed me in that he truly wasn't trying to become a pro the way that I wanted." He also feels Briggs submitted in the Wilson fight.

"I tried to prepare Shannon to know that at some point, when he was in a competitive fight, he was going to be faced with a choice: to deal with what was going on and finding a way through it, or finding a way to get out of it. Shannon made the wrong choice."

The last straw for Atlas was when he saw that the attention Briggs was being paid by his financial backers and other hangers-on was undermining the fighter's dedication and that Briggs himself contributed to it.

"Shannon had a false sense of success and it all became too much," Atlas said. "I felt betrayed. He didn't give it the same run for the money that I did."

The idea that Briggs is more interested in living the life of a successful athlete than he is in actually being one is fueled in the minds of some by Briggs's devotion to hobbies outside the fight game. When not in the gym, he's often composing or recording rap music, or modeling for photos that will appear in magazines that have nothing to do with boxing. His skills as a fighter are not his only wares, and one suspects that when his fighting days are over, he will not be among those who fight on because he has squandered his ring earnings. He has options, but insists that boxing will come first.

"I am in this business to become heavyweight champion of the world. There is no second place," he said. "I'm in this to go down in history as one of the best, not just as a guy who makes good money."

The trainer charged with getting him there now is Miami-based Carlos Albuerne, who has worked with Roberto Duran, among others. Albuerne practices a style considerably more relaxed than that of his predecessor.

"I love boxing now," said Briggs. "There was a time that I wasn't happy in my boxing life. Now I love going to the gym. We work hard but we laugh and joke around sometimes and it's fun. I'm learning every day and getting in great shape."

Despite Briggs's obvious natural talent, Albuerne's task is challenging. For all his speed and athleticism, or maybe because of it, Briggs still makes mistakes that underscore his lack of experience against real opposition. He relies too heavily on his speed to get his power punches home, and frequently over-commits to punches, leaving himself off-balance in the process. As Wilson showed, he's not hard to find with the jab—or with the hook or right hand for that matter. Head movement is not his strong suit. Against competition like Bowen, who was Briggs's third straight knockout victim since the loss to Wilson, Briggs doesn't need anything but his natural ability and his emotion. When the quality of his competition will improve is the question. Some important people are tired of waiting to find out.

"I'm very exasperated with the whole Shannon Briggs situation," said HBO Sports Vice President Lou DiBella. "I felt what happened to Shannon in the Wilson fight could happen to any young fighter and that he was still talented enough and had enough of a name so that it wouldn't hurt him."

So DiBella did what any fight fan would ask him to: He scheduled Briggs for some serious competition on the network's *Boxing After Dark* series.

"We had a number of good opponents for him to face – Michael Grant, Kirk Johnson, Joe Hipp – and he pulled out of each of them," said DiBella. "To me, that was such a great opportunity for him. If he had won, there was a chance that he could have fought Foreman. He can't be out there claiming to be the future of the heavyweight division by beating Melton Bowen. I have to wonder where his head is at, if he's motivated to be a fighter."

Briggs' response: "It wasn't my fault those fights were canceled. I'll fight anybody."

So it falls back to the manager, Marc Roberts, who by now is used to people asking him when his star fighter will step up. "By September or October of this year, the bottom line will be in and everyone will understand that Shannon is big news," he said, possibly the most manager-ish thing any fight manager has ever said. "He will fight a top 10 or 12 guy—Grant, Tua, Savarese, Hipp, or Johnson."

Briggs chimed in. "This is the year for Shannon Briggs. I know I'm the best heavyweight in the world. You're gonna see the real Shannon Briggs and all hell is gonna break loose. I'm here to stay. Get used to me."

We demand a lot of our future heavyweight champions. One gets the sense that by year's end, we will know if, in this case, looks were deceiving.

Epilogue: Briggs outpointed George Foreman to win a piece of the heavyweight title in 1997 but lost it to Lennox Lewis in his next fight. He retired with a record of 60-6-1 (53) in 2016.

CONTENDER STAR
ALFONSO GOMEZ

HIS ONLY FEAR IS GOING
BACK TO HIS OLD LIFE

ORIGINALLY PUBLISHED IN *THE RING*, JANUARY 2008

SOME FIGHTERS GAIN the love of millions because they are themselves inside the ring, where nothing can be hidden, and are experts at hiding who they are outside of it, where whole industries are built around obscuring reality. Julio Cesar Chavez and Mike Tyson come to mind. Others are loved as much for their social and political accomplishments as for their pugilistic ones. Muhammad Ali and Joe Louis are prime examples. Still others are dipped in whatever the magic elixir is that makes some men excel both in life and in the ring, their skill matched only by their charisma and their charisma matched only by their skill: Ray Charles Leonard and Oscar De La Hoya.

Alfonso Gomez, who we imagine will have beaten the well-worn Ben Tackie by the time you read this, is not likely to make anyone forget Tyson or Chavez or Ali or Louis or Leonard or De La Hoya. Hell, he might not make anyone forget Grady Brewer by the time the dust has all settled. But he is making his mark today not only as a fighter who is as eminently likable outside the ring as is any fighter of his era, but also as a guy who can fight a bit after all—and not just for a guy from *The Contender* TV show—but for a fighter. His win over

Arturo Gatti in July suggested he is not quite the reality-show creation some in the fight business would prefer him to be, and also that he is possessed of a coolness in the ring few would associate with his cuddly, aw-shucks humility. The manner in which he dispatched Gatti, whose autograph he asked for (and received) in the run-up to the fight, implied a fighter who, like most other fighters, has some demons with which he is dealing. Nice boys don't do what he did to Gatti.

"No, I have no demons," Gomez told *The Ring*. "But I grew up poor, in a poor neighborhood. I saw our family lose our car because we couldn't afford it, saw us get kicked out of our house and go through foreclosure. Remembering that motivates me because I don't want to live like that ever again." That fear is indeed a demon of sorts, the same one that drives some men into prisons and crack houses, and others into gyms and boxing rings and schools and careers. Gomez doesn't realize that not all demons are bad.

"Beating Arturo Gatti makes me even more determined than I was, because being rich and successful and a champion used to seem so far away," he said. "Now it's so much closer, so I don't want to go back to the way it was. I have to dedicate myself 100 percent because every victory brings me closer to what I have been looking for. I have to look spectacular because now I have to get the people to believe in me. I don't have demons, but I have a lot of motivation. If I mess up now, I go back to where I started, and I don't want to do that."

That cash-starved past is not as far back as you think. Gomez made $350,000 for beating Jesse Brinkley in *The Contender* season-one semifinal, but went through it quickly. The Gatti fight put him back on his feet financially, but for a while it was like he was a kid back in Mexico again—and not in a good way.

"I learned a hard lesson about money," he said. "Because I wasn't used to having money, because I had never had any before, I just spent it. Bought myself a nice house, bought my mother a nice house, bought myself a hot Chrysler. I thought the money I made that first year of *The Contender* would just always be there but it wasn't. Right before the Gatti fight, I was in real financial trouble. If I had known then what I know now, I probably could have doubled that money, but because I had never had money before, I didn't know what to do with it other than spend it. I won't make that mistake again."

That he has a chance to make it again—indeed, that we know him at all—is due in large measure to the very first *Contender* episode, when he shocked his teammates and most of the viewing audience by calling out tournament favorite Peter Manfredo. It was one of the best moments of the first season and went a long way toward establishing Gomez as a fan favorite and also toward revealing something about his character.

"Out of all the fighters we've had on *The Contender*, he was the most popular from Day One," said Gomez's promoter Jeff Wald, who is also the show's executive producer. "Everybody loves him, and not just fight fans. I'll give you an example: During that first season of *The Contender*, my wife would take my daughter to school, and all the women there, all these 30-and 40-year-old women, would talk about Alfonso and how much they loved him.

"Look at what he did that year," Wald continued. "He was an alternate, wasn't expected to do anything. And what does he do? Challenges Manfredo, in his first fight, the guy everybody expects to go all the way. And he beats his ass. He beat him with balls, smarts, and skills."

It is among Gomez's favorite memories from his time on the series, and he loves to tell the story.

"Going into *The Contender*, I knew a lot of the guys, but I didn't know Peter Manfredo," he said. "I knew Ishe Smith because I had fought him, and I knew some of the other guys from seeing them around. But I didn't know anything about Manfredo. All the other guys were afraid of him. Everyone thought Ishe Smith was the best guy on our team, and Manfredo was the best guy on their team. I saw him train and work out, and I could see he was strong, but I believed I was the best fighter there. At the moment, we were going to decide who was going to fight who. Joey Gilbert on our team was so afraid to fight that I just volunteered to fight Manfredo. I didn't want my team to lose the first fight, and I wanted to prove I was the best fighter there. My teammates didn't want me to, except for Ishe, who told me I could win. But that was one of the best decisions I ever made."

But to every upside, there is a downside too. Gomez, like many of his *Contender* alumni, has struggled against the perception that he has gotten more exposure and money than his talents deserve, and that he and the other *Contender* fighters, and the show itself, are neither good for the sport nor representative of how it really operates. Indeed, you would not have to work terribly hard to find someone in the industry to agree with the assertion that Gomez is little more than a likable clubfighter. It's a characterization that makes Wald bristle.

"This clubfighter stuff pisses me off. Go back and listen to what Emanuel Steward, who has no love for *The Contender*, said about Alfonso after the Gatti fight. He said Alfonso would have beaten Gatti in his prime. Gatti still had skills in that fight; he was still a warrior, and he had no quit in him, and Alfonso did everything right. He fought Gatti smart."

Still, Wald doesn't appear in any great rush to move Gomez, 17-3-2 (8), up the ladder unless he sees a style matchup he likes. He acknowledges he wouldn't have taken the fight with Kermit Cintron had Gomez, and not Jesse Feliciano (with whom Gomez has a 1-1-1 series going) been offered it because of the "size difference" and what he sees as Cintron's limited drawing power. But Gomez "has the potential to go the distance," Wald said. "Do I want him to fight Paul Williams right now? Probably not. But I'd love a fight with Ricky Hatton. Or Paul Malignaggi. I'd like Julio Cesar Chavez Jr. too."

Indeed, had Gatti beaten Gomez, Chavez was next for him. Gomez ruined that and said afterward that he'd like to take Gatti's place against the son of Mexico's greatest-ever fighter. "There's been a lot of talk, but he hasn't fought the level of competition that Alfonso has fought," Wald said. "But Chavez in Los Angeles would mean something. That would be big. With his fans out there, and the fans we would bring in, it would be big."

Such a matchup would clearly be the biggest of Gomez's career, but would not cause him to lose any sleep. He claims to be one of those rare fighters who never gets nervous before fights, never has to battle back the anxiety-driven nausea that visits even the greatest fighters in their dressing rooms. Talking to him, seeing how he carries himself, watching how relaxed he is in the ring, you believe him when he tells you. He has no reason to lie.

"I'm never scared. I think, what is the worst that can happen? I lose? I've lost before. I can handle it. There will be other fights. I get knocked out? So what. I just go in there and do my thing. And I know it'll be all right because I've dedicated myself 100 percent in the gym. I was only nervous before a fight once in my life— against Jesse Brinkley in *The Contender* finale because I knew what was at stake: The winner was getting $350,000 and the loser $100,000. That made me nervous. But other than that, never."

That wouldn't surprise Gomez's manager, Gary Gittelsohn, who says Gomez is "extremely confident and knows his place in the world." Like Wald, Gittelsohn believes it was Gomez's decision to challenge Manfredo that set him apart from the other contestants on the show and continues to set him apart today.

"He made a tremendous statement when he did that," Gittelsohn said. "It showed he believed in himself enough to call out the favorite of the group when he didn't have to, and really endeared him to the viewers. It made him the fan favorite."

That confidence is what Gomez believes makes him likable and approachable. He's always had it, both in and out of the ring. "I'm upbeat all the time, I like to laugh," he said. "I didn't get into all the drama on *The Contender*, and people saw that. It's always been like that. I may not be the best-looking guy, but because I'm confident and don't care, the girls like me. I wasn't the most popular kid in school, but in every gym I've ever been in, everybody liked me and liked my style, liked the way I fought. I've only had 20 fights and 12 or 13 of those fights have been the best fight of the night, even though they weren't the main event."

It's not a stretch to predict that Gomez's personality will bring him success after his fighting days are over. He graduated with a B.A. in Music Engineering from the Musicians Institute in Hollywood and has a recording studio in his home, where his brothers, who have a band, record their music. He's interested in acting and has interests outside the ring and plans to pursue them someday, one assumes with the same humble confidence with which he enters the ring. He credits his parents with instilling in him the confidence to believe he could do whatever he wanted with his life.

"From the time we were little kids, my parents always planted the seeds of success in our heads. They always told us we could be whatever we wanted to be in this world, that being poor was temporary and someday we'd have everything we ever wanted," Gomez said. "They said, 'You can do everything you want' and we started believing it, and once you believe it, you can go ahead and do it. I thought everyone believed that; that everyone dreamed of being successful and famous and having money, but I found that's not the case. Not all parents teach their kids that. We were very lucky that our parents did."

It's hard to say how far Gomez will go in this hard business. However far it is, it'll be awfully hard not to root for him as he tries to prove his parents right.

Epilogue: In his only shot at a world title, Gomez was stopped in six rounds by Canelo Alvarez in 2011. He retired in 2015 with a career record of 25-6-2 (12).

HE ONLY LOOKED THE PART

MICHAEL GRANT'S LONG ROAD FROM HEIR APPARENT TO JOURNEYMAN

ORIGINALLY PUBLISHED IN *THE RING*, DECEMBER 2010

IN MID-AUGUST, patrons of Route 287 or of The Garden State Parkway, heading northbound, away from Atlantic City and the depravities of the Jersey shore, were besieged by the startling presence of billboards advertising a prizefight in Newark, the state's oft-maligned Essex County hub.

"The Big Challenge," the signs beamed. On one side was an image of Tomasz Adamek: white, soft, almost pasty, his brown hair shaved into more or less a crew cut. Not at all imposing. Almost sheepish. Next to him, Michael Grant, clearly much larger, black, bearded and muscular, his skin shimmering like a thoroughbred's after a warm-up run on a crisp October morning.

The billboards were the work of Main Events, Adamek's Totowa-based promotional outfit, which is headed by Kathy Duva. To Duva and her staff, Adamek has been a godsend. Once one of the game's premier promoters, the company took a hit with the retirement in 2007 of the late Arturo Gatti, a reliable, if regional, box office draw. Fernando Vargas, another star, quit the same year. Main Events' other high-profile fighters—Evander Holyfield, Riddick Bowe, Lennox Lewis—were from another era and long since gone or irrelevant.

With Adamek, Main Events found a fighter with a strong ethnic link to the community, a rare and precious thing these days. New Jersey, especially in its northern regions, has a burgeoning Polish presence.

Adamek's home away from home has been The Prudential Center in Newark, the crown jewel in Newark Mayor Corey Booker's ongoing gentrification initiative. It is where Adamek beat Steve Cunningham, Jonathan Banks, Bobby Gunn and Jason Estrada. The shows all had the feeling about them of a raucous party, with Polish songs and antics and all manner of loud and joyous revelry. The fans that came to cheer on Adamek (5,000 or so the first couple times, then 9,000, then 10,000 strong) could not be faulted. They'd suffered long and hard with Andrew Golota. They deserved a winner. Adamek, so far, has been a winner.

Grant was selected ostensibly because his great size—6'7", 250 pounds, give or take—approximates that of the Klitschko brothers, the twin towers of the heavyweight division, at least one of whom Duva hoped could be convinced to meet Adamek next year. If Adamek, a dwarf of a heavyweight as heavyweights go these days, could figure out a way to deal with Grant, maybe he could with the Klitschkos too. Big is big.

For Grant, it was manual work, a laborer's chore, playing stand-in for a fully realized and successful giant. Wladimir Klitschko, the younger of the two brothers, is the world heavyweight champion, a role that was supposed to have been Grant's. He was the "heir apparent," an outdated term now but one that seemed invented for him in the late 1990s when he was undefeated, getting paid more by HBO than many world champions, and streaking toward a shot at Lewis, presumably the outgoing king. By now, Grant's story is well known.

An outstanding all-around athlete, he never picked up a pair of boxing gloves until he was 21 years old. In a business where the best practitioners can hook off the jab before they can ride a bike, he got an irreparably late start. The hope and the wish was that his great size, athleticism, and appearance—he simply *looked* like a heavyweight champion—would compensate. For a while, it did.

Grant was managed early on by Bill Cayton, who 10 years earlier had co-managed Mike Tyson to early and catastrophic success, and Craig Hamilton, a Long Island boxing memorabilia collector. Grant did away with the usual heavyweight flotsam and learned the rudiments of the game under Don Turner, a veteran trainer credited by some with orchestrating Holyfield's upset wins over Tyson.

Under Turner's tutelage, Grant more or less sailed past his first 25 opponents, no small feat given his lack of experience. By 1998, he was facing ranked, higher-quality heavyweights such as David Izon, Obed Sullivan, and Ahmed Abdin, and the formula held. He was still winning and playing to moderately good crowds in Atlantic City, but his team, by then, knew something was missing. And it wasn't just experience.

"I think for a long time a lot of us that were with Mike wouldn't accept what he is and what he isn't," Hamilton told me a couple weeks after Grant dropped a unanimous decision to Adamek in Newark.

"Michael is not really a fighter. He's not a guy that ever liked fighting. He knew he could do it. And as we went along the trip with him most of the time, when he got to a certain level, most of the guys he fought were truly better fighters than he was technically, but it didn't make any difference. He was just too much for them physically. He would just beat them down."

Hamilton said that even as Grant was winning, he thought his fighter could do more, given his athleticism and size. It was a long while before he realized Grant just didn't have the mentality of a true fighter.

"It was because we could see the fabulous potential there. With everything in his arsenal, we felt like if there was just some way to get more juice going in this guy. But you're really not going to get that from someone who doesn't like the sport to start with."

Still, Grant was doing well, beating the guys HBO and his management team put in front of him. When he ground down tough

Lou Savarese over 10 rounds in New York on HBO, the title shot was a near certainty. By mid-1999, *The Ring* rated him among the world's top-five heavyweights. His team took one more big fight — against Golota, the skilled, hard-punching, and emotionally fragile Pole who twice threw away victories against Bowe when he could not or would not stop hitting Bowe low and was disqualified.

On the same night and in the same ring where Stephan Johnson took a light jab from Paul Vaden, went to sleep and never woke up again, Golota hit Grant with a right hand in the first round and dropped him hard. Another knockdown followed. But Grant stood up and muscled his way back into the fight. He gradually wore down Golota, and, after getting dropped himself in the 10th, Golota told referee Randy Neumann that if this was the way things were going to go he preferred to not continue.

Those who doubted Grant all along felt vindicated by what they saw as proof that he had a weak chin. His supporters pointed to the heart he showed getting up from two first-round knockdowns. To then-heavyweight champion Lewis, Grant was suddenly irresistible. A title shot was proffered and accepted, and, from all appearances, Grant was confident. He had reason to be. After all, he was undefeated in 31 professional fights.

"I know that people say that because Andrew Golota dropped me with a right hand, then Lennox Lewis is going to do even worse to me with his right hand," Grant said shortly before the Lewis fight. "But keep in mind, he's only Lennox. He's not a machine. He's flesh and blood, just like I am. And as far as I'm concerned, the only thing he has on me is experience, which doesn't bother me since I've fought experienced guys my entire career ... Lennox will bring out the best in me."

You know what happened then. Lewis destroyed Grant in two rounds. Afterward, Turner told Hamilton, who is about 6'2" and in the 240s: "If Grant were the same size as you, he'd be 0-31." And then the wheels really came off. Hamilton said it was bound to happen sooner or later, but the crash started with the Golota fight.

"Michael is a tremendous athlete. Really gifted," said Hamilton.

"But you have a person here who has tremendous insecurities. So what you do when you're bringing him along is try to build his confidence. But it's not something you can really do with a person. It's like power: You either have it or you don't. When Michael came to us, he was not the most secure, confident guy. Golota hit Michael with a perfect shot in the first round. Whatever confidence he had up to that point was gone. His chin was gone."

A switch in trainers after the Lewis fight, from Turner to Teddy Atlas, didn't help. (It rarely does.) Jameel McCline stopped Grant in the first round. When Atlas later obtained for Grant a fight on ESPN, they had him spar 1970s journeyman and part-time ESPN analyst Scott LeDoux. LeDoux feinted a jab to Grant's body. Grant, showing how little he had developed as a fighter, dropped his hands, and LeDoux, who was in his 50s, demonstrated how easily he could have caught Grant with a left hook.

In June 2003, Dominick Guinn stopped Grant in the seventh round in Atlantic City, signaling the end of Grant's days as a serious heavyweight. Atlas and Grant subsequently split. So too did Grant and Hamilton. Jim Thomas, the Atlanta-based attorney who advised Holyfield throughout Holyfield's championship years, had been co-managing Grant along with Hamilton by that time and elected to stay on when Hamilton left. Grant generally is loath to speak of that period, though he allows that he believes he could have used a few more fights before facing Lewis.

"Was I rushed? Only with the Lewis fight," Grant said in early September. "I was rushed on that Lewis deal. He had everything. He was a smart, very smart champion."

Not surprisingly, Hamilton and Grant disagree on this point. Hamilton told *The Ring,* "Michael knew all of his options. He wanted Lewis. He could have lost to John Ruiz for a lot less money and then there would have been no Lewis fight. He certainly wasn't rushed. He was never a person who wasn't going to stand up and say what he felt about anything. If I believed that him fighting another three fights after the Golota fight would have helped him beat Lewis, I would be the first to say it."

It's 10 years since the Lewis fight, and Grant is 38 years old. He's softer around the middle than he was then, as we all are, and the beard is gone. He's still an Adonis. He's had eight fights in the seven years since Guinn wrecked him at Boardwalk Hall, winning all of them. But the victories were all but empty; the opposition was soft. He's not the heir apparent anymore, but, as he prepared to meet Adamek, it must have felt like old times. Boxing writers scrambled to get close to him, to hear and record what he had to say. Others made repeated calls to his cell phone, and, if he didn't know them or feel like calling them back, he didn't.

His trainer for the last four fights, Eddie Mustafa Muhammad, told anyone willing to listen that Main Events made a big mistake putting Adamek in with his guy. Grant, ever true to form, was more philosophical than pugnacious.

"I didn't know I'd still be boxing 10 years later," he said before the Adamek fight. "I thought by this time I'd have some belts and been retired at an early age.

"It was good for me to go through what I went through in this whole span. It brought experience, patience, things that were probably missing in my arsenal. Now these years have accumulated and those things are now part of me—patience and experience. I am happy, and happy I am still here in one piece."

In the last days before the fight, Grant could be seen on the roof of The Best Western Hotel across from The Prudential Center, reading the Bible or silently shadow boxing. He had to know, of course, that in towns all around him armies of Adamek fans were gathering to cheer his defeat. And it didn't matter to them if it was easy or not, bloody or not, and, in truth, the more violent it was the better.

When the night arrived, the arena filled slowly. The preliminaries were witnessed by mainly empty seats, but, as the main event drew near, more and more red shirts filled in the gaps until a crowd of 10,972 was on hand. Hordes of young Polish men, rowdy and happy with beers and smiles and chunky girlfriends, some with funny hats that matched their shirts, sang and clapped one another on the back and chanted "Goral! Goral!" even before Adamek was visible.

Then they were in the ring, Grant forcing a scowl and Adamek bouncing in and out while the crowd roared and sang and waved their signs and hats. It is one of the many counterintuitive things in boxing that a shorter man in the fight must make himself shorter still to be effective, and this is what Adamek struggled to do throughout. It was a struggle because it is not in his nature to get low and box and move. As a cruiserweight, he was a predator, but, against heavyweights, and especially against Grant, he had to punch and get out of range, punch and get out of range.

It was Grant's job to either keep Adamek outside, where only Grant's punches could score, or to catch Adamek coming in. Yet over and over, Adamek jumped in with the same combination—jab, right-hand to the body, left-hook to the head—and time again, from the early through the middle rounds, it landed. And you wondered how Grant, in his 50th professional fight, could not see it coming.

Meanwhile, Grant jabbed and looked for ways to land the right hand. And waited. And plodded. And looked. And scowled. And got outworked. Finally, at the end of the sixth round, he caught Adamek coming in with the right he had been waiting the entire fight to land and it buckled Adamek. But the bell rang before Grant could press his advantage. As he turned toward his corner, Muhammad was already climbing through the ropes, pointing wildly at Adamek, his eyes wide with excitement and hope that this sudden success would inspire Grant to open up. It had already been an exasperating night for Muhammad trying to convince Grant to throw punches. At one point, he asked Grant why he was posing like he thought he was on the cover of *Cosmopolitan* magazine.

Now, in the corner, Muhammad hollered at Grant. He cursed. He pleaded. It was useless. He couldn't make Grant a fighter, not in a corner in the middle of a fight. Not ever. It was too late for that. And the athlete that Grant always has been was not going to beat Adamek, who is *all* fighter. Fighting is *in* Adamek. It is not in Grant, and all the cajoling in the world wasn't going to put it there. Muhammad could not make Grant believe in himself. It wasn't going to happen, but he tried.

"It was very, very frustrating," Muhammad told me. "It took a lot out of me. I said, 'Michael, if you don't want to do it for yourself, do it for your family.' He just gave me a blank stare. It's a shame. You spend eight, nine weeks with a guy, and you're telling him what to expect and what to look for, then when it happens, he falls into another gear. He doesn't want to put out. He didn't execute. Adamek was there for the taking. He was there. Michael just didn't execute."

Amateur psychologists will venture where Muhammad won't: Grant didn't execute because he didn't believe he could, because he believed that if he tried he would fail, and not trying your hardest and saying you'll do better next time is infinitely easier in the present than believing in yourself and taking the gamble. If you gamble and lose, there is no excuse. There is no "I'll do better next time." When you lay it all out and lose, there is nowhere to hide the failure.

This doesn't make Grant a loser. It makes him a man who does not have in him what makes very good fighters who they are, even if he has it on the outside.

Grant had a moment or two down the stretch that almost quieted the crowd, and, in the 12th, he raged after Adamek like a man suddenly energized. But it was too late, and he knew it. The judges scored the bout for Adamek 118-110 (twice) and 117-111. *The Ring* scored it 117-112 for Adamek.

Two weeks afterward, Grant allowed that he was concerned about having enough gas in the tank by the late rounds and paced himself accordingly. He regretted it. "I should have went and just put it out there," he said. "I was worried about later on, and I shouldn't have did (*sic*) that. Every day since the night of the fight, I've been down on myself. I learned from it. And I won't ever accept it again. Next time I'm bringin' it."

Grant is well past the time when talking like a fighter will make him one. We all are permitted the fantasy that one day soon we will wake up and be as we imagine and hope ourselves to be, but prizefighters, like undiscovered rock stars, do not find the secret in middle age. And "next times" rarely work out.

We are who we are.

Meanwhile, reviews of Adamek's performance were mixed. Few judged him capable of staying with either of the Klitschkos, and by the time he and Grant returned to their lives and tended to their bruises and scrapes, the billboards in Jersey were already advertising the next big thing. It's the way of the world.

RIGHT PLACE, RIGHT TIME, RIGHT MAN

HOW GLEN JOHNSON RUINED ROY'S RETURN

ORIGINALLY PUBLISHED IN *THE RING*, FEBRUARY 2005

IT ALMOST WAS FITTING that it worked out the way it did for Roy Jones. Not that he was knocked unconscious the way he was, because whether or not you like him, it's always at least a little unsettling, or should be, to see a fighter in that condition – even one as difficult to like at times as Jones always has been.

What was fitting was that the fighter who put him in that state, Glen Johnson, is Jones' polar opposite – if not necessarily as a man, because we never really got to know Jones the man, then certainly as a prizefighter and performer. The point is driven home further by the recognition that Johnson didn't just beat Jones, didn't just knock him cold with a single punch; he brought to a striking end the Roy Jones era.

It's over. After more than a decade of more or less uninterrupted championship dominance, after obtaining titles in four weight classes, after years and years of general recognition as the best practitioner on the globe, Jones is done. Make no mistake; despite his typically self-indulgent, mysterious, and non-committal declarations to the contrary a week after the fight,

Jones is through as a top fighter and probably as a fighter altogether.

The bloom is well off the rose, and the fitting part is that Johnson, a man of sincere modesty and one who never would be caught referring to himself in the third person, a guy who not too long ago lost four straight fights, did it to a man who, until this bout, probably hadn't lost four straight rounds.

The Jones era was ended by a fighter who couldn't get a break when he should have, who never took for granted what he could do in the ring, and, most critically, did not walk away when lesser men surely would have. The bad decisions alone that Johnson has suffered would have forced most out of the gym and into the comfortable banality that the rest of us endure. Not Johnson.

"I always believed in myself," Johnson, 41-9-2 (28), told *The Ring*. "That I was getting ripped off didn't mean that I didn't have the talent or skill; it meant that I was getting ripped off. I spent so much time and effort in this that I cannot just walk away from it. I'm not the kind of person that can live a street life, so I would have to learn another profession. I have responsibilities that I have to take care of. I have kids and all of the bills that come along with trying to live."

Jones never talked that way. Even before the titles, even before the multimillion-dollar HBO contracts, before his ego exploded and he created a blanket of smug isolation between himself and the fight media. That it ended with a loss to Johnson, who said after the fight that he's not the best fighter in the world, merely one who is willing to fight the best fighters in the world, is the nicest kind of symmetry.

You could argue, and some will, that it was Antonio Tarver—who has a lot more in common with Jones, as a performer, than Johnson does—who did it really, and not Johnson. After all, it was Tarver who pushed Jones seemingly to within a combination or two of losing their first match in November 2003. And it was Tarver who was the first to lay out Jones with a single shot, when he did it in their rematch in May '04. But the question must be asked: Who among us wouldn't have given Jones an excellent chance of winning in the rubber match? Who among us was ready to concede with certainty that it wasn't a lucky punch, or that Tarver's odd assortment of physical blessings hadn't conspired to accomplish what no other fighter would or could? And most importantly, who among us now would give Jones a chance in a third match with Tarver, after seeing what Johnson did? That's the difference. Tarver began the debate; it was his own misfortune that it was Johnson, and not he, who finished it.

The outcome was no great surprise to Johnson, nor was the fact that Jones, 49-3 (38), fought the way that he did. "He was exactly what I thought he would be," Johnson said. "He got off his shots. He worked to get outside so he could get his shots off, but I kept close to him and kept up the pressure. That took him off his game. I needed to go out right away and set an example and let him know that this was the kind of fight it was going to be. I had to make it known loud and clear right away."

Johnson did that, rushing Jones in the first and staying close to him until knocking him cold with an overhand right in the ninth. His activity and work rate had him in the lead on all judges' cards at the end, while Jones appeared passive, even by his standards.

"That's the way he always fights," said Johnson. "The reason he was not throwing a lot of punches was because I wasn't letting him. He was not comfortable. If I was on the outside, he would have been comfortable and peppering me with combinations. But because I was so close to him, I was shutting him down."

It was and remains a remarkable level of confidence expressed by Johnson, considering where he's been. Regardless of whether Jones had been stopped by Tarver in his previous fight, Johnson was an underdog and he deserved to be. This is a fighter who lost, in consecutive outings, to Sven Ottke, Syd Vanderpool, Silvio Branco, and Omar Sheika. As recently as 2002 and 2003, he dropped decisions to Derrick Harmon and Julio Gonzalez. The pattern isn't recent; after getting stopped by Bernard Hopkins in July 1997, he lost consecutively to Merqui Sosa and Joseph Kiwanuka.

Clearly, not all of Johnson's hardships were borne of scorecards ill-completed and nefarious goings on. There just seemed never to be very much special about him, and it was not until his two battles with

Clinton Woods—who was wholly unknown before Jones took him apart two years ago—that Johnson's skills and gumption were taken seriously. It is worth considering that he was getting things done that no one was noticing.

"Johnson's talent is being consistent and steady," said noted trainer and ESPN2 *Friday Night Fights* commentator Teddy Atlas. "His talent isn't the kind that we look at a lot these days because we notice things that are very obvious—things like speed and athleticism and power—but there are other kinds of talent that aren't so noticeable, like being consistent and steady, and that's the kind of talent Johnson has."

That particular talent was evident throughout Johnson's big night, particularly in the fifth round. That was when he startled Jones with a right hand high on the head while Jones was trapped in a corner. And Jones, in one of the more impassioned moments of his career, let loose with a blistering combination of blows that Johnson took squarely. Earlier in his career, Jones threw such combinations frequently. Lately, he's only thrown them only when desperate, as he was in the last two rounds of the first Tarver fight. But they aren't as effective as they used to be, and Johnson, well, he might as well have been shooing fruit flies from his face.

"He never hurt me," Johnson said. "You know going into the ring that you're going to get hit. That's why we do our sit-ups and the roadwork we do so we can withstand the hard times that come during the fight."

Indeed, Johnson's ability to withstand the hard times during a fight had been proven over the course of his career -- not only during the losses, but during the harder wins. And it may be that quality rather than just Jones's erosion that precipitated the upset. The criticism that Jones' grit never was really proved, that he never really had to display mettle in the way that less gifted fighters must almost from the outset, was valid. But it's a tricky question:

Would you rather be ordinarily talented and as a result struggle through a hard business, or be supremely talented and never have to show the grit? Should a fighter be thankful for ability that overwhelms average competition, or wish for tests that force him to stretch?

"When we see so much flash and ability, sometimes we don't see the guy with a critical eye the way we should, and we just say, 'That's extraordinary,'" offered Atlas. "But the competition for Jones was pretty shallow. We were having so much fun looking at this guy with so much ability, but the great fighters always got tested, and Roy never got tested."

Conventional thinking says that Jones is getting hit and stopped now because, at 35 years old (the same age as Johnson, by the way), he no longer has the speed and sense of anticipation and reflexes that allowed him to get away with the mechanical and fundamental mistakes he's made throughout his career. It's true; one only has to look at the career of Muhammad Ali to see that unless you get the basics down, you're going to get hit a lot as you age, regardless of the kind of magic your genes allowed when you were 24. Atlas says it's that and more.

"It's also the intimidation factor. The opportunities to land the right over Roy's left, or to hit him with shots because of the mistakes he's always made were there before, just not as much. But there weren't guys around who were professional enough to just throw the punch. Jones' speed and ability influenced those guys. They got intimidated, and when you're intimidated, you hesitate before you throw the punch and then the chance isn't there anymore. They weren't professional enough. That was always there and ready to be a Pandora's Box for Roy."

Atlas attributes about 20 percent of Jones' seemingly sudden demise to his age, some percentage higher than that to the quality of opposition — Tarver and Johnson being, in Atlas's opinion, better than most guys Jones has faced — and a certain percentage to the fact that "sooner or later it had to happen that someone was going to capitalize on Roy's mistakes. It was a matter of time."

Johnson was the one to do it. Whether the win will translate, most preferably, into a big fight with Tarver, remains to be seen. Maybe it doesn't. Or maybe it does and his steadiness isn't enough to overcome

Tarver's greater talent, and he reverts to the guy who lost all those fights.

You get the sense it won't diminish Johnson's standing much, even if that's how it turns out. He ended an era, and that's something you can take with you.

Epilogue: Johnson split a pair of close bouts with Tarver and fought most of the top light heavyweights and super middleweights of the era over the next 10 years. He retired in 2015 with a record of 54-21-2 (37).

IBEABUCHI SHOOTS DOWN BYRD

IS IKE THE SECOND COMING OF MIKE?

ORIGINALLY PUBLISHED IN *KO*, AUGUST 1999

YOU COULD HEAR the cash registers singing their special song the minute Chris Byrd hit the mat. Throughout the alternative reality we call the fight game, the tough talk stopped mid-mumble, half-smoked cigarettes dropped from the mouths of thieves and mere scoundrels, and a lot of butts were lifted up all at once out of a lot of metal folding chairs. Old, wise fight guys and some young, dumb ones, too, knew what it meant when Byrd crashed from Ike Ibeabuchi's left uppercut bomb and was stopped moments later. It meant big money, and if they hadn't said it before, they were saying it now: *We Like Ike.*

They said it because with that one meaty punch (forget the right that followed it and the others that compelled a terrified official to call it off with a second left in the fifth round), Ibeabuchi registered his success with dollar signs -- great, big green ones, the kind that light up the eyes of promoters, television suits, and young women of ill intent. It was also the kind of punch that sent high-minded heavyweights back into the gym for some extra schooling, and to hell with that community college application they were holding onto just in case.

Because with some luck, maybe they could find a big punch, too, and sometimes -- not here, but sometimes -- a big punch is all that stands between an ordinary fighter and a fighter who can afford to have a glove-shaped swimming pool installed in his living room. A big, power-punching heavyweight like Ibeabuchi means huge money, more than a sweet scientist like Byrd could command in a hundred years.

But there is always a downside, even for hulking heavyweights who are on the precipice of fame and unlimited riches. For even as Ibeabuchi celebrated in the ring that served as the podium for his grand re-entrance into big-time heavyweight boxing, even as one of the game's most powerful men, HBO executive Lou DiBella, was telling ringsiders that Ibeabuchi reminded him of a young Sonny Liston (maybe DiBella was more right than he knows), there was sadness in the big Nigerian's eyes. He posed for the cameras like a heavyweight prince is supposed to, and smiled and politely answered the questions he would be asked several times over. He was surrounded by dozens of people, most of them laughing, pounding his gargantuan back, strutting, the way a lot of fight guys do these days. But he was alone.

Gerry Cooney, who in another lifetime was a big heavyweight also regarded as a banger of substantial potential, once told me that the best part of boxing was the time immediately after a victory when everyone is congratulating you and all you have to do is smile, say thanks, and lap up the praise. It's a small window that closes when you shut your eyes that night and remember that if you don't win again next time, everything you've done up to that point is shot to hell. But Ibeabuchi doesn't even allow himself that window, at least going by the countenance he wore in the ring. And based on the stories we've heard, that's no great surprise.

You know by now the tale that began two months after Ibeabuchi jumped out of promoter Cedric Kushner's god-awful "Heavyweight Explosion" shows and into David Tua's face in June 1997. He out-willed Tua in a wonderful brawl that night, and we should've known then, when we saw him soak up Tua's best hooks and smile, that he was a troubled man. What sane person could do such a thing?

Anyway, then came Ibeabuchi's arrest in August for charges of kidnapping and attempted murder. To summarize: When his girlfriend left him, the fighter grabbed the woman's young son, fled with him in a speeding car, and rammed into a freeway overpass at 65 miles per hour. Some said he was trying to kill himself, some said he was trying to hurt the boy. Either way, he failed at the former, but succeeded at the latter, and was briefly jailed. He discovered then that it helps to have friends and promoters with deep pockets and Rolodexes full of good attorneys because people work a whole lifetime to find a heavyweight who can fight like Ibeabuchi and so will go to fantastic lengths to keep him earning.

Still, twice he violated bail restrictions, was re-jailed, diagnosed with, at least, manic depression, and disappeared from boxing for a full year. If the story had ended there, we might be inclined to think that Ibeabuchi had been driven temporarily insane by a woman—Lord knows he wouldn't have been the first—but there was still the Tua fight as evidence of something deeper, then the incident that occurred while in training for the Byrd fight. To wit:

While sparring with cruiserweight Ezra Sellers, Ibeabuchi suffered a small cut on his eyelid. After the session ended and Sellers had his hand wraps removed, he went over to Ibeabuchi to apologize for cutting him. Ibeabuchi saw that Sellers was wearing a ring, which Sellers had just put on, and accused him and assistant trainer Jay Wilson of conspiring against him. He attacked the two of them, kicking and wrestling both to the ground. Reportedly, both Sellers and Wilson filed criminal complaints against Ibeabuchi, but later dropped them.

Some would call this a minor incident, no different from a pair of football teammates getting it on during a scrimmage under a sweltering August sun. Others detect a pattern. Ibeabuchi's trainer, Curtis Cokes, the fine welterweight champion of the 1960s, broke up the fight that day.

"They got into a little altercation in the gym," Cokes told me. "It wasn't really anything. It happens all the time when guys are in the heat of battle and they get into a shoving match. Everyone was in the gym the next day.

"Everybody blew it out of proportion, but it wasn't that big of a deal. I've seen fighters where you have to get in the ring and break it up after the bell has sounded. They're just being competitive and fighting," Cokes said. "Heck, I like to see a guy with a little fire in him in the gym. That makes me know that he's really trying to do his job. I see it all the time." Cokes' view is corroborated by Wilson, who, despite the incident, worked Ibeabuchi's corner for the Byrd fight.

"Is he difficult [to work with]? At times, he is," Wilson told me. "But this was the same thing that happens in all gyms." Wilson didn't offer if he'd ever been attacked by a fighter before, but one has to suspect that if fighters assaulting trainers were as common as he and Cokes would have you believe, there would be a lot fewer trainers around.

Whatever the case, neither the cut nor the incident helped Byrd once Ibeabuchi, 20-0 (15), started catching him with lead rights in the third round. For the first two rounds, Byrd, 26-1 (14), did what he does best, slipping and dodging Ibeabuchi's bigger blows and looking for all the world like a 208-pound Pernell Whitaker. But "The President" enjoys hand speed that no fighter of his dimensions should be allowed to employ, and when he trapped Byrd on the ropes, where Byrd can hide without detection from slower foes, Ibeabuchi teed off, landing the uppercut heard 'round the boxing world. The significance of the victory cannot be overstated.

In case you haven't noticed, the heavyweight division is heating up, and we're not talking about Lennox Lewis and Evander Holyfield preparing to waltz to another dreary tune that, with any luck, will result, officially, in an undisputed champion. We're talking about Tua and Hasim Rahman, who surprised us by meeting once and who we hope will meet again; we're talking about Lou Savarese gutting it out against Mount Whitaker, and then maybe against Michael Grant in June; about Kirk Johnson finally taking a small step up with a hard-fought victory over Al Cole. The young guns are fighting one another. Ibeabuchi's timing could not have been better.

"I think he is in a very enviable position," said television commentator and longtime boxing reporter Dave Bontempo. "Ike can develop nicely but quietly. The pressure is low. He's not at that point where he can't have a bad showing. Ike's in a great spot; he's in a stalking position. He has to be taken seriously, but he doesn't have the pressure of the very top guys."

That's if he can control whatever demons he has that have plagued him up to this point. In the weeks before the Byrd fight, rumors circulated that Kushner, wanting to ensure that nothing would prevent Ibeabuchi from meeting Byrd, hired a keeper to shadow his fighter wherever he went and keep him out of trouble.

"It wasn't to keep him out of trouble," Kushner said recently. "Some of us [promoters] have what we affectionately call a 'watchdog,' someone to make sure the fighter gets whatever he needs and gets taken care of and to make sure he gets on the right plane. I do that with all of my fighters -- there's always someone I have direct contact with in the camp."

Kushner addresses with equal diplomacy Ibeabuchi's growing reputation as a "difficult" fighter.

"The pressure of training has a lot to do with how one acts," he said. "The sacrifices are supreme and very significant. It's almost unnatural what one has to do for 60 to 75 days until a bout. If one has to act a little differently during that time, that's understandable."

Cokes also denies any major problems with the fighter.

"All the sportswriters seem to like to write about guys who have a bad reputation outside the ring. Ike's got some problems outside the ring, but no more or less than anyone else. It's just written up more about Ike because he's a Nigerian and really doesn't understand some of the rules and regulations we have in the States. He's no better or worse than any other guys."

The evidence suggests something to the contrary and makes us wonder what it is about heavyweights—some marvelously gifted, some less so—that makes them so susceptible to what we will call emotional instability. Recent examples are many: Andrew Golota, who twice fouled out against Riddick Bowe in fights he was clearly winning, and, if that wasn't enough, showed up for his title fight with Lewis two hours late and hopped up on painkillers; Oliver McCall, who is best-known for his mid-fight meltdown against Lewis, but who on other occasions too entered the ring close to tears.

Then there was Bowe, who didn't have enough self-control to keep from slugging an unsuspecting Larry Donald at a press conference, joined and then quit the Marines, and then reportedly tried to kidnap his family; and, of course, Mike Tyson, who recently throttled and kicked in the groin a pair of middle-aged men who made the horrid error of conferring with the fighter's wife roadside following a harmless fender bender.

Perhaps Cokes is right and we've blown Ibeabuchi's struggles out of proportion. Maybe he's no less stable than anyone else, but because he's one of the best young prospects in the game, he's under the microscope. Maybe none of it has any bearing on what he can do in the ring, that he is exactly what he appears to be. And if that's the case, God help the rest of the world's heavyweights.

Epilogue: Ibeabuchi was arrested in July 1999 and sentenced to prison for a string of charges related to sexual assaults. He was released in 2020 and in 2025, at 52 years old, he fought in Lagos, Nigeria, winning in three rounds.

BACK FROM THE BRINK

THE BOXERS THAT COLD-COCKED COCAINE

ORIGINALLY PUBLISHED IN *KO*, MAY 1998

PRIZEFIGHTING IS a hard business for hard men (and sometimes women). Those who enter its cold arena are drawn to it not so much by a simple thirst for competition, for surely the world is full of less severe contests that don't require the will and courage of fighters. They are drawn to it by an unrelenting desperation in their hearts, a burning need, sometimes, to right some unidentifiable wrong committed long ago, without their consent.

They most often enter the arena from the ranks of society's lost masses, from the destitute cities and destitute worlds that soil the landscape of existence. The upper-middle-class roots of Ray Leonard, Marco Antonio Barrera, and Muhammad Ali, among others, notwithstanding, the best fighters are spawned from poverty and destitution. They know well the searing cries of unwilling violence and the heartache of grinding poverty. It makes them better in the ring, for he who has little to live for has nothing to fear. Despair defines the souls of the world's best fighters.

It is no coincidence, then, that many of these powerful, desperate men who are driven to bare their essence in a prize ring often find themselves mired and powerless in the throes of drug addiction, where a crack pipe or a coffee table adorned with a string of powdery white lines promises sweet escape, a reward for their dark persistence. Indeed, some of the very characteristics that make for a great fighter—desperation, obsession, anger—serve the addict in good stead.

The list is long of fighters who have watched impotently from behind a blanket of fog as their careers vanished. The most recent notable is Aaron Pryor, who went from star to homeless junkie in what seemed like the bat of an eye. But lesser fighters have suffered as well. Little Mike Ayala was high on heroin when Danny "Little Red" Lopez stopped him back in 1979. His brother, Tony, a superstar in the making, couldn't stay away from the booze and it ruined him.

The careers of Tyrell Biggs, Johnny Bumphus, Rocky Lockridge, Pinklon Thomas, Michael Dokes, and a ton of other guys you've never heard of and might have had they not become addicts, were cut short by their compulsions.

Tommy Morrison's well-publicized bouts with alcohol abuse continue now, in his retirement. Bert Cooper aged decades in a few short years, and Oliver McCall has lost millions. Even Peter McNeeley, who exists just barely on the fringes of fistic celebrity, appeared in the headlines recently when he publicly grieved the drug-related death of comedian Chris Farley, whom he had befriended while the two endured a course of drug rehab together.

Few activities are as physically and emotionally demanding as a prizefight, and there is only so much strength a man can muster when he is torn between the insanity of the ring and the insanity of addiction. History mandates that the two cannot co-exist, at least not for very long. Existence in one world precludes existence in the other, and it is the rarest of men who can successfully inhabit both until finally, painfully, the choice is made to fight—and to live. It is rarer still that, having made that decision, the fighter can recapture that which he was before the need to escape overwhelmed him. But for four fighters -- Vince Phillips, Kennedy McKinney, Johnny Tapia, and, in a different way, William Guthrie, the road has opened, the brink beaten back, the demons defeated.

For Phillips, the problems started back when he was in the Army, where, as he put it, "Me and Kennedy [McKinney] were partners, runnin' buddies." He had always smoked marijuana back home in Pensacola, Florida, but cocaine became the drug of choice by the time he left the military at 24. Soon after, he and McKinney would disappear for long stretches at a time, while those around them—promoters, managers, fight game stewards who know the rules of the co-existent worlds—could see Phillips wasting himself and tried to help. It did not work, though Phillips knew himself what was happening.

"Whenever I'd get high, I'd hear a voice saying, 'Maybe this ain't for me.' But I would not listen. I just kept getting high. When Kennedy won the title [in December '92], I started celebrating and didn't stop until January '93."

The low point came when Phillips was suspended by the Nevada State Athletic Commission after testing positive for marijuana following a first-round knockout of Julio Flores. He had been on the verge of a match with Charles Murray for the title vacated by Pernell Whitaker. Now the shot was gone.

Over the next couple years, Phillips fought the good fight, clean for a while, then high, clean, then high. Then it happened. "I went on a cocaine binge for 90 days," he said. "Then I heard a voice say, 'Come on home.' And I listened. I've been sober now since May 16, 1993."

Ask him if the losses he's suffered in the ring since, losses to Anthony Jones, Ike Quartey, and Romallis Ellis, ever made him falter, ever made him seek consolation in the sweet scent of escape, and he doesn't hesitate.

"Jones was my first loss, and I was six months clean. I could have said, 'What's the use? I'm going to get high.' But because I did not, things just kept getting better. God tests you to see if you're strong enough. That was the first pitch. Ball one. The loss to Quartey was the second pitch, and I didn't get high that time, either. Ball two. Then came the Ellis fight. Ball three. Then God gave me ball four, against [Kostya] Tszyu, and I hit it out of the park."

Phillips' upset knockout win over Tszyu netted him the title most think he would have won four years earlier, had he only listened to the voices. These days, Phillips, 38-3 (26), stays clean by attending Cocaine Anonymous and Narcotics Anonymous meetings, whether he's home in Florida or training in Las Vegas.

That's not always enough, however.

"I have a sponsor named Michael Howard," Phillips said. "When things get bad, I call him. We get a cup of coffee together and talk. Now, instead of going out, I reach out." He credits both his boxing family—that includes his agent Akbar Muhammad, manager Bill Miller, and trainers Kenny Adams and Terry Stotts, as well as his real family—fiancée Yvette, and children Vince Jr., 11, Laquan, 7, and Amanda, 6, as "the people who keep me together." He also seeks help from one more avenue. "Every morning, I get up and give my will to God and ask Him to help me stay sober today."

If Phillips' story is one of ultimate triumph after a downward spiral, then McKinney's is one of a rollercoaster ride with valleys and peaks in equal numbers. McKinney was thought by most to be used up going into his bout in December with pound-for-pound entrant Junior Jones. Most thought McKinney, 33-3-1 (19), would succumb to Jones's superior firepower. Instead, "King" displayed some fireworks of his own, stopping Jones in the fourth round. While the win netted him only the low-rent WBO title, it opened the doors for some big-money fights down the road and gave his career new life. The victory was a long way from McKinney's days of hanging with Phillips, when the two would disappear to crack houses and Las Vegas nightclubs to get their fill of the ride they thought would never end. It almost did end when McKinney checked himself into a drug treatment center in April 1989, but he relapsed shortly after being released.

Another stay a short time later brought similar results. Finally, he tested positive for cocaine after struggling to a split-decision win over trial-horse Joe Martinez, and the Nevada State Athletic Commission suspended him for six months.

McKinney put the time off to good use, entering the Methodist Outreach Center in Tennessee. He walked out 90 days later and has been clean since. For McKinney, making good on his decision to come clean required inspiration. It came from what he calls "a good, strong family base. My family really helped me overcome it. To see my mother with tears in her eyes, telling me not to throw away the God-given gifts I have ... My family was so important. They helped me every day. Also, when I had my second son, I realized I never wanted to have other kids come up to him in school or something and say, 'Your dad's a crackhead.'"

McKinney has a formula for staying clean. While not unique, it is effective. "I go to meetings twice a week and pray, pray, pray. I pray every night and ask God to relieve me of any urges that come my way."

Three years after kicking the habit, McKinney did indeed recapture all that had been lost in those dens of hopelessness, stopping Welcome Ncita in 11 rounds to win the IBF junior featherweight title. After five successful defenses, he lost the belt to Vuyani Bungu, and in his next significant bout was stopped by Barrera in a magnificent war of attrition and valor. It was the kind of fight, and the kind of performance, even in defeat, that spoke volumes about McKinney, about the depth of his heart and his resolve. Still, it was a loss and some wondered if it would signal a relapse. According to Charles Carpenter, McKinney's manager, it did not.

"Anyone who knows an addict or has an addict in his family knows that it's a day-by-day process," Carpenter told me. "Any event, sad or happy, can trigger a relapse. But Kennedy realized he did not want to be a failure. He realized that if he didn't grasp the opportunities he had, he could end up being a bum and he didn't want to become that."

Carpenter signed on as McKinney's manager a year ago after serving as his legal adviser for four years. He is confident that McKinney has licked for good the ghosts that haunted him in the past. "He's really a good family man now," said Carpenter. "He really cares for his wife and his two boys, and that helps him stay focused. Our strategy with Kennedy has been to keep him busy. After the loss to

Bungu [in their April '97 rematch], we had him back in a fight in 30 days. He does his best when he's in training or looking forward to a fight. His trouble always came between fights. When he didn't have a fight coming up, he had a lot of time to kill, and didn't handle it real well."

Carpenter and negotiator Murad Muhammad are working on a deal with Frank Warren to match McKinney with Naseem Hamed in the spring. The outcome, be it peak or valley, shouldn't matter. McKinney's long rollercoaster ride has already brought him back from hell.

Tapia, the IBF junior bantamweight champion, knows too of the depths from which McKinney and Phillips have risen, for he is a kindred spirit. He is also, in a sport filled with pathos and emotion, the game's quintessential tortured soul. We know too well the story of Tapia's childhood, which came to an early end with the brutal rape and murder of his mother. Though he claims to have little recollection of the time, its remnants are etched in his face: in the lines around his mouth, in the permanent sorrow in his eyes. We see every bit of his agony in those eyes, and the only time we don't is when he's embroiled in combat.

Only in the ring is Tapia distracted enough to fully block out the memories, for in that place, the urgency of the moment affords him no time to think. The ring is no place for melancholy, and so it is with a sense of great irony that one comes to the realization that Tapia knows no other true sanctuary, yet for a time, he sought its comforts in no great way.

Back in 1991, Tapia was the hottest thing in the junior bantamweight division, with a 22-0 record and a title fight calling in the near future. But the lure of cocaine was greater than his need to be in the ring, and the fighter tested positive for the drug three times over the course of a year. He was suspended for 3½ years by the New Mexico Athletic Commission as a result. Tapia spent those years away from the comfort of life inside the ropes, the only place in which he ever felt at home. He landed in jail more than once, and during one 65-day stint, cleansed himself of the drugs that had taken his career.

He prayed for another chance upon his release, and got it after passing repeated urinalyses and getting his license restored. Despite occasional run-ins with the law, he has been clean since December '93.

When one surveys the recent history of the sport's most noteworthy comebacks -- by George Foreman, Evander Holyfield, Vinny Pazienza, and others -- the one forged by Tapia, 42-0-2 (24), must rank among the most impressive. He rates among the world's best pound-for-pound fighters, and, in besting Danny Romero in last summer's superfight, elevated himself higher than many thought he would ever get. He still wears the face of the doomed, but for now, the only place he gets high is at home in the ring.

Current IBF light heavyweight titlist Guthrie doesn't share the stories of Phillips, McKinney, and Tapia, not exactly. If he spent weeks and months at a time lost in a drug-induced fog, he's not saying. He is willing to say that he toiled in the drug world as much as any of them, but his role was different. Drugs were his business rather than his passion, and he learned early on that that vocation carried more to gain, and more to lose, than even the business of boxing.

Never mind that Guthrie was an accomplished amateur who won the National Golden Gloves title in 1985. Forget that even as he was making his mark as a young, hot pro that he was still running the con, and was 8-0 before the cops caught up with him and changed his life.

Guthrie was reared in the desperate streets of St. Louis and lived in the Pruitt-Igoe Housing Development, an area notorious for drug trafficking. He took to dealing as readily as he did boxing, and by the time he was sent away for a three-year stretch to a federal penitentiary in Marion, Illinois, he had amassed greater wealth than most fighters will ever see. His riches came, however, with a heavy price.

"I dealt with death every day," said Guthrie. "There were lots of low points. I would lose a friend, lose a friend, lose a friend. Every day, someone would get killed, guys that I knew. Death was everywhere."

It was during his three years in prison that Guthrie grappled with the larger questions of life and decided where his would take him. "I was sitting in prison and thinking, 'Was this what I wanted for my life? To be in prison? To die?' That was an extreme low for me, but if I had the chance, I wouldn't change it unless I could also change the path that took me there. It was a blessing that changed my life altogether. It gave me the chance to get control over my life. In order for me to move forward, I needed to study my past so I could deal with my present, and plan for my future. It gave me this reality: I was dead, but I still had life. I really got a chance to understand life, and freedom, and what friendship and death really mean."

Guthrie, 24-0 (21), got out of prison in '93 and never looked back, winning the vacant IBF title last July with a third-round kayo of Darrin Allen. These days he deals in peace and purpose when he's not battling other light heavyweights.

"There is another purpose for me in life," he said. "Until I find out what it is, I'll continue to do the right things for my family, and if I can help other children along the way, I will. I've had close calls with death, and I think all the time about why I was spared. I think about it every day."

For Phillips, McKinney, Tapia, and Guthrie, the biggest fights they have won't be on pay-per-view. They are the ones they'll fight with themselves. One day at a time.

CAN CHAVEZ JR. LIVE UP
TO HIS FATHER'S LEGACY?

ORIGINALLY PUBLISHED IN *THE RING*, OCTOBER 2010

THE BIGGEST SURPRISE TO come out of Julio Cesar Chavez Jr.'s win over John Duddy in June should not have been how much better Chavez allegedly was compared to previous performances. Whether he actually is better now than before is a matter of conjecture to be explored later.

No, the real surprise was that even by night's end, Duddy's famously delicate and handsome face, despite the steady pounding it received, wasn't pumping scarlet plasma into the San Antonio night like so much crude oil into the Gulf of Mexico.

This is not to say that Junior isn't a prodigious enough puncher to bloody up Duddy like others have, or that somehow Duddy, too, was better than he'd been before. Skin can be temperamental that way, but try telling that to generations of Irish and other fair-skinned, sharp-boned pugs whose fragile capillaries burst apart at the first hint of insult.

Chavez didn't have to cover the canvas in crimson to change the tide of sentiment that was riding against him, most of it held by fight game snobs (see "media") who refused to believe that a kid with no amateur fights needed 40 pro bouts before he was good enough to go in with someone as basic and easy to hit as Duddy.

It wasn't possible either that the progeny of a fighter as great as the peerless Julio Cesar Chavez could be anything more than the gimmick of yet another greedy promoter ringing dry the moldy rag of nostalgia. And really, you couldn't blame the cynics for that. Of all the many sons (and alas, daughters, too) of men who have fought at a high level and have thus been compelled to try to do the same, no more than a small handful can be described in words more favorable than mediocre, timid, or, to put it charitably, insincere.

Indeed, a short while before Chavez beat Duddy by commanding decision in front of a reported 8,172 at the Alamodome, Sal Sanchez II, purportedly the nephew of featherweight great Salvador Sanchez -- with the telltale afro and little else to recommend him -- was more or less manhandled by Tomas Villa over eight rounds. That Sanchez tried hard until the end and didn't crash at the first sign that it would be a rough night marks him as something of a rare bird among his breed.

And certainly Chavez's previous outing, a dismal decision win over club fighter Troy Rowland, after which Chavez was suspended for testing positive for a diuretic, did little to sway those who believed he was the latest in a long line of circus acts created by Bob Arum. Arum, you will recall, is the one who, not terribly long ago, gave us the wonderful twin gifts to boxing that were Mia St. John and Butterbean. So there was precedent. Regardless, this much is true: Chavez met the best fighter of his career and turned in what could be seen as his best performance. That is not insignificant.

"Chavez seemed to me to really make a quantum leap in that fight," veteran broadcaster Barry Tompkins, who called the fight for Top Rank pay-per-view, told *The Ring*.

"Not only in terms of his ring savvy, but he did step up in terms of his opponent. It is perfectly fair to say that Duddy is by far the toughest guy he's fought. I think he came in there with an idea of how he was going to win and took the fight away from Duddy. He showed a lot more maturity than I thought he had."

On that point, opinion would seem unanimous. Saddled with the reputation of being a lazy, half-ass worker in the gym -- a characterization whose accuracy Arum asserted in the weeks leading up to the fight—Chavez, 40-0-1 (30), started against Duddy in an unusual posture for him: moving and jabbing from the outside.

This was no doubt the influence of "Trainer to the Stars" Freddie Roach, who took over Junior's training just four weeks before the fight and promptly said he wanted him to work more from the outside, where he could use his height and reach. Chavez, Roach said, fought too much like his father. (*If only!*)

At any rate, after three rounds of letting Duddy, 29-2 (18), walk into looping right hands and left hooks (as opposed to *walking him into* those punches, and there is a difference, boys and girls), Chavez, 160, let his genes take over and started backing up Duddy, Derry, Ireland, with more hooks and right hands. Each one that landed made a sound that approximates a wet sponge hitting a sidewalk.

As most of us know, and with apologies to Billy Conn, when you've got an Irish fighter going in reverse, your work is almost done. Chavez, Culiacan, Sinaloa, Mexico, was wobbled with a hard right hand in the sixth but otherwise remained in control, even if Duddy, 159, never gave up and, in some rounds, gave almost as good as he got.

"John is the toughest fighter I've faced so far," Chavez, 24, said later. "He kept the pressure on and really pushed me farther than I've been to this point in my career. But I knew coming in that he was going to be challenging, and I was happy to walk away with the victory." The scoring, which was non-controversial by Texas standards, was 116-112, rendered by Glen Crocker, 117-111 from Julie Lederman, and a fairly ridiculous 120-108 from Juergen Langos, who found not a single round to give Duddy. (*The Ring* scored it 117-111).

Another curiosity was the appointment of referee Jon Schorle, whose appearance in a bigger fight could only mean that Lawrence Cole, son of Texas commissioner Dickie Cole, had been kidnapped and was being held by guerillas somewhere on the other side of the world.

The only thing that assured the judges of a meaningful night's work in the end was the admirable obstinacy of Duddy, who, at a still relatively young 31, has taken a volume of punches in the last several years disproportionate to his age. It is regrettable that a fighter as polite and well-mannered and good-looking as he is cursed with such stubborn mediocrity.

"Julio fought a good fight. There was a lot of pressure on him and he performed and answered all the questions I asked of him," Duddy said afterward. "I took him into deep water. And yes, he can swim."

What remains to be seen is if the same will be true when Chavez's competition gets stiffer than Duddy, and let's face it, a fight against anyone in the top 10 at 160 or 154 will be a considerable upgrade. It is worth mentioning only in passing that the WBC laughably made Chavez the recipient of a ranking that puts him in position for a shot at the excellent Sergio Martinez, its top-rated junior middleweight and *The Ring* middleweight world champion. Even Chavez's most ardent supporters wouldn't push for that fight.

"They'll never do that fight in a million years because Julio Cesar Chavez would get killed," said Martinez's promoter, Lou DiBella, his reputation as boxing's greatest practitioner of understatement firmly intact. "We would go to Mexico for that fight. But I have no reason to believe Arum or Chavez's brain trust would consider that fight. That fight's a murder."

DiBella, who in that analysis (and for maybe the first time ever) cannot be accused of exaggeration, said if it were up to him, he would match Chavez with the son of another legend.

"Do you want to put equivalent talent in the ring and have a huge promotion? Why not Chavez and Ronald Hearns with their fathers, who are real legends, in the background?" DiBella said. "Look, Chavez is an attraction, and I don't think he's talented. I don't blame the people of Mexico for embracing him; he's the son of a legend."

That may seem harsh to some, but as well as Chavez handled Duddy, he remains a work in need of serious investment if he is to come close to fulfilling the wishes the Mexican people have for him. Forget about attaining the fistic status his father reached; fighters like Chavez Sr. come along once a generation if we're lucky. Junior, while demonstrating against Duddy a nifty step to the right to set up right hands, is far from a technician or a thinking fighter. For one, he is straight up and down, with very little upper-body movement or bend at the knee. His defense is predicated solely on blocking punches with his gloves. Okay for a clubber of Duddy's ilk, but against any worthwhile 154 or 160-pounder, a little head movement goes a long way.

Roach, whose services Junior maintains he solicited independently, is credited with improving Chavez's conditioning and focus, which Junior's former trainers, uncles Miguel Molleda and Rodolfo Chavez, were apparently loath to do. This is not hard to imagine: The elder Chavez was hardly a Spartan when it came to training and soared to heavenly heights regardless. He was a natural wonder. Junior appears something less, based on Roach's statements early in camp that the kid was having trouble mastering the moves Roach showed him as they worked the pads. But as camp wound down, the trainer seemed satisfied with his new student's progress.

"There were a lot of warning signs about how he is lazy and doesn't want to work, and would he last a week with me?" Roach said. "But he is a great kid, great to work with and is very disciplined. He gets up in the morning and does his roadwork every day, comes in the gym and sparred up to 12 rounds with three sparring partners. Overall, it was a real good experience and we enjoyed each other's company, and it was a pleasure."

Interestingly, Junior contradicted reports that Chavez Sr. was unhappy with the decision to leave his uncles for Roach.

"We had talked about it, and he said that maybe I needed somebody to take me to the next level," Junior said before the fight. "We had thought about some guys and thinking about doing something.

"When I told him about Freddie Roach, he got very excited," Chavez continued. "Freddie is not going to waste his time with a nobody or someone that has no talent. By Freddie taking me, my father felt that Freddie gave me confidence that he would take me to that next level. He is very happy."

In the crush of bodies that flowed into the ring following Junior's win over Duddy, the elder Chavez, looking waxen and puffy in a black tux and mandatory red "Team Chavez" headband, gave and received his share of hugs. But there came a moment not long into the celebration when the old "Lion of Culiacan" stood alone across the ring, watching his son take in the cheers and adulation.

They used to cheer for him that way, of course. He was a king everywhere he went in Mexico. There was no one bigger. The people loved him. No, it was more than that. More than love. They *worshipped* him.

They still did, of course. But it wasn't the same. *He* wasn't the same.

And it was hard to know, as Julio Cesar Chavez watched his son bask in the glory of his first big win, if it made the father proud or hurt him more than any right cross or left hook ever did. Or both.

Either way, if Freddie Roach can do for Junior what he has for Manny Pacquiao, among others, the rejoicing in Mexico will be loud and long-lasting.

Epilogue: Chavez Jr. won a middleweight world title in 2011 and made three defenses before losing on points to Sergio Martinez. He subsequently fought sporadically and poorly over the next several years and never contended again.

THE FIGHTER'S JOURNEY

WHY I FOUGHT

A JOURNEY OF BROKEN
BONES & DISCOVERY

ORIGINALLY PUBLISHED IN *RINGSIDE SEAT*, FALL 2017

"Do you want me to stop it? Billy, look at me! Do you want me to stop it?"

"Huh? No."

It's 1981. I'm 15 years old, fighting a Puerto Rican kid in the St. Mary Elementary School auditorium in South Amboy, New Jersey. I can't make a fist with my right hand. It throbs and burns when I try. Something's broken.

"Are you sure?"

"Yeah."

"Then get out there and box and move against this kid. Stop punching with him. You don't have to. Just box and move!"

"Okay."

The bell rings for the second round. I don't box and move. I go after him and punch. As long as I keep punching, I know I've got a chance. Soon, I find that every time he rushes in, he's open for a left hook, my best punch. So I let him come. It lands every time. Late in the third, I'm against the ropes, and he runs right into one. He sags.

Finally!

He backs off and I chase him across the ring, throwing hooks.

Every one lands. Two, three, four. He falls backward like he was pushed off a cliff.

I hear a crowd of men whooping and hollering, but their cheers are muffled, as though coming from another room or another time. I ignore them. He gets up at "nine," wobbling. He's really hurt. The referee waves me in. I'm surprised he's not stopping it. The kid can barely stand. *Fuck it.* I launch another hook and it lands perfectly, right on the point of the chin. He goes to sleep in the middle of the ring. Doctors and his corner guys race in and kneel around him. He's asleep a long time before he comes to.

Back in the locker room, I look at myself in the mirror. My face, chest, shoulders and upper back are blotted with pink and purple welts and abrasions. Blood trickles from my nose. I don't understand why. I don't recall getting hit.

I've been asked a couple times if my experience as an amateur boxer makes me a better boxing writer. I don't know. I've only ever been a boxer and then a writer. So I can't answer. I would have to know what it feels like to be a boxing writer without having boxed, and it's too late for that. It's been too late for a long time.

I was nine years old when I opened a copy of *Sports Illustrated* and saw a photo of heavyweight champion George Foreman training for his upcoming fight with Muhammad Ali in Zaire. I was a shy, anxious kid, and for reasons I could not identify, much less understand, I excelled at attracting the attention of the many and varied neighborhood bullies and sociopaths roaming the middle-class subdivision in which I lived. It was not uncommon for me to race home from school as fast as my feet would carry me, a gaggle of grammar-school hooligans hurling insults and taunts of the type found exclusively in the vocabulary of rough kids in 1970s New Jersey. I'd crash through the door at home, panting and red-faced, both elated at having survived another day and depressed at the thought of having to do it again tomorrow.

My mother: "How was school?"

"Fine."

In that photo of Foreman, whose deep scowl and bulging biceps projected a kind of strength, power and malevolence I could only dream of, I found everything that I wanted to be. In 1974, the heavyweight champion of the world was still seen as a kind of king among men, an extraordinary physical specimen whose size, strength and fighting prowess propelled him to a plane far beyond that to which ordinary men, such as my decidedly *un*-athletic father, or, for that matter, other men I'd seen around the neighborhood, could ever aspire.

No one told the heavyweight champion what to do; he told *other* people what to do. The heavyweight champion certainly never ran from anyone. He made *other* people do the running. That was for me. Never mind that Foreman was African American, 6'4" and prodigiously muscled, while I was morbidly and disconcertingly white, skinny, red-haired and freckled. Moreover, there was nothing in my physical makeup that suggested I would be anything beyond average size.

Nevertheless, before long, it was George Foreman *this* and George Foreman *that* and push-ups and sit-ups and weight lifting and roadwork (what other people, civilians mostly, called "jogging") and an instructional book titled *Boxing for Boys*, that I must have signed out of the school library a hundred times by the time I moved on to junior high.

My parents did not discourage this obsession, but drew the line at buying me a heavy bag for Christmas, despite its repeated appearances on my annual list. A factory machinist and a waitress, they earned modest wages and a good bag was beyond their means. The money I earned from an afternoon paper route wouldn't cut it either, but I would not be deterred. I sought out and befriended one of the least popular kids in school because I knew his father worked for the post office, and, unless T.V. had been lying to me, postal workers had easy access to all manner of duffel bags and canvas sacks and such, which, when stuffed with crap from around the house, would fill in quite nicely for a professionally-made *Everlast* heavy bag.

A week later I had my heavy bag packed lumpy with old newspapers and rags and hanging from a tree in the backyard. I never hung out with that kid again. Looking back, I know this deceit was unsavory to say the least, but as I saw it, having a heavy bag was non-negotiable if I was going to be the next George Foreman, and these were desperate times. Sorry, Phillip.

Though my paper route didn't make me prosperous enough to buy a heavy bag, it did afford me the means to buy boxing magazines at the local newspaper stand and soon I was there every couple weeks to see which new ones had come in. I consumed them—*The Ring, Boxing Illustrated, KO, International Boxing, World Boxing*, etc. I ordered dozens of back issues, too, to learn the sport's history. My father brought the *Newark Star Ledger* home with him after work every night, and I would scan the sports section for Rob Lawin, the boxing columnist, and the great writer Jerry Izenberg, who covered sports with a prose so lyrical as to be almost musical. Then it was to the TV listing of upcoming fights and fight results columns.

I didn't know it at the time, but all of this reading was teaching me how to write about boxing – and about life. The best work of Nigel Collins and Steve Farhood and, to a lesser degree Bert Sugar, opened my brain in places I hadn't known existed and became templates to which I would refer, over and over, sub-consciously or otherwise, over the next 40 years. The best *Sports Illustrated* writers, Mark Kram, Pat Putnam, Ralph Wiley and Ed Schuyler, showed me that coverage of a mere fistfight, when in the right hands, could read like a kind of poetry. These great works would soon be joined by the boxing books of George Plimpton and A.J. Liebling and W.C. Heinz and others, including all the boxing biographies I could find. This education was as essential as pounding the homemade heavy bag in the backyard or skipping rope in the carport. I just didn't know it yet.

I cried myself to sleep the night Jimmy Young sent Foreman into retirement in 1977 (I was 11), but there was so much boxing to fill the gap. There was Larry Holmes's title reign and the last days of Muhammad Ali. The light heavyweight division was packed with exciting, fearless brawlers such as Matthew Saad Muhammad and

Eddie Mustafa Muhammad, Dwight Muhammad Qawi and Marvin Johnson, and later-stage Victor Galindez. Marvelous Marvin Hagler was kicking ass up and down the middleweight division and Danny Lopez, Salvador Sanchez, Wilfredo Gomez and Edwin Rosario were lighting up the smaller weights, along with Aaron Pryor, Alexis Arguello and Ray "Boom Boom" Mancini.

Sugar Ray Leonard, Roberto Duran and Tommy Hearns were household names and how could it be otherwise? Fights—*big* fights— were on free network television all the time, either on Saturday afternoons or Friday nights, in prime time. How could anyone *not* be a fight fan?

In early 1980, I read in the local paper about a boxing gym that was six miles from my home and decided it was time to see if I really wanted to box, or be content with fantasy and the heavy bag in the yard. By this time, my childhood anxieties and fears had given way to a blinkered rage and sullenness of a type not uncommon among young men of questionable breeding.

I craved competitive, violent, physical contact, but up until then, I wasn't convinced yet that I had the courage to get in a ring. I had dabbled in other sports: Pick-up football games were great, but I was too antisocial for organized football, plus the jocks were assholes. I'd made the wrestling team in junior high but when the going got tough on the mat, it was all I could do to keep from balling up my fists. Baseball was too esoteric (*plus, jocks*), basketball not violent enough. I took a deep breath, called the gym and found that it was open from 6:00 to 8:00 PM on Mondays, Wednesdays and Fridays. I asked my father to drive me one night after dinner. He did.

While my father idled in the car nearby, I stood frozen at the heavy, gray steel door at 88 Jackson Street listening to the gym noises coming from inside. I heard the thumping speed bags, bells ringing to start and end rounds, gloves pounding on heavy bags. I heard male voices, some laughing and joking, others shouting instructions. A part of me wanted to run back to the car and spend another year pretending I would be a fighter someday.

I pulled open the door and stepped into another world, one that was at once exhilarating and terrifying. I tiptoed in and stood at the end of a corridor next to a wooden desk with a sign-in sheet on it and stared, open-mouthed at the activity exploding around me. The gym's proprietor and head trainer, Tony Gabriel, a stocky, hardboiled man in his early 60s, walked over and asked what I wanted.

"Um, can I train here?"

"What?" He squinted to hear me over the speed bags.

"I want to be a boxer. Is it alright if I, ya know, if I work out here?"

"You want to be a what?"

"A boxer. A fighter."

"A fighter?"

He smirked and shook his head, which I would learn was his favorite way to express the low opinion he held of every would-be fighter who walked into his gym.

"Dues are $5.00 a week. The locker room and showers are over there. When you come in, you sign your name right here on this paper. See? When you leave, you sign out. That way, if someone wants to know if you were here, I can show them. See?"

"Yes."

My head spun as I walked out back to my father, dozing in the car. I didn't know what to expect in the weeks ahead, just that everything was about to change. My dad brought me back the next Monday and three times a week until he died about 18 months later.

Gabriel wouldn't let me do anything but skip rope the first four weeks. No shadow boxing, no hitting the bags, no sparring. I figured this was the way he tested new guys, found out how bad they wanted to be fighters. Ha! He had no idea I'd been jumping rope for a year in my carport. I could skip all night. If he thought this would drive me out of the gym, he was wrong. This old prick didn't know who he was dealing with. I'd have cleaned shit out of the toilets with my tongue if it meant I could keep coming back.

One night toward the end of the fourth week, another trainer, a guy in his 30s with a head full of black, curly hair, sat and watched me skip, smiling and shaking his head, apparently in admiration of my willingness to skip rope for two hours straight.

Danny Thomas had an easy smile and generous spirit and I immediately liked him. Some weeks later, when Gabriel introduced me to a kind of shuffling footwork that probably was in vogue at the turn of the century, Danny gently took me aside and showed me how to get up on the balls of my feet and move more fluidly. This and other small grievances led to a rift between the two that eventually prompted Danny to leave the South River Knights of Columbus gym and open the New Brunswick PAL several years later. I went with him.

Danny taught me everything he knew and I did my best to absorb it. He was patient, encouraging, and, at significant personal expense, generous with his time. When he told me six months into our time together that it was time to start getting fights, I was terrified but agreed. Along with the other fighters from our gym, we started attending amateur fight cards around New Jersey.

And so it started: A decision win in Hamilton followed by a points loss in Edison. A win in South River, then the knockout win over the Puerto Rican kid in South Amboy. After three months off to heal my broken right hand, a knockout loss in Trenton. More time off for a broken nose gotten in sparring, then a win in Aberdeen. This was all in preparation for the state Golden Gloves tournament in Elizabeth, where I won my first fight by knockout but lost a decision in the next round.

I realized over this time that when I was able to lose myself in the fight, to forget who I was, things went well. I knew how to fight and was always in shape. And I could punch. Just as frequently, the anxiety and self-doubt that were remnants of my grammar school nightmares prevented me from performing.

When Sugar Ray Leonard was at his best, a writer asked him if he ever doubted himself in the ring. He replied that when he signed for a fight, he always thought: 'There's no way this guy beats me.'

When I had a fight coming up, I thought: "There's no way I beat this guy."

It continued: A win in South River, then two wins in the Golden Gloves to get me to the middleweight finals, which I threw away probably because I thought that if I won I'd have to keep going, keep fighting. And I didn't want that anymore.

By this time I was 17 or 18 and starting to acknowledge what I had known all along: I never would be George Foreman. I wouldn't even be Duane Bobick, and not just because I stopped growing at 165 pounds. It wasn't in me. Really, it never had been.

Around this time, teachers in my high school started to praise my writing. This was fairly shocking, as I hated school and most of the teachers. I did the absolute minimum needed to pass my classes, and in some cases not even that—but I excelled in English and journalism. During my freshman and sophomore years, I'd spend my lunch period every day in the library and, after quickly running through the boxing books, turned to the great fiction writers on the shelves, temporarily escaping the many horrors of adolescence. The results of this reading began to show.

One day, my Advanced English teacher handed me a paper I had written, which she had graded an "A." I had a black eye from the previous night's sparring session. She shook her head. "If only you really cared about school," she said, and gently advised me to stop boxing before I got my "brains scrambled." The more praise I received, the more important writing became. I couldn't pass Algebra I, but I could write the shit out of a paper analyzing Jean Paul Sartre's trilogy of novels on existentialism in pre-war France.

These years also brought a steady girlfriend, a small band of good friends, and the discovery of the power of cheap beer and its attendant merriments. All these things started to fill the holes in me that once had been filled by boxing. When I started fighting, I needed it. It did for me things that 20 years of therapy couldn't have. It's not hyperbole to say that it saved me, even if I don't know from what.

Now there were other things. I didn't need it anymore. I fought a couple more times after the loss in the Golden Gloves finals, mostly for Danny, who I believed I had let down. Both losses. After all the years he spent on me, he deserved better. After the last loss, he told me I should retire because I wasn't listening to him anymore. He was right.

Because boxing gets in your blood, 10 years later, at 28 years old, I got back in the gym and trained for a comeback (still trying to be George Foreman). Danny was there for me, as always. It was a disaster, but it helped me to close the door, finally, on that part of my life.

So I couldn't be George Foreman; maybe I could be Jeff Ryan or Bobby Cassidy or one of the other guys who wrote for the boxing magazines I'd been reading for 20 years. Maybe I could be Phil Berger or Michael Katz or Ron Borges. Maybe that's what I was supposed to be doing all along.

I started writing and submitting boxing articles to magazines and attacked it with the same doggedness and stubbornness I had employed in the gym all those years. A couple pieces came back, rejected, like hooks I had tried that were blocked or slipped at the last moment. I adjusted. I regrouped. I went in again. Another miss. I obsessed. Worked. Tried again...

And then one got through. And then another. It was my great fortune that Nigel Collins was running the family of fight magazines that I had grown up reading. He took me under his wing and taught me everything I needed to know—just like Danny had—and for a solid 15 years made me the best writer I could be.

I talked to Danny recently. He lives in Florida now. We reminisced for a while, and he told me I was a better fighter than I thought I was. Just like old times. "But," he added, "You're a better writer than you were a fighter."

I'll take it.

It's 2017. I'm 51 years old. It's January, and 37 degrees outside. I'm in my backyard, hitting the heavy bag. It's 8:30 at night, dark. I see my breath and the light flashing from the television inside, where my wife watches a detective show. My kids are doing homework. I pound the bag with hooks and smile as it swings merrily. The punch is the last thing to go.

Before long, my nose runs. I'm winded and my shoulders and knees ache.

I can't figure out how to fix a transition in the book I'm writing. There are too many bills and the bad days bring new anxieties and reminders of the terrible inevitabilities that await all of us. It's a fucked-up world. We're all just hanging on. I slam another hook into the bag. And then another. As long as I keep punching, I know I've got a chance.

FEAR AND LOATHING
IN NEW JERSEY

A GOLDEN GLOVES ODYSSEY
TO THE END OF HOPE

"THEY'RE GOING to match everyone up soon. I'll be right back. Stand next to someone you think you can beat."

I was in downtown Elizabeth, New Jersey in a back room of the old armory on the corner of Magnolia Avenue and Walnut Street, one of 20 welterweights waiting to fight in the opening round of the 1982 New Jersey Golden Gloves amateur boxing tournament, novice class. My trainer, Danny Thomas (no relation to the actor), had just run off to talk to someone on the other side of the building.

Stand next to someone I think I can beat?

I'd need a bus ticket back to the suburbs. In every corner of the room were hard, tough kids from the roughest cities in Jersey -- Newark, Camden, Elizabeth, Trenton, Hamilton, Paterson, Plainfield. They looked like grown men. All black or Hispanic. I was 16. I'd never felt so skinny, so vulnerable. So white.

I scanned the room. *Nope. Nope. Nope. Nope. Fuck no! Nope. Nope.*

An old guy with a clipboard and wearing a New Jersey Golden Gloves shirt appeared from the back of the room. "Alright everybody, line up!"

Shit! I scanned harder.

Then, I spotted him -- on the other side of the room, a kid even whiter and skinnier than me. And he looked even sadder and more terrified than I imagined I did. *Jackpot!* I darted across the room and grabbed the spot to his left, so close that our arms almost touched. I wasn't taking any chances. No one was going to wriggle between me and my little skinny white boy. I snuck a good, hard look out of the corner of my right eye. Inspected him.

Yeah. I got this.

The old guy with the clipboard started going up and down the line, tapping guys on the shoulder as he went: "You and you. You and you. You and you." But he wasn't tapping the guys right next to one another. He was skipping two guys in between.

"You and you. You and you. You and you."

I didn't get the little skinny white kid. For a while I didn't look down the line to see who I'd drawn. I didn't want to know. Plus, if he was looking at me, he'd see me looking at him and that would be a whole new problem – who looks away first? Do I smile and nod? Dirty-look him? But everyone was breaking off, going back to their little corners of the room. It would probably be my only chance to get a good look at him until we got into the ring. I glanced over.

Fuck.

Fear is one of the great fetishes among those who study fighters and fighting. You can understand it. A man of average temperament and intellect sees another man climb a set of steps, pass through ropes onto an elevated, brightly-lit platform to fistfight another in front of a crowd of onlookers and wonders: *How is he not terrified?*

Cus D'Amato, the boxing savant and revered trainer and manager of Hall of Fame champions Jose Torres, Floyd Patterson and Mike Tyson, among others, dissected and articulated the mysteries of the complicated relationship between prizefighters and fear better than probably anyone. It is one of the many outrages of modern commercialism that so many of the quotes attributed to him have been hijacked and repackaged as "self-help" gimmickry. Nevertheless:

"The first thing I do with a young fighter is explain fear; most people don't know much about fear. They think it's a sign of being 'yellow.' But fear is normal. It's like fire. If you let it get out of control, it will destroy you and everything around you. If you can learn how to control it, you can make it work for you. Fear is just nature's way of preparing you to fight."

It's a hard thing to control. A cameraman filming a 1983 documentary about the Catskill Boxing Club captured a teenage Tyson, of all people, in full panic mode, sobbing in the arms of assistant trainer Teddy Atlas before taking the ring in an amateur tournament. Speaking on the subject decades later, Tyson said that the hyper-aggression he showed before a fight in his championship days was a mere mask -- his method for handling the fear of being humiliated: "I was always scared to death. A big part of fighting is being afraid."

A lucky few were immune to it and didn't need it. Legendary heavyweight champion Rocky Marciano was so calm before fights that he napped in his locker room during prelims. Promoter Bob Arum once said the sensational multi-division champion Manny Pacquiao anticipated a fight the same way others might a game of basketball. And when asked if he ever felt fear before entering the ring, 1960s heavyweight champion Sonny Liston, the Tyson of his time, replied, "I always feel that the other fellow should be nervous, so there ain't no use in both of us being nervous."

But those are the exceptions. No less a brute than former two-time heavyweight champion George Foreman confessed to being so terrified of Joe Frazier leading up to his title challenge of Frazier in 1973 that when he stared Frazier down during the referee's instructions, he feared that if Frazier's gaze dropped, he would spy Foreman's knees shaking.

It's an odd thing to hear from a man recalled as one of the most intimidating heavyweights ever, but Foreman claimed fear was a part of every contest.

"In boxing, I had a lot of fear. Fear was good," Foreman said long after his fighting days were over. And it was the one time that he wasn't afraid that things fell apart.

"For the first time, in the bout with Muhammad Ali, I didn't have any fear. I thought, 'This is easy. This is what I've been waiting for.' No fear at all. No nervousness. And I lost."

The 1950s heavyweight contender Lou Nova practiced yoga to help calm his nerves in the locker room before big fights. Max Baer was said to have been so terrified before his fight with young phenom Joe Louis that he refused to leave his dressing room until threatened by former champ Jack Dempsey. After Louis stopped him in four rounds, Baer said, "I define fear as standing across the ring from Joe Louis and knowing he wants to go home early."

Some guys never even make it to the ring. The fear overtakes them. In 2001, musclebound former Olympian Jeff Lacy was scheduled to make his super middleweight pro debut against Kevin Butts of Toledo, Ohio. After the weigh-in, which was presumably the first time Butts saw Lacy up close, he approached Lacy and said to him, "Good luck with your career," then left town in the middle of the night.

Ray Mancini, lightweight champ in the 1980s, said on the subject, "You have to have fear. Not fear of the opponent. Fear of the unknown, not knowing what's going to happen. My ritual was, I'd look in the mirror when they called me out, knowing I wasn't going to look like that when I came back. You prepare yourself."

I'd had four or five fights by the time the Golden Gloves competition came around, so I knew already what it was like to be afraid before a fight. To walk into an empty high school gymnasium or ballroom or Knights of Columbus Hall and see the rows on rows of empty wooden folding chairs, knowing they'd be filled, their occupants staring up at the ring, empty now, but soon I'd be up there trading punches with another kid, trying to not embarrass myself, fighting for ... *what exactly*? Then the long wait in the locker room, the monotony interrupted only by the doctor's physical and the weigh-in, the steady drip of nervous sweat trickling down my flanks, the urge to piss.

And then, as in a dream, I'm in the ring, all the faces on me, my opponent staring at me from the other corner, the bell rings, we approach one another, someone lands a punch. And with that, all fear is gone.

Danny returned from his errand. "Who'd you get?"

I pointed to the opponent I'd drawn.

"Jesus. Why do we get all the monsters?"

I could go into a long description of all of the physical attributes Harold Crawford possessed that compelled Danny to react the way he did. Suffice to say Crawford was exactly the opposite of the little skinny white kid I had hoped to draw. And it was at this point that I stopped being afraid. What sense was there being afraid when I knew precisely what would happen? This wasn't pre-fight jitters, or what Sugar Ray Leonard called "butterflies." You have to have hope to be afraid. No hope meant no fear.

A couple weeks earlier, Danny and I watched the best and most experienced fighter in our gym, a junior middleweight, get blown out in the first round by a guy from the same gym as Crawford and who looked just like him. Our guy quit boxing, just like that. That would be me. For Danny's sake I'd go in there and try, and when Crawford knocked me cold, they'd wake me up, Danny would drive me home and I'd never box again. Just like that.

And that was the best-case scenario. I might even end up in the hospital. Broken nose, broken jaw, concussion, who knew? Maybe some injury that would rule out ever boxing again. And wouldn't that be perfect? That way, even if I wanted to box again, they wouldn't let me. I could save face by telling everyone that I still wanted to fight but the doctors wouldn't allow it.

It would be over. No more bloody noses, no more aching hands or black eyes, no more being afraid. No more trophies either, and no more seeing my name in the newspaper or being respected (or better yet, feared) at school or in the neighborhood. No more people asking me when I was fighting again, no more thrusting my hands overhead and hearing a crowd cheer for me. No more "Great fight kid!" No more soul-cleansing, late-night pushups or early-morning runs, no more feeling like a god when landing the perfect punch. But that was okay.

This was it. I accepted it. I sat on a bench in that room listening to the crowd's cheers and their boos, their laughter and chatter, instructions hollered from the ninth row because everyone in a fight crowd is an expert: "Jab! Jab! One-two!" And their boasts: "I told you that motherfucker could punch! I *told* you!" When a big punch landed or, one of the fighters knocked to the canvas, the collective "ooohh," deep and in perfect unison, rumbled and vibrated down through the wooden floors and up through the rafters of the old armory and out into the New Jersey night where the rest of the world was mundane and desultory and stunk of truck fumes but at least it was safe. Or, at least the fear not so acute.

All around me, nervous fighters who still had hope were warming up for their turn, shadow boxing, getting gloved up, nodding to last-minute instructions, stretching, pacing, and when they got the call they walked out shiny with sweat and anxiety and they couldn't have known it then but at that moment they were more alive than they had ever been or ever would be.

The armory's stillness that had greeted them hours before had been replaced with the energy of a thousand or more heads turning and straining to see them, evaluate them, sniff out their fear or examine the cut of their shoulders or calves or cheekbones, any sign that might give away whether they were worth betting on or against, whether they would run and stall, or charge in, flailing away. Whether they would bleed. Whether they would fight. In what other walk of life could a man be scrutinized so, and then have the chance, so fleeting, to disappoint or to defy, or to shock?

My fight with Crawford would be one of the last of the night. The wait was long. They came in two-by-two after their fights were done, a couple with head tipped back, pinching bloody towel to nose, others unmarked, smiling. Whispers. Sighs. Excuses. Exalted or despondent, winners or losers, all betraying a barely concealed sense of: *Relief*.

How I envied them.

———————

Suddenly I'm in the ring. Danny is next to me. The referee motions to Crawford and me to join him in the center for final instructions. I obey but my eyes remain on the canvas, delaying the confrontation until the last possible second, until after the first bell, when I will have no choice. The referee goes through his spiel:

"No hitting below the belt. No wrestling. When I say 'break,' take a full step back. ..."

A voice tells me to look up at Crawford. I listen to it.

A head taller, he glares down at me, his mouth twisted upward, brow forced down in an angry scowl. Like he can't wait to get his hands on me.

"In the event of a knockdown, go to the furthest neutral corner and wait there until I tell you to come out."

I look back down at the canvas. A beat passes. The voice comes back: *Who the fuck is this motherfucker scowling at? Look back up at him!*

A fainter, more familiar voice: *Do not look back up at him. Repeat: Do not look back up at him.*

I look up anyway. Our eyes lock.

I can hear my heartbeat. *One. Two. Three.* Crawford's scowl melts away. He looks down at the canvas.

This motherfucker. I've got him.

"I want a good clean fight. Return to your corner and come out at the bell."

I'm bouncing in my corner. I feel light, fast, strong. Danny massages the back of my neck. "Look at that long body, Billy. You've got a lot to shoot for. Hook to that body."

I hit Harold Crawford harder than I'd ever hit anyone. It was over in 42 seconds.

Three weeks later we were back at the armory for the next round of the tournament. I drew Jaime Erazo from Paterson. Ordinary looking kid. Stocky, but long-armed. I tried to get into the same awful mindset I'd had for Crawford. As painful as it was I was willing to endure it if it meant getting the same result.

I couldn't do it. I couldn't manufacture it, couldn't talk myself into hopelessness. I realized then that it had to be real, authentic. It had to be organic. I went in with run-of-the-mill prefight jitters, hope and fear, fear and hope, and was awful. Lost a split decision. I was never as good again as I had been the night I had lost hope. It's a wonderful thing but sometimes it gets in the way.

SAY GOODNIGHT
TO THE BAD GUY

WALTER COWANS AND
THE ECONOMIES OF LOSS

THEY FOUND Walter Cowans with his head in an oven, in his mouth the rubber tube that in happier circumstances had carried the oven's gas to its burner. The tube had been threaded through a hole Cowans had poked in the plastic bag he'd placed over his head and then tied around his neck. You can call the bag overkill, but to those who knew Cowans, it made sense. He'd aborted several suicide attempts over the years. He wanted to make sure this one stuck.

Eight days prior, Cowans, 36, had been stopped in the second round in St. Louis by a St. Louis patrolman named Sam Hill, who went by the nickname "The Punching Policeman." Hill was undefeated at the time but turned out to be better at policing than punching. The loss was the 102nd of Cowans' career against 26 wins, but don't imagine that it was that final defeat that drove Cowans to take his place among the great majority. After all, when you've lost 101, what's one more? Nor should you fret that too many blows had rattled loose Cowan's brain to such an extent that he didn't know what he was doing.

Walter Cowans always knew what he was doing. He knew it when he tied that bag around his neck in May 1999, and he knew it when he beat me stupid in a dilapidated gym in the armpit of New Brunswick, New Jersey in 1980.

"I don't think anyone could make Billy look bad."

Scotty looked back at me from the passenger seat of our coach's '70s-era Volvo and smiled. My gym mate and frequent sparring partner, Scotty was our club's "Golden Boy"—just a kid, 15 years old like me, but he could slip and slide and bob and weave under, over, and around punches like a 40-fight pro. It was something to see. He was responding to our coach's admonition that we shouldn't worry if the guys we were on our way to spar that night made us look bad -- they were more experienced than we were. We'd sparred a lot, but neither Scotty nor I had had our first official fight yet.

We were headed to Willis' Gym in New Brunswick, about a 15-minute drive from South River, up Route 18, then to Route 1 and to Hiram Street in the heart of the town's poorest and shittiest neighborhood, the type of neighborhood in which all the real boxing gyms are found: Boarded up windows on wood-framed, lopsided houses, rusted-out, 12-year-old cars on cinderblocks, crushed cigarette butts on burnt orange grass, graffiti everywhere, dumpsters over-flowing with trash, and then, incongruously, a shiny, late-model luxury car.

I had never been to any fight gym other than our little club in South River, a mostly white, working-class town in central Jersey, six miles from where I grew up in Parlin. The only times I'd seen neighborhoods like the one in New Brunswick came when I was a kid and my parents would take my sister and me to visit relatives in Newark and Irvington. From the safety of the NJ Parkway, we'd zoom by neighborhoods that looked just like the one that Willis' Gym was in, and inevitably, my parents, who'd grown up around there, would grumble over how the area had gone to hell and it was a good thing they'd got out when they did.

The interior of Willis' Gym was as if someone had taken all the shit and detritus and misery that was outside, remolded it into boxing equipment, wrapped it in duct tape, and moved it indoors: creaking wood floors, the ring canvas stained with blood, spit, probably some puke and who knew what else, miles of tape holding together a pair of heavybags. If something was wood, the paint was peeling off it. If it was metal, it was rusty, bent. The aroma was that of a thousand dirty jockstraps, a thousand more handwraps that had never seen water, much less soap, and just the right amount of desperation. If you'd told me the place was built and furnished in the 1920s and had remained untouched since, I'd have believed it. In other words, it was a perfect fucking fight gym.

I was there to spar a kid named Walter Cowans. We were about the same size, 125 pounds, give or take, and the same age, or close to it. He'd had five or six fights, and his trainer and the gym proprietor, Ed Willis, a gentle, soft-spoken man in his 60s, and mine, Danny Thomas (no relation to the actor), had talked about Walter and me fighting if we seemed pretty evenly matched while sparring in the gym. That was the way it worked. That's how good trainers found opponents for their kids.

In the gym, I changed, loosened up, shadowboxed, wrapped my hands. Danny buckled on my headgear, tied on the big gloves, put in my mouthpiece, smeared my face with Vaseline. Mr. Willis, as everyone called him, did the same for Cowans. I bounced in the corner waiting for the first bell. "Just relax," Danny said. "Hands up, chin down. And jab."

"You'd stick the barrel [of a gun] in the guy's side. And the guy would look in your eye and know you was serious," Cowans told writer Rick Reilly for a 1989 *Sports Illustrated* feature, describing how he used to rob people in the street when he was a teenager and gang member in New Brunswick in the early 1980s. He stole anything he could get his hands on and carried a straight razor when he didn't have a gun. He was delighted to tell Reilly how he used it. "You jab a guy and he doesn't even know his face has been sliced."

Cowans had gained notoriety as one of the game's most prolific fighters, and, not coincidentally, perhaps its most prolific loser. By the time Reilly profiled him, Cowans' pro record was 11-54-1. He fought nine times in 1989, a rate almost unheard of in modern prizefighting, and, uncharacteristically, went well over .500, winning seven times. But winning was never Cowans' goal. He'd already decided by that time that he wanted to be in the record book for having more professional fights than anyone, ever.

Cowans had learned early on that winning was not for everyone. After moving from Jersey to Wisconsin, he got a manager, turned pro, and promptly lost six straight fights, two to a fighter named Victor Flores. Was it because Cowans couldn't fight? Hell no.

"About a month later, I'm watching TV and I see this Flores guy fighting Jackie Beard, who was the NABF champ at the time," Cowans told Reilly. "And I'm thinking, 'Wow, why are those guys sticking me in fights like that?'"

It was already too late for Cowans, in so many ways, to be a special fighter, a champion, or a contender. So he became a journeyman, or what they call a "trial horse" in the fight game—a guy who fights everyone, fights often, and is used primarily to build the record of other, superior, better-connected fighters who might have a future in the sport. For Cowans and fighters like him, win, lose, it doesn't matter. What matters is going the distance. If he goes the distance he can fight again the following week and get paid. If he gets stopped he gets suspended. He gets suspended he doesn't get paid. He doesn't get paid he can't pay the rent. And fighting was the only job Walter Cowans had.

"He relied on his purses to live more than any guy I'd seen," Stan Johnson once told me. Johnson, former boxer, ex-convict and all-around man of ill repute, a hat-trick achieved in the fight game more often than any other legal business one can name, took over Cowans' management and the two barnstormed all over the Midwest: Chicago, Detroit, Green Bay, Saint Paul, Gary, South Bend, Grand

Forks, Madison. Occasionally, they hit Brooklyn, Tucson, Pittsburgh, Miami. The fights, and especially the losses, piled up—five in 1990, eight in '92, another five in '98. Breaking up the losing streaks were pockets of wins—five straight losses, two wins. Three losses, three victories, then six more defeats. Two wins, then another losing streak. It didn't matter to Cowans as long as the checks kept coming in.

"If you needed a fighter who would go six or seven rounds, you called Walter Cowans because he would give you those rounds," Johnson said. "He was a promoter's dream that way. I used to get excited when a guy would hurt him and then really go after him hard because I knew Walter would use every trick in the book to get out of the round. He was very slick defensively. Most guys couldn't hit him with two punches in a row."

Inevitably, some guys did and when he got stopped, Cowans simply assumed a different name and showed up at the next stop as Darrell Green, or Mark French, or "Big" Jeff May, or Raheen Muhammad. He fought men in weight classes two or three above his own. A few states that were sticklers caught onto it and banned him— New Jersey did. So did Illinois. But most of the time, nobody gave a shit. They let the man make a living. You have to be fearless to live that kind of life, and that's what Cowans was.

"He never feared anybody," Del Porter, proprietor of the Ace Boxing Club, where Cowans trained, told writer Pete Ehrmann. "If I got a call from a promoter saying he needed somebody for a guy with 23 straight wins, Walter would take it in a minute."

Johnson agreed.

"He wasn't afraid to get in there with anybody. I remember when he fought against a big middleweight one time, a big undefeated kid at the time, and Walter wasn't nothing but a welterweight then."

That was probably Cowans' loss to Mike Evgen in 1989, for which Cowans made about $3,500 (equivalent to about $9,000 in 2025), which Johnson said was his biggest purse.

"Walter was an opponent; he knew that," Johnson said. "He knew his place in the chain. He knew he was never going to be no more or

WILLIAM DETTLOFF

no less than that. That's what he was and he made a nice living but he pissed it all away on [women] and drugs and material things.

"He was a skilled guy. But as Vince Lombardi said, winning is a habit. So, unfortunately, is losing. Walter played that role and that was cool with him. He didn't mind. He accepted his role. He was who he was and he accepted it."

"Billy, you gotta throw some punches. Come on, let your hands go."

Danny wiped away the blood pouring from my nose but he couldn't do anything about the ringing in my head from the three-minute beating Cowans had just given me. And the second round was about to start.

"Okay."

"Come on now. Hands up, chin down. Relax. Let your punches go."

"Okay."

I went back out to the middle of the ring, put my hands up, my chin down, tried to relax and got my ass handed to me for three minutes. It was even worse than the first round. When the bell rang, Danny waved to Mr. Willis.

"That's it, we're good. That's all."

Thank Christ.

While Danny shook off my headgear I looked across the ring and could just about make out an exchange between Mr. Willis and Cowans, who looked angry. It was something along the lines of:

Mr. Willis: *Why didn't you let up a little?*

Cowans: *Why, so that motherfucker can do to me what I'm doing to him?*

He was right, of course. He was under no obligation to go easy on anyone.

As a pro, Cowans made few friends. "He had a very difficult personality. He had trouble with just about everybody," Jack Cowen told ESPN in 2008. Cowen booked dozens of fights for Cowans in the '80s. He said Cowans was always angry. "He was just a very difficult guy. He had all kinds of problems. He was very capable in the ring, but the street life got to him."

———

We went back to Willis' Gym for sparring plenty over the next couple years and I took a couple more beatings, but none like the one I took that day from Walter Cowans. He won the state Golden Gloves tournament that same year and beat some good fighters. When Willis' eventually shut down, Danny and I left the South River gym and Danny opened the New Brunswick PAL not far from where Willis' was. One night Cowans showed up looking for sparring. He had grown into a big, solid, broad-shouldered welterweight. I had too. Danny asked if I wanted to spar with him.

"Sure."

I'd like to say I avenged the beating. I didn't. I held my own. The following night I watched while he sparred a guy two weight classes lighter than him. The little guy was giving him hell. When Cowans couldn't take the embarrassment anymore, he started kicking the guy and had to be dragged out of the ring.

———

"He was addicted to drugs," Cowans' mother, Sydney Ramseur, told *The Milwaukee Journal Sentinel* after Cowans died. She said he'd started smoking weed at seven years old and was a teenager when he upgraded to crack. "He would stay clean when he boxed because that was more important to him. But when he was done boxing, he would use drugs again."

Depends on your definition of "clean." Stan Johnson said he watched Cowans smoke a joint while wrapping his hands right before a fight and walk into the ring high as hell. He said he'd never seen a fighter do that before.

Porter, the trainer, knew Cowans was in trouble toward the end. "He would call two, three, even four times in the middle of the night, all strung out from cocaine, and say, 'I gotta get ahold of myself,'" Porter told *The Sentinel*. "I'd say, 'Walter, get on your knees and talk to God. He'll listen.'"

I doubt he took Porter's advice. The Walter Cowans I knew was not the kind of guy who took advice from anyone. He always knew exactly what he was doing.

THE LURE OF THE COMEBACK

AND WHY IT'S SO HARD TO RESIST

ORIGINALLY PUBLISHED IN *RINGSIDE SEAT*, Fall 2022

NOT LONG AGO, I came across a news item about former middleweight champ Kelly Pavlik considering a comeback. Turned out to be a false alarm. Still, my first thought was: "What took him so long?"

Pavlik last fought in 2012, and despite persistent rumors that he was returning, he still hasn't pulled the trigger. Good for him. He's 40 now, or thereabouts, and even considering how many athletes perform at a high level these days in their middle 30s, the window has pretty much closed for him. It's too late. He won. He waited it out. He knew if he waited long enough, time would decide for him. It's a good strategy. Pavlik didn't need the money. "It's just the itch," he said at one time.

It's more than that, though. They make creams and ointments that will knock out an itch in two seconds. They don't sell in stores what it takes to keep a man away from boxing once it's gotten into him.

"Billy!"

"Billy!"

I stood in my corner waiting for the bell to start the second round of my "comeback" fight. It was 1992. I was 28 years old. I turned around and looked down at my trainer, Danny Thomas, calling my name.

"You're stinkin' out the place! Come on!"

He was right.

I started boxing in South River, New Jersey at 15 years old. I fought in smokers and in Golden Gloves tournaments held in high school gymnasiums and church halls and armories. A couple were in fancy banquet halls: silverware and champagne glasses clinking, blood and sweat sprinkling the carpet, the aroma of steak, perfume, Vaseline. A chandelier over the ring, noses bloody and red. Sweat. Anxiety everywhere.

Most of the time the crowds were a few hundred people. For the Golden Gloves tournaments, which were still a big deal then and held in Elizabeth, it was a thousand or more, some years close to two.

Despite my trainer's best efforts, I was a mediocre fighter. I was easy to hit. My nose bled on contact. I fought tight, which caused me to tire quickly, no matter how hard I worked in the gym. And for all but my first couple of fights, I over-relied on my left hook. If I couldn't land it, I was out of ideas.

Because boxing makes no sense, all of these flaws conspired, under the right circumstances, to produce exciting fights. Three times an opponent and I were awarded "Best Fight of the Night" trophies at the night's conclusion, each because I had spent the first round or so getting those flaws painfully exploited before forgetting who I was and coming back in the bout's second half to win.

There's not a fight crowd in the world that won't cheer on a kid who goes from getting his ass kicked to doing the ass-kicking. They eat it up. That's what they pay to see. They go nuts for it. I grew up in a house where praise was non-existent. I guess lots of fighters have. To go from that to hearing a few hundred or a thousand people cheering, screaming for you, jumping up and down, high-fiving each other, is surreal.

And they're cheering for you.

Not for your team.

For *you*.

And when you climb down the steps, they pound your back, one by one, strangers all:

"Great fight, kid!"

"Shit, how long is your reach, kid?"

"I knew I shoulda bet on you!"

An older heavyweight in our gym pulled me aside after a card in South River, where I came back and beat a visiting fighter from Trenton.

"How old are you again?"

"15."

He shook his big head. "Jesus Christ."

I lost a decision to Jaime Erazo from Patterson in the quarter finals of the Golden Gloves tournament in '82. I was terrible, but it was a good fight, back and forth. The judges gave it to him by a point. I was walking back to the locker room, head down, when a middle-aged guy with a kid, maybe eight or nine years old, stopped me. He had a pen in his hand and a pad.

"Hey, good fight, kid. My son here would like your autograph. Is it all right?"

I was 16 years old.

Are you kidding me?

———

Muhammad Ali famously described the later rounds of his third fight with Joe Frazier this way: "It was like death. Closest thing to dyin' that I know of." What kind of insanity compels a man who has felt the darkness this keenly to return to the scene again and again? Ali fought 10 more times after that fight and frequently spoke to the press about the pain of boxing and of getting into condition. Why did he keep doing it?

You can say for the money, but Ali was arguably the most famous man on the planet by the time he and Frazier visited hell together via Manila. There are lots of ways for the most famous man in the world to make a good living that don't involve almost dying. Why did he keep doing it? Because everything good that ever happened to him – and there was enough good for several lifetimes – happened to him because of boxing.

If you get a fighter talking to you and he's honest, he'll say he has a love/hate relationship with the sport. It hurts even the great ones, deeply, sooner or later. And I'm not talking about the business and the missing money, the back-stabbing and bad decisions. I've never felt another pain like the pain that comes from getting smashed on the bridge of the nose with a straight right when sparring, or catching a hook to the pit of the stomach when there's two minutes left to go in the round and there's no way you're stopping because if you do the rest of the guys in the gym will know you never were tough enough for this shit in the first place.

But the inverse is true as well: When you are the one landing the perfect hook to the body or the counter-right over the jab or the uppercut you've been practicing for weeks on the pads, there is an accompanying bliss that resides somewhere beyond shrieking crowds or claps on the back or cheers born of bloodlust and beer. You are already divorced from any awareness that you are injuring another man; he may as well be a heavy bag. When you do it right, the way it should be done, the way your heroes do it and you see his pain, there is a real beauty to it. It goes deep.

By 1984, my senior year in high school, I was tired of fighting. I wanted to chase girls, drink beer, drive fast cars, hang out with my friends. I didn't need it anymore. It showed in my last couple fights, which I pissed away through apathy. I was still doing it only because I felt bad abandoning Danny, who had invested so much in me over the years. But he agreed it was time.

"You don't listen anymore," he said.

So just like that, I wasn't a fighter anymore. But if I wasn't a fighter, who was I?

A couple years went by. Those things I'd stopped fighting for, the partying, the girl-chasing, the cars, had become routine. There had to be something else, right?

Of course there was: I could fight again. That would fix everything. And this time I would do it right. I'd relax in the ring. I'd move my head more. I'd be smart. I'd get in even better shape. I quit smoking and drinking, started running.

I went back to the gym in South River. Danny had moved on, but the old man who ran the gym took his place. I felt out of place among all the kids but also kind of like returning royalty. Most of the kids there would never have a single fight; they were just there to work out. Soon, I was sparring and doing all right. Then I sparred an older guy named Larry who had a back as wide as an old Buick and a murderous right hand. I held my own in the first round, but in the second, he slammed home that right hand on my nose. The blood poured. There was a long way to go in the round, and he wasn't taking it easy.

What the fuck am I doing here?

I quit again. Another year went by. Same old shit every day. There had to be something else, right? Was it all just working, drinking, banging? Really? Was there nothing else?

I went back to the gym. I told myself I just didn't give it enough time the last time. If I had stuck with it longer, it would have come together. I couldn't expect to walk in and just get it all back. Everyone knows that. By then, Danny had returned and welcomed me back. I threw myself into it. A couple weeks later, Ricky Meyers showed up at the gym looking for sparring.

Meyers was a hotshot amateur from Woodbridge, a few towns to the North. He ended up going pro and fighting a few times on ESPN, even beating Micky Ward on points in 1991 and later Ray Oliveira. He could fight. Danny asked if I wanted to spar with him. "Sure."

In the third round, I threw three consecutive jabs from the same exact distance at the same exact speed. Lunacy. He slipped the third one and came over with a right hand.

What the fuck am I doing here?

I was gone again. This time for good. I wasn't that 16-year-old kid anymore who lived for this. There had to be something else out there that would do for me the things that boxing had. I just had to find it.

A year later I was off the Marlboros and booze again and training for a comeback at a gym in Brick, about 20 minutes down Route 9. (I was ashamed to go back to the old gym after ghosting Danny the way I had.) New trainer. New surroundings. It was the home base of Frank Savannah, a local amateur middleweight who, a couple weeks before I showed up, won the state Golden Gloves title. He eventually turned pro, got signed by Main Events and put together a decent career before Dana Rosenblatt stopped him in 1994.

My new trainer: "Wanna spar Frank?"

Me: "Sure."

I picked up a pack of Marlboros and a six-pack on the way home.

Former heavyweight title holder Chris Byrd was so damaged and in so much pain from his days as a fighter that he frequently contemplated suicide and found relief only through smoking copious amounts of marijuana. Nevertheless, he spent much of 2020 and 2021 promoting a return to the ring that, fortunately, never happened. He was 52 years old.

It took Sugar Ray Leonard four comebacks over 10 years to be convinced that it was over, the nail in the coffin a derisible knockout loss to an aged Hector Camacho.

Nigel Benn, middleweight terror from the 1980s and '90s, announced a comeback in 2019 at the age of 55. He sought "closure." An injury scuttled it. Fellow Brit Ricky Hatton suffered severe depression after retiring from boxing and, like Byrd, contemplated suicide. (Hatton killed himself in 2025.) One-time middleweight belt holder Sergio Martinez retired after losing to Miguel Cotto in 2014. He announced a comeback in 2020 and has fought four times since. He is 47 years old.

Tyson Fury quit boxing after winning the heavyweight championship against Wladimir Klitschko in 2015. The three years of inactivity that followed featured drug and alcohol addictions, depression, anxiety attacks, massive weight gain and an aborted suicide attempt. While Fury concedes depression and anxiety have always plagued him, boxing provided a respite. He fears what will happen when he can't do it anymore.

"I'm very worried because I can't let go—just like most of the great champions throughout history. Look at Floyd Mayweather. The guy's 45 years old, taking fucking fights against YouTubers and stuff because he can't let it go," Fury said in the lead-up to his fight against Derek Chisora on December 3. "It's a very difficult thing to let it go. Very difficult.

"I do not know how to quit. I'm going to be like Roberto Duran, fighting at 59 years old. I don't know anything else. I'm going to mess up this undefeated record ... now I know why all the greats get hurt."

I got married in 1990. Couple years later bought a house in a good neighborhood. Put up a heavy bag in the garage. Got a decent job in an office. Life was good enough. But at night, when I tried to sleep, my mind would go immediately to the little glories of my days as a fighter and, more importantly, to what I would do differently now that I was older and wiser. Not that I was going to do anything about it, of course. It was too late. I was domesticated. I could never fight again. Those days were gone. Just memories now.

But each night the memories and fantasies would return. I'd try to ward them off, think of other things—work, sex, money. I knew not to give in to them. I remembered the pain. Other nights, I would nestle into them like they were a warm blanket. They kept coming. Sometimes I'd lie awake wishing I were too old to ever do it again, that I were 40 or 50. Yes, I'd have given up 10 or 20 years of my life just to be done with it, finally, and know that even if I wanted to do it again, I couldn't.

But I wasn't 40 or 50. I was 28 and in the right light you could still see the outline of a six-pack when I took off my shirt. And I shook the whole damn house when I visited the heavy bag. Sometimes I would jump out of bed and shadowbox in the mirror in the middle of the night, my wife sleeping soundly, oblivious. I'd tell myself: *Fuck it. I'm doing it.* But the next morning would restore sense, as mornings so often do: What was I thinking?

This went on for a long time.

Finally I gave in and went to the old gym. Danny was back, training a whole new generation of kids. He agreed, reluctantly, to train me. I promised myself that this was it. The final time. And I wouldn't quit until I had an actual fight. No matter how bad it got in sparring, no matter how many times I asked myself what the fuck I was doing there, I wouldn't quit, I would see it through to the end. Otherwise, I'd have an excuse to try again. This had to be the last time.

I worked hard for six weeks. Lost 16 pounds, got in great shape. The South River Knights of Columbus Hall, right next to the old gym, held a card every year in May. The timing was perfect. I'd never lost when fighting on that show. The night of the fight, I got matched up with a kid from a local gym. I waited in my corner for the opening bell. My friends were in the crowd. My wife, too. I thought: "Well, this is what you wanted. Let's see what happens."

I remember reading a quote from Archie Moore. He said that when you're in shape, mentally and physically, you don't feel the punches. It's true. I've experienced it. I'd come out of fights where I was shocked when the locker room mirror greeted me with a reflection lumped up and bruised, though I couldn't recall ever getting hit.

It hurt every time this guy touched me. And he walked through my best left hooks.

Halfway through the first round: *What the fuck am I doing here?*

Danny stopped it after I got up from a second-round knockdown. He'd known all along how it was going to go down. "I knew you had to get it out of your system," he said.

So did I. And finally, I was free.

THE BUSINESS

THE GOOD WITH THE BAD

ORIGINALLY PUBLISHED IN *RINGSIDE SEAT*, SPRING 2022

THE FIGHT GAME isn't for everyone. First, of course, there's the violence, and those born without early exposure to it or a physiological affection or craving for it have no use for it. Even those who meet these standards are known, on occasion, to lose their taste for it as they age, a frequent side effect of which is to lecture younger versions of themselves as to its many dangers.

But violence—in the world and in sport—isn't particular to the fight business. The blood and occasional gore do not account for its standing among commercialized "sports entertainment," as a kind of Wild West, the outlaw of the major sports, even if it is not as major as it once was. The administration of professional boxing is so distinct from other popular American sports such as football, baseball, and basketball that it may as well not exist.

Sports leagues in America are such prolific money-making machines that their team owners see themselves, rightly, as manicured executives running large, multi-billion-dollar corporations. Their interests lie solely in the profit margins and they employ the conventional strategies and techniques their moneyed fathers and grandfathers used to build their own corporations.

It is why every NFL player says the same thing after every game. It is why every pronouncement, every public answer, every process, is reviewed by attorneys and public relations suits. It is why press have to go through several layers of intermediaries in order to speak with a player. There must be assurances that the player stay "on message" and the questions not too taxing or provocative.

This rigidity is inherent in every corporation and this includes the NFL, MLB, and NBA. The fealty to regulation provides a kind of comfort but squashes any attempts at independence, at individuality. There is no freewheeling. There is no sense of danger, of the unexpected. You trade that for banality and commercials starring Hollywood celebrities. It's like watching a sitcom: You know everything will be all right in the end

By contrast, following prizefighting is like walking a tightrope without a net. Corruption is rampant. So too is incompetence, and they are not mutually exclusive. The goal is the same: make money. But there are few, if any, rules that govern how one is permitted to achieve that. Create a new weight class? Sure. Start your own sanctioning body? No problem. Name multiple "world champions" in the same weight class and assign them different designations? Why not? Who's going to stop you?

You can start main events at midnight if you want. Charge $100 for a pay-per-view card for a bunch of trash fights and one potentially good one that could end at any time and also might suck. No one has any real way of knowing. Wrap your guy's hands in bits of plaster in the locker room. Who's going to notice? The guy from the athletic commission is the treasurer's nephew and wouldn't know gauze from a hole in the ground.

Want your lawyers to work in conjunction with the promoters behind the scenes so the fighter thinks he's being protected but really isn't? Go for it. What's he going to do about it? He can barely read.

Your fighter just got knocked out or got a bad decision? Screw it. Get a mic in his face and turn him loose. So he tells the promoter to go fuck himself (James Toney), or says the ref has a gambling problem (Juan Manuel Lopez). Who gives a shit? It's boxing!

Watch for long enough and you get the sense that everyone's just sort of winging it. There is no safety net. Anything can happen. A guy bites his opponent's ear off (Mike Tyson). A fighter attacks his opponent's trainer (Juan Manuel Lopez). A trainer attacks a fighter (Leon Lawson). A nutjob (James Miller) flies a paraglider into the ring in the middle of a heavyweight title fight and gets his ass handed to him at ringside.

It's not for everyone. But when the lights go down before a big main event and you know anything can happen, and then it does, there's nothing that beats it. Nothing comes close. And this lawlessness that it lives on, barely, is what gets you there, almost by accident, to a place that no other sport can.

The fight game is an absolute mess. And that's part of the fun.

THE TIES THAT BIND

ORIGINALLY PUBLISHED IN *RINGSIDE SEAT,* SUMMER 2021

THERE IS NO SHARPER editorial on the irrationality of the human spirit than the coming together of otherwise disparate humans over two fighters knocking loose one another's brains in the name of sport. If you've ever attended a prizefight and seen several thousand people rise as one in response to a furious exchange or sudden knockout, you know what I'm talking about.

It matters little, in most cases, how many in the crowd are black or Jewish, Irish or Mexican, English or Sudanese. The Ukrainians in the crowd will rise with the Russians, the Polish with the Portuguese, the Zambians with the Filipinos. The electricity and adrenaline explosion produced during the course of the right kind of prizefight lifts them all together -- Democrats and Republicans, atheists and believers, the righteous and the merely moral, the indefinable mass. They are overtaken. They can't help it. It is a reflex of the feral.

Certainly, there are those swept into the game who are motivated by national or ethnic pride and root primarily or even exclusively for their "own kind," and indeed, when prizefighting was at its zenith in terms of its popularity in America, this kind of rooting tribalism sustained the business. The immigrant classes fighting their way into the American sporting consciousness in the 1920s and '30s—the Jews versus the Italians, the Irish versus the blacks, the Italians versus the Irish, all fighting their way out of the ghettos, or trying to, so strongly invested in "us against them" that, as Jack Newfield once wrote, "rivalries [were] built on ethnic tension, and you could get ten thousand people for a fight between two neighborhood heroes."

Still, even he who arrives at a prizefight waving the flag of his countryman is helpless against the weight of emotion that is fueled by the special kind of back-and-forth violence or sudden apocalypse the right kind of fight produces, and, importantly, even if his own man gets the worst of it. We've all seen a partisan crowd go mostly silent when their hero takes a steady beating, but that's not the same as watching him happen suddenly on a violent end.

When an aged Joe Louis challenged Ezzard Charles for the heavyweight title in 1950, Louis was perhaps the most beloved prizefighter ever, and the crowd mostly watched in mournful silence as Charles battered him. In the 14th, a right hand made Louis shudder and do a little sidestep. The crowd, overwhelmingly rooting for Louis but helpless against the emotion brought on by the possibility of seeing him stopped, cheered wildly before, one presumes, regaining their senses. Due largely to Charles' gentle temperament, Louis lasted the distance.

I watched the Larry Holmes-Muhammad Ali fight in 1980 on closed-circuit TV in an armory in Elizabeth, New Jersey. It was a big crowd and most of its members chanted "Ali! Ali!" in the early rounds, before it became clear he had no chance. I didn't see a single section of the crowd rooting for Holmes, and yet, at least once late in the fight when it appeared Ali was about to be stopped, the crowd, helpless against its collective instinct, rose and cheered before sitting back down on their metal folding chairs and mourning the slow torture of a living legend. No one cheered for Holmes when Ali's corner surrendered, rather anti-climactically, between the 10th and 11th rounds.

Whether or not we know it, the weakness we exhibit in the face of all of boxing's sweet brutalities lies in the subtext of everything we do when we watch this sport, no matter who we are, with whom we align or what we believe. We should keep this in mind so that we all can come to a greater understanding of that which thrills us and ails us and, incomprehensibly, brings us together for a short while.

FIGHTERS AND WRITERS

ORIGINALLY PUBLISHED IN *RINGSIDE SEAT*, WINTER 2019

Such is the nature of fight game journalism that one who spends a fair chunk of his adult life mixed up in it finds that every story is at once both old and new. Every feature of the life of, say, Jack Dempsey or Henry Armstrong has been written over yet again, the same dates and details chronicled and celebrated so that one could recite them by heart, the only difference to be found in the flavor of the writer's prose. The lies fighters tell are all the same - the failures, the glories, the robberies, the accidental truths, the rags-to-riches-to-rags plotlines virtually interchangeable regardless of the decade, era, or even the century.

The freshness of each story is found in the nuggets of new truth unearthed by skilled investigators and fashioned anew by writers uninterested in fallacy, legend, or convenient untruths. There is not so much lost to history if only we take the time to look, and the best news is that new history is created again, over and over, every time the lights switch on over a ring and two gloved men take a step forward. It is no wonder there is ever more material as it involves boxing.

All journalism is truth-seeking, and the best writers reveal perhaps more truth than is preferred. They confront the very way we interpret what we see and how we experience fights with omnipresent media selling us things we neither require nor want merely for the hope of selling to us again next time. They search for secrets long hidden, for others buried right out in the open, mourn what could have been, and raise a glass for that which has been lost and will never return.

It is possibly the nature of journalists, and maybe boxing journalists especially, to gravitate toward the maudlin, but even in the stories that render us guilty by association, there are small things over which to rejoice, because nothing is gained in this world without pain, and nothing that is lost matters if it didn't bring joy to begin with.

A writer new to this terrain might worry that all of this scholarship would leave him desperate for material. He needn't suffer for long; there's not a sport on this planet with a history riper for exploration, a history that creates another chapter or sentence, at least, every time a man bashes another on the head, be he brute or artist. It's trite to be sure, but boxing really is the gift that keeps on giving.

For good reason, the business of prizefighting has nearly always been viewed by the upper class as another of the many senseless and backward rituals of the unwashed underclass. There can be no explanation beyond backwardness and unevolved barbarity for such a strong, collective interest in a spectacle as base and damaging as what we see when two otherwise intelligent, highly-trained, sentient human beings try with all their being to punch the other into unconsciousness for —and this is where it is especially dumbfounding —the entertainment it provides.

One suspects and hopes that should the species survive another millennium, the version that replaces ours will have evolved such that its members will look back upon our affection for legalized brutality with a kind of disgusted bewilderment, the way we do the to-the-death battles of the gladiators in ancient Roman times.

That it has taken many centuries for the species to move from the routine fatal barbarism of the Coliseum to comparatively benign unconsciousness as a method of victory is either heartening or discouraging, depending on one's point of view. In either assessment, it is evident that evolution will not be hurried.

Nevertheless, coverage of the sport and its participants has contributed mightily to the stores of what our most educated minds categorize as "literature" and surely that must count for something.

Many of the important authors of modern times wrote with affection and clarity about the business and sport of boxing. Ernest Hemingway, Norman Mailer, W.C. Heinz, Pete Hamill, A.J. Liebling, Joyce Carol Oates, Roger Plimpton and many others, some more accepting of the violent and sad nature of man than others, have explored our attraction to and revulsion at the fight game. In many cases, the best analyses are mere reportage; even to the unwashed among us, fighting as the great metaphor for life goes not unnoticed and one inevitably comes to the conclusion, if unhappily, that boxing is no more brutal than life itself and thus earns its place in the literature of our world.

BEHIND THE SCENES:
EMILY PANDELAKIS GIRTEN

IT DOESN'T HAPPEN BY ACCIDENT

IN ITS MOST RUDIMENTARY FORM, a fistfight occurs spontaneously, birthed organically through some threat or grievance severe enough to compel two people to ball their hands into fists and try to hurt the other to such a degree that one is the winner and the other, by necessity, the loser. Someone observed long, long ago that watching such an event excited something in the human spirit, switched on some neural circuit once necessary, perhaps, for survival of the species, and thus was born prizefighting as commerce.

And here we are today, a thousand or more years later, and this primitive circuitry remains intact, as evidenced by, if nothing else, the crowd of onlookers that immediately gathers around two humans punching it out, be it at a playground, bus stop, school cafeteria, street corner, highway, Walmart, ballgame, or PTA meeting. The pull to watch remains irresistible, revealing the happy truth that evolution will not be hurried, and also that given enough time, modern people can complicate almost beyond recognizability even the basest human acts.

Modern prizefighting, in this context regrettably meant to include various mixed martial arts contests, features administrative and marketing elements that couldn't have been envisioned in the wildest fantasies of those who first came up with the idea of making people pay for the pleasure of watching one punch another on the head. Indeed, there is an entire sub-industry whose purpose it is to market it to the masses and then, to the degree possible, ensure a satisfactory product has been delivered to onlookers, making them, in the best world, return customers.

Emily Pandelakis Girten got into the sport the way most do – by accident, which by most accounts is how all the best careers are born. Today she is so sought after as a publicist and operations guru that in a sport that everyone, including boxing insiders, claim is on life support, she finds herself forced to turn down work and expand her team – which consists in the main of herself and her husband.

"So, my schedule right now, I've got, for example, an MMA show. So I'm running everything from the ticketing and consignment tickets to getting the cage, getting all the fighters' medicals situated, all the paperwork with the commission, all of that stuff. And I do that for World Fighting Championships (WFC). So we have six shows the next eight weeks that we're doing."

She speaks quickly and with authority, with little to no chit-chat. Her manner is direct and concise. She is, after all, busy, and estimates that 85% of her workload is event management and the remainder in public relations.

We're used to watching fights and assuming that the myriad things that have to happen before the opening bell somehow just fall into place, that, for all we know or care, gremlins or some such wave a wand and put it all together. Nonsense, of course. None of it happens by accident. Everything is managed every step of the way. It has to be.

"And then for TGB Promotions I do their shuttles, their ground transportation. And then for Top Rank, I help with licensing. For Lou DiBella, I do PR. For Hitz Boxing, I handle marketing collateral, contracts, commission, and medical paperwork primarily. So, it's just kinda different for every client."

Pandelakis Girten is one of those fearless souls who learns as she goes and can navigate people and adverse circumstances through sheer doggedness and persistence, training be damned. "I've always worked in small businesses. I did work in the government for a very short period of time, but everything else was small businesses," she said recently.

"And I've always been a type to kinda learn very quickly on the fly without anybody telling me how to do things. I worked in software and project management, but I also did documentation and marketing and 10 other things. And that's kind of always been my strength, is the ability to do a lot of different things."

How many different things, you ask? It depends on the client, but for any given show, she might select photos for the fight poster and work with the graphics person to put it together, build a website for the promotion, order tickets through the venue, book the ring (or cage) and the round-card girls, a photographer, ambulance and any other staff that's needed on site.

She'll get the insurance, work with the local commission, get the fighters' medicals done and their licensing, book security, get fighter information for the ring announcer, find out what songs each fighter will walk out to, what size gloves they will wear and the names of the people working their corners.

Tired yet?

She'll order, pack, label and take the gloves with her to the venue, and maybe arrange and manage airport transportation for the fighters and their teams. She'll attend the weigh-in, check in the fighters and have them complete any last-minute paperwork, have their photos taken, finish any remaining ticket orders, print labels for all the commission seats, and label envelopes for the will-call window. When the show is over she might write the fighters' checks and update social media with the results.

This is a long way from Pandelakis Girten's earliest plan to be an Egyptologist. While taking college courses, she started working as a secretary for a software company, then at 19 gave birth to a son. Eventually the software company recognized her abilities, expanded her role and had her working in marketing and conducting software implementations and traveling, which effectively ended her days as a college student. She stayed with the software company for 15 years until a chance meeting at a boxing gym changed her course.

"I was dating a guy and I was really in shape. I was a personal trainer, and he said, 'Hey, you should try boxing.' He took me to the Central Boxing Gym in Phoenix (AZ) and Jose was the manager."

"Jose" is Jose Benavidez Sr., father of Jose Benavidez Jr. and David Benavidez, both fighters of import in the middleweight and light heavyweight divisions, respectively, at this writing. Benavidez started training Pandelakis Girten, they became friendly, and before she knew it she was putting Benavidez Jr.'s videos on MySpace and YouTube. Before long she was pitching stories to local media and getting the Benavidez boys on radio shows and podcasts and fielding requests from local newspapers, all the while making important connections in the industry.

"And then, you know, it just grew from there. I just had access to those people because of Junior's talent. That's why I love them all forever. We got to be really close friends. Him and his wife lived in my house. Like, we were super-duper close, still are. And that's kinda how I started."

One day she called Cameron Dunkin, then a manager of several high-profile fighters, and tried to sell him on Jovan Young. Dunkin said he wasn't interested but that she should keep calling. "And I did," she said. "And finally, he hired me and I learned, very quietly, a ton about management operations from him, and that's how I got into more of the operations stuff."

Pandelakis Girten said that she and Dunkin, who died in 2024, had a good connection and that he mentored her, which gave her legitimacy in the business. Through their association she learned everything there is to know about how the back-end works involving the bigger fighters and the deals they make. But knowledge takes one only so far. It's showing up, as the saying goes, that gets the job done – no matter what the job is.

"I find myself being able to wear a lot of hats and do a lot of different things, and I think that's very valuable in this business. I don't mind being the janitor. I don't mind doing, you know, grunt work even now after all these years because it has to get done as part of the show. I'm flexible with my time and my travel.

"But it was a lot of years of not making any money and, in fact, almost getting my house foreclosed multiple times," Pandelakis Girten said. "But right now, I think, you know, I just have a good reputation. I answer my phone. I'm actually known for that. Like, people say, 'Emily always answers her phone.' I think that I'm just good at what I do, and I enjoy it. I'm passionate about it."

Pandelakis credits her association with David Benavidez in particular with expanding her reach. He is generally recognized as one of 10 best in the world at this writing, and after running through the super middleweight division is on the verge of adding to his collection of big-fight victories, now at 175.

Like most others in boxing, Pandelakis Girten laments what appears a self-inflicted downturn in boxing's reach these days, caused mostly by the sport's inattention to the exposure and development of young fighters. She notes correctly that today's biggest stars became what they are through repeated exposure on cable television—namely HBO and Showtime—which no longer broadcast boxing. Even ESPN recently ended its association with Top Rank, leaving boxing, for the first time ever, without a television presence.

There may be some reason for optimism: Streaming giant Netflix has gotten into the business, broadcasting the Mike Tyson-Jake Paul event, which garnered a reported 108 million viewers, and Terence Crawford's win over Canelo Alvarez, which was watched by a reported 41 million. And while many scoffed at Top Rank's decision to stream Naoya Inoue's fight against Murodjon Akhmadaliev on Facebook, it exposed Inoue, one of boxing's best practitioners, to a huge audience.

"They had all those viewers, 13,000,000 viewers. When has he ever been seen by that many viewers?" Pandelakis Girten said. "So, I think, the Netflix deal where you get to watch it for free, is good. Anything that gets it into people's hands at a moderate or low price is going to keep things going. I think we just need to focus in that direction and stop longing for HBO and Showtime to come back. I wish they'd come back, but we can't build our business on that model anymore."

Pandelakis Girten has other ideas she thinks would help restore some of boxing's luster, such as putting out a line of boxing action figures and trading cards, which she would put into the hands of every kid who attends a show. She wants to get more of her clients endorsement deals, stay the hell out of matchmaking, which she did briefly ("it's the worst job in the business") and continue doing whatever it takes to make sure that when she's involved in an event, everything that can go right, does.

"It's much more boring than anybody thinks," Pandelakis Girten said. "Everybody thinks it's a glamorous job, but it's like just a bunch of paperwork." That may be so, but without it we wouldn't get to watch people try to separate one another from their senses, and then where would we be?

ON QUITTING

ORIGINALLY PUBLISHED IN *RINGSIDE SEAT*, SPRING 2021

WE CAN ARGUE until the cows come home over the appropriateness of using "quit" to describe what BJ Saunders did after the eighth round of his fight with Canelo Alvarez on May 8, but no matter how you slice it, he chose not to continue. That's literally what quitting is. The question that's at the heart of all the back and forth is this: Was the reason for his surrender justified? The simple answer would seem yes, given reports that Alvarez's right uppercut fractured Saunders' eye socket in several places. But the answer isn't that simple. The important ones rarely are.

I don't necessarily blame any fighter for calling it a day when it gets to be too much, for whatever reason. This is a hard business. Every fighter decides for himself or herself what the line is. For some, it's a busted hand, for others a swollen eye, for others still, a bad cut. That's fine. It's their life. But there's a flipside, and it's this: That fighter will never be great. That's what he gives up when he quits: potential greatness.

There are exceptions, of course. They're mostly reserved for fighters at or near the end of their career, or for fighters who later proved that their surrender was an anomaly -- see Alexis Arguello and Erik Morales against Aaron Pryor (in their rematch) and Manny Pacquiao (in their rubber match), respectively. See Julio Cesar Chavez in his rematch with Frankie Randall. See Roberto Duran against Ray Leonard (II and pretty much III, also), and Israel Vazquez against Rafael Marquez (I). There are more.

But those are the exceptions. Most of the time, when you see a guy quit, you know he'll never be great, and it's okay because a lot of fighters don't care if they're great. They like the attention and money and women, but if they can make enough to buy a house and give their kids a decent life and then get the hell out without getting their brains scrambled, that's a good deal.

You can't blame them. But they'll never be great. They'll be forgotten as soon as their career ends and no one outside their circle will think about them again until they drop dead. To most fighters, that doesn't matter. And so what? That's their choice. Good for them.

But are these the guys you watch boxing for? Are these the guys who got you hooked? Was it a fight where a guy got injured and quit that made you a boxing junkie, or was it Ward-Gatti? Or Corrales-Castillo? Or Foreman-Lyle?

Maybe it was Rocky Marciano stopping Ezzard Charles with his nose split down the middle, or Carmen Basilio going 15 rounds with Sugar Ray Robinson with an eye so swollen he looked like a human fly. Maybe it was Naoya Inoue fighting through a fractured orbital bone and a broken nose to beat Nonito Donaire.

We watch sports, and especially boxing, for the heroics. We watch it for the risk. We watch it for the drama. We watch it for the danger.

If you don't hold the fighters to a standard that's higher than the one to which you hold yourself, why are you watching? If you want to see someone quit from something that also would make you quit, why are you watching? If you want to watch people quit things when they get too hard, just go outside and look around. Or get a mirror.

Most fighters, and you can't blame them, draw a line: "This is how much I will endure. No more than this." BJ Saunders probably thought he didn't have a line. Most fighters think they can and will endure anything in pursuit of victory until that anything arrives and their instinct for self-preservation kicks in.

A few, a *very* few, have no line. And at the end, when everything else is gone, the crowds and the money and the friends and the women, they'll still have that and they will be remembered for it.

Those fighters are rare. They should be celebrated. And you can't celebrate them without thinking less of the others. And that's the way it should be.

BOXING AND THE RISK-
TO-REWARD RATIO

ORIGINALLY PUBLISHED IN *RINGSIDE SEAT*, WINTER 2023

IN DIRECTOR RON HOWARD's 1982 comedy *Night Shift*, the two lead characters, Chuck Lumley and Bill Blazejowksi, played by Henry Winkler and Michael Keaton, respectively, find themselves in a crowded Manhattan jail cell after being arrested for running a prostitution ring out of the city's morgue. Lumley is distraught and lashes out at Blazejowski for convincing him to join the sex trade.

"Oh, come on, we *have* to be pimps," Lumley mocks him, assuming a falsetto voice. "Let's be pimps!"

Blazejowski's response is perfectly nonsensical: "Well we couldn't be doctors!"

I thought of this line after reading reports about 1970s heavyweight contender Joe Bugner, who, as reported by Colin Hart in February in *The Sun*, has advanced dementia at age 72 and no recollection of a career that saw him in the ring with Muhammad Ali, Joe Frazier, Earnie Shavers, Ron Lyle, and others.

"He will be 73 next month yet believes he's only 38," Hart quoted Bugner's son, Joe Jr. "He happens to be in his own little world."

Such is the nature of the various brain diseases and conditions that cause dementia that, as recently as 10 years ago, Bugner exhibited no signs of cognitive decline. In 2013, he was interviewed by *The Ring's* Tom Gray, who reported, "at 63 years of age (Bugner), sounds like he's never taken a punch in his life, despite having endured three decades in the prize ring."

Following Hart's revelation came the usual laments over the ravages boxing heaps on its participants, the need for reform, and the warnings to young men (and women) who are attracted to its glory and brutality. The subtext to all of it is and has always been: Why would anyone do this?

Why would anyone be a fighter?

Well, to quote Bill Blazejowski: They couldn't be doctors.

There is a naive and pervasive sense among a certain class of boxing observer that fighters come from (and return to when they are through) environments where they could be anything they want -- doctors, lawyers, business executives, scientists, artists, etc., but for reasons known only to them, chose one of the hardest and most dangerous sports in the world.

Does that make sense? How many people do you know of who left a promising career in law or education or medicine to become professional fighters?

It's true that fighters *choose* boxing, but in most cases, their career options are depressingly few. By a sizable majority, fighters come from poverty, from violence, from broken homes, from the foster care system, from reformatories, from jails and from factories because boxing gave them a shot at something better.

How do you tell a talented 16-year-old kid who sees his friends killed in the streets and wants to be the next Floyd Mayweather that he shouldn't fight because he might get dementia when he's 72? When you were 16, did you care what things might be like when you were 72? Or 62? Or even 52?

And it doesn't have to be that bleak. For every fighter who gets early-onset dementia or something worse from his career in the ring, there are many others who make it out undamaged.

Murray Sutherland is one. He fought at light heavyweight during

Bugner's era, more or less, and faced all the killers of his generation—Matthew Saad Muhammad, Michael Spinks (twice), Thomas Hearns, Richie Kates, Eddie Davis, Bobby Czyz. His story is typical.

"I worked in a factory, eight-hour shifts, days, then afternoons, then nights, over and over, as a machinist," Murray said in 1981.

"The whole time I kept saying I wasn't going to do this the rest of my life. People would ask me what else I could do. I used to say I didn't know, but I sure as hell wasn't going to work in a factory the rest of my life."

And he didn't. He saw the world. He fought champions. He made a hell of a lot of money. He lived.

Of course, it's not just economics. The destitute number in the millions and they're not all fighters. A man must have an aptitude for it, a craving for violent contact that is mostly physical or biological and that he has inherited from someone or something. He has to want it. No man can be a boxer against his will. He has to love it. He has to need it.

I get the sense Joe Bugner needed it more than loved it, as he was a little passive for American fight fans. In his biggest fights, against Ali and Frazier, he more or less fought to survive -- except for a moment late in the Frazier fight in '73 when he walked Joe into a perfect right hand that shook Frazier to his bones.

In the few seconds that it appeared Frazier might go down, Bugner must have felt like the king of the world. Surely that is worth something.

IN THE AGE OF CORONA BOXING IS THE KEITH RICHARDS OF SPORTS

ORIGINALLY PUBLISHED IN *RINGSIDE SEAT*,
SUMMER/FALL 2020

WHILE THE MOST popular sports in America flail and mostly flounder trying to get their business model together in the Age of Corona, it is prizefighting, the niche sport that has been dying for almost as long as it has existed, that is innovating its way into something resembling normalcy.

As of this writing, NBA executives and agents are lobbying the league to cancel the remainder of the season as multiple players test positive for the Coronavirus. College sports are in a shambles as universities scramble to organize rosters without fully opening up.

Major League Baseball commissioner Rob Manfred recently told MLB Players Association executives that the season will be cancelled if the sport doesn't do a better job of managing the virus. This after 21 members of the Miami Marlins tested positive. Even the NFL, a financial juggernaut and by far the most popular spectator sport in America, is on unsure footing as the season approaches, with many players opting out.

Meanwhile, in the bizarro world that is professional boxing, Top

Rank and *ESPN* just completed a seven-week summer series that included 13 cards and 70 fights— many of them evenly matched and competitive. Doing business almost exclusively in "The Bubble" in Las Vegas, they navigated 19 positive Covid cases and 12 cancellations but still put together and televised almost 400 rounds of boxing.

It's true that the ratings were not great; the average number of viewers per show was somewhere in the low-to-mid 300,000 range, with Miguel Berchelt's non-title win over Eleazar Valenzuela peaking at around 418,000. Still, unless my high school math teachers were lying to me, 300,000 is better than zero by, well, 300,000.

A couple weeks after the ESPN series ended, boxing delivered as only it can, with shows from Premier Boxing Champions on Showtime, Eddie Hearn's Matchroom Boxing on DAZN, and the return of Srisaket Sor Rungvisai in Thailand, all in one day. The previous week featured announcements concerning several fights of import, including Errol Spence-Danny Garcia, Vasily Lomachenko-Teofimo Lopez, Leo Santa Cruz-Tank Davis, and Canelo Alvarez-this guy or that one.

At least there's movement. Things are happening. Liars in suits are negotiating. Most of it is bullshit, hyperbole, and obfuscation, which is a way to say that boxing is starting to feel like boxing again. That's more than you can say for a lot of things.

Like Keith Richards, boxing survives largely in spite of itself. It always has. Remember that in the late 19th and early 20th centuries, the sport was illegal in most of the United States. It might have stayed that way if not for America's entrance into World War I and the ascendance of Jack Dempsey. Since then it's survived gangsters, greed, mismanagement, Butterbean, Hollywood, the American Medical Association, more gangsters and greed, the banning of 15-rounders, Don King, the afore-mentioned mainstream sports, silver belts, Ferdie Pacheco, the WBO, fighter-deaths, day-before weigh-ins, widespread brain injury, "super" champions, John Ruiz, "interim" world champions, and dalliances with open scoring and standing eight-counts.

Pandemic? *Please.*

The fight game will survive because people enjoy watching other people punch and get punched. That's really all there is to it, which brings us to the Mike Tyson-Roy Jones exhibition scheduled for November 28 at Dignity Health (*really?*) Sports Park in California and available on PPV for a reported $49.99. You may have noticed that on social media and elsewhere, the majority of interested observers fall generally into one of two camps.

The first of these is the one whose members have been storm-trooping message boards with exclamations that are typically some variant of "Iron Mike is back, bitches!" In the minds of these, it is forever 1988. The inevitable decline that began in the '90s never occurred, nor did the ensuing 15 years of retirement. Tyson is forever 25.

The other camp is made up of purists who are shocked—*shocked!*— that the fight game, the oldest and noblest of the violent arts, would degrade itself with such a blatantly lurid sideshow as two 50-something former superstars sparring in overstuffed gloves and headgear. What would Pierce Egan think?!

I don't know if I'll pay $50 to watch Tyson and Jones waltz together. There are worse things to waste money on. When faced with these types of choices, I often ask myself: If these two guys had a fender bender in the street or a parking lot and were getting ready to throw hands, would I stop and watch, or would I drive away?

You bet your ass I'd watch. You would too. That you're thinking about it right now is the key to the game's survival, even during a global pandemic. There are some things we just can't do without.

A GOOD FIGHT RUINED

A SAD TALE OF INCOMPETENCE
AND CONTROVERSY

ORIGINALLY PUBLISHED IN *THE RING*, NOVEMBER 2011

THERE IS ALMOST NO GREATER delusion than the one that holds an absolute good could exist in a sport in which a participant's goal is to produce brain injury in his opponent. But within the context of modern-day prizefighting, the Abner Mares-Joseph Agbeko matchup, going in, was as close as one could reasonably expect to come. There simply was nothing to dislike about it, even by a media whose affection for concussion and redemption, not necessarily in that order, is surpassed only by its love of drama, reconditioned or manufactured, and rampant finger-pointing.

Mares-Agbeko was the final anyone who'd been enamored of Showtime's neat little bantamweight tournament was hoping for, secretly or otherwise, and the tournament itself was a more concise, less-bloated version of the super middleweight tournament so cursed almost from inception that one is forced to marvel at its happy conclusion. That Agbeko, 28-3 (22), chose to stay in the tournament after suffering sudden-onset sciatica, which postponed the final, reinforced the suspicion and the hope among believer-types that the fight was something along the lines of preordained.

Important too was the business reality that the winner would put himself in position to face Nonito Donaire, who, by most credible accounts and despite his small physical stature, is being groomed to become the next Manny Pacquiao (non-Filipinos need not apply). There still would be the matter of Panama's Anselmo Moreno to deal with, but the unwashed masses would be happy to learn that some legal or promotional entanglement or another would prevent him from playing along, and Donaire versus the winner of Mares-Agbeko would be The Next Biggest Little Thing Ever.

Lastly, Mares, 22-0 (13), has the kind of charisma and story and smile that helps sell tickets and with the right promoter and attention —he has been a Golden Boy fighter since turning pro — it is believed in some quarters that he could be made into a kind of mini-Oscar De La Hoya, and what's wrong with that? You couldn't blame anyone for crossing his fingers with the hope that Mares could do it, though without The Golden One's troubling tendency to say or tweet things that get his minders and other associated suits into trouble. (And you wonder why Bob Arum kept him on such a short leash in the beginning. He knew.) But there would be time later for all that.

In the vernacular of modern sport, the fight couldn't miss. So long as the two of them made it to the ring and weren't besieged by a swarm of locusts or frogs falling from the sky or some other such Biblical disaster, everything would come together nice and tidy, and we all would go to bed afterward feeling good about our beleaguered little sport. And then along came Russell Mora and everything went to hell.

By the time it was over, judges C.J. Ross, Adalaide Byrd, and Oren Shellenberger had given Mares, Montebello, California, a majority decision win by scores of 113-113 and 115-111 (twice), but that is so incidental as to be irrelevant. (*The Ring* scored it for Mares, 115-112.) The real story was the ruination of what should have been a bright night for boxing and, as you surely know by now, how Mora screwed everybody — Agbeko, Mares, Showtime, the fans, and really, anyone who enjoys a good fistfight fought fair and square. Yes, in a rare display of clarity, the attendant sanctioning body ordered a rematch—isn't that nice of them—but the damage already has been done.

It wasn't just the low blows—55 of them, according to boxing writer Thomas Hauser, who watched the fight a second time, which is not recommended for the overly empathetic — that Mora more or less ignored. It wasn't the blown knockdown call in the opening round, during which Agbeko's feet went out from under him as though he were on ice skates, even though a Mares punch had barely grazed him.

It wasn't just Mora's constant hectoring of Agbeko, Bronx, New York, via Ghana, to stop pulling Mares' head down, a way to say that Agbeko himself was causing Mares to hit him low. It wasn't even the final, terrible insult -- the Mares left that slammed into Agbeko's groin right in front of Mora. Or when you thought finally Agbeko would get some justice, better late than never, Mora counted over Agbeko, giving Mares a second undeserved 10-8 round and all but guaranteeing Agbeko's defeat.

It wasn't any of those single events that ruined everything; it was the sum total of all of them, and, when you heard later that Dana Jamison from Don King's office had warned Nevada Commissioner Keith Kizer that Mora is a "Golden Boy referee," it made it all worse, even if it was a baseless claim. And Kizer, who doesn't excuse himself to go to the restroom before running it by legal counsel first, made it worse, as he makes many things worse, by being overcautious, saying that Mora is a good referee who had a subpar night.

"In a situation like this, the referee needs to get with me and also with some of the senior referees here in Nevada, which I'm encouraging, to learn from this performance and improve in the future," Kizer told Kevin Iole at *Yahoo.com*. "He'll need to take his time coming back and build himself back up. I have a very high confidence he'll be able to do so."

One is compelled to wonder where Kizer was while Mora was having this subpar night and why, if he saw it unfolding as such, he never chose to pull Mora aside and straighten him out. He had 48 minutes in which to do it, after all. It was a long fight. He couldn't take him aside between rounds after, maybe, the 22nd low blow? Text him? Have his attorney draft him a letter? Why sit back and let him continue to screw up on a grand stage?

Also, you could be forgiven for asking what Mora needs to learn, exactly. What a low blow is and what it isn't? Isn't that lesson pretty much covered the first day of referee class and wrapped up before lunch? "Okay, class, here's the belt line. A punch landed above it is legal; below it is illegal. See here? Watch my hand. Legal, illegal. Above, below. Legal, illegal. One more time: Legal here, illegal there. Any questions? Good. Next lesson: how to tell when a round has come to an end. First, you'll hear a bell ..."

One can only imagine what a "training session" between Mora and Joe Cortez, the most senior of Nevada's senior officials, might sound like: "The first thing you have to remember, Russell, is I'm fair but I'm firm. Next, here's the belt line. A punch above it is legal, below it illegal. Remember that, from class? Sure you do. Here legal, there illegal. Got it? Hey, did I tell you I was inducted into the International Boxing Hall of Fame? No? Here's how it happened ..."

Such was the severity of Mora's incompetence that he made sympathetic characters of two of the fight game's most dependable villains -- Showtime's abrasive Jim Gray, whose sarcastic postfight interrogation of Mora was received as brilliant payback, and Don King, who in better days had the juice to name the referee he wanted and got him, every time.

"What I saw was either total incompetence or corruption," King said. "Choose whichever you'd like. I've been around a long time, and I've never witnessed anything like that. It's so outrageous. The last one, Mares hit him directly in the [groin], and he was down, writhing in pain on his knees. And the referee called it a knockdown. It was so outrageous and makes you question everything you hold holy." As the old saying goes, or should go, you know you done fucked up when Don King is calling you on your bullshit.

Another sign is when Showtime's terminally agreeable Al Bernstein tells the viewing audience your performance is the worst he's seen in 15 years. Bernstein's usually cheerful and unflappable call grew more exasperated as the fight wore on and his postfight wrap-up was almost halfhearted. You couldn't blame him. It should have been a banner night for Showtime, a celebration of a little tourney pulled off more or less flawlessly with the crowd's favorite, Mares, the winner. All they needed was a referee who would do the job right.

You could make the argument that Agbeko, though the official loser, gained something in a tainted defeat he would not have had with a clean, close decision loss or even a victory: the public's sympathy, which, temporarily at least, is a powerful ally. And to be clear, he did not perform overly well over the fight's first half, missing many punches and relying too heavily on sweeping left hooks that Mares, 117 ½, was only too happy to block and counter. Agbeko, 118, was a half-step slower at least over the fight's first half, and, except for a big right that wobbled Mares in the fourth, he was continually outfought until the fight's latter stages, when he stepped forward and threw straight right hands in earnest.

"This was a very big fight tonight, and I am a champion. And I don't know why I have to fight two people in the ring all the time," Agbeko said after the fight.

Low blows aside, Mares fought well throughout, using his quickness and straighter punches to beat Agbeko to the punch and his feet to jump in, stab Agbeko with a hook or right, and then jump back out again where he could watch Agbeko's counter hook sail by. He was everything you wanted a bright young star to be if you were in the star-making business and if you didn't mind that your star likes to hit guys in the balls over and over.

Mora made all of it moot, made sure that in the main, it is he who will be remembered when fans look back at Mares-Agbeko I. It made for an awkward time for the sport's contrarians. Even the most disagreeable among them could muster no defense for Mora and were forced into the fold of the majority, an uncomfortable place to be sure. It couldn't be helped. Some things are just too obvious.

· · ·

Epilogue: In the rematch three months later, Mares won a unanimous decision by three scores of 118-111. The referee was Lou Moret.

INSIDE THE DIAZ-
MALIGNAGGI CONTROVERSY

WHAT REALLY HAPPENED AND WHY

ORIGINALLY PUBLISHED IN *THE RING*, DECEMBER 2009

STRICTLY SPEAKING, there was very little that was unusual about what happened on August 22 in Houston, Texas. A hometown boy won a decision over an out-of-towner in what most agree was a reasonably close fight.

Really, measured against the ever-fluid and relentlessly entertaining standards practiced in the prizefighting business, it was utterly mundane. Even if you want to say the out-of-town kid got robbed – and there's not even universal agreement there – that's pretty humdrum in this sport. It always has been.

What made Juan Diaz's win over Paulie Malignaggi noteworthy was the length to which Malignaggi went to forecast what he saw as a loss that was both virtually inevitable and profoundly unjust in its architecture, and the degree to which his prediction came true. It was uncanny.

Malignaggi couldn't have predicted the outcome more accurately if he were the sole owner of the world's only functioning time machine and used it to travel ahead to the moments that came right after he gave Diaz what was, in the eyes of a substantial majority, a thorough boxing lesson.

The happenings of the fight are by this time widely known and almost secondary in terms of their importance, but they deserve a general recounting nonetheless. Malignaggi, 26-3 (5), used his legs and an accurate, stinging left jab to control and out-maneuver Diaz in many of the rounds and, along the way, opened two cuts around Diaz's left eye. Diaz, 35-2 (17) chugged ever forward, as is his wont, but found his famously high punch output significantly impeded by Malignaggi's movement, jab, and ability to shut him down inside. Still, Diaz's hooks and power punches were more readily noticeable and appeared harder than Malignaggi's jabs and occasional right hands. And when Diaz landed, the Houston crowd, bless their boxing-loving hearts, reacted as one would expect them to react.

The unanimous decision for Diaz, 137 ¼, was rendered by judges Raul Caiz, Donald Sutherland, and Gale Van Hoy by scores of 115-113, 116-112, and 118-110, respectively. A majority of the boxing press had Malignaggi, Brooklyn, New York, 138 ¼, winning in the vicinity of 115-113. *The Ring* scored it 116-113 for Malignaggi.

A poll conducted by *fightnews.com* in the days following the fight found that approximately 60 percent of respondents thought Malignaggi deserved the decision, while the balance was evenly split between those who thought Diaz won it and those who believed it could have gone to either man.

In Malignaggi's mind, the seeds of the official vote were sown during negotiations for the fight, during which he and his camp say he gave ground on all the important financial and strategic considerations. He accepted the location, the Toyota Center in Houston. He accepted a small, 18-foot ring, which clearly benefited the aggressor, Diaz. He took a maximum weight of 138 ½, which he hadn't made in several years.

These concessions, according to Malignaggi's camp, were the result of leverage Diaz had, largely because his promoter is Golden Boy Promotions, whose relationship with HBO guarantees its fighters dates—and, consequently, larger purses—that are rarely available to fighters aligned with other promotional companies.

"Diaz had a guaranteed date (on HBO)," Lou DiBella, Malignaggi's promoter, told *The Ring*. "Paulie Malignaggi didn't. Paulie wasn't going to get on television without an opportunity. And the opportunity that presented itself was Juan Diaz."

Malignaggi agreed.

"If DiBella Entertainment had other dates (on HBO), I would not have gone to Houston," Malignaggi said. "But because Golden Boy has all the dates, I would not have had another chance at another big fight until 2010. If there were any other options, no doubt about it I wouldn't have gone to Houston to fight Juan Diaz. But there were no other options. You have to take what you can get. I'm not in a position where I want to fight until I'm 35. I had to take any opportunity."

So with the cards already stacked against him in ways and by means that are not at all unusual in the fight game, and indeed whose acquisition can and should be viewed as part of a good promoter's job, Malignaggi rested his flagging hopes on what he says he was promised: neutral officials.

What he got were Caiz, from California, Sutherland, from Oklahoma, Van Hoy, from Texas, and referee Laurence Cole, also from Texas and the son of Texas Department of Licensing and Regulation (TDLR) boss Dickie Cole.

Before attempting to discern how "neutral" these judges were, it's important to discuss Malignaggi's recollection of how the alleged promise of neutral officials was made, and by whom.

"I was at the Empire State Building at the (Floyd) Mayweather - (Juan Manuel) Marquez press conference," Malignaggi said. "Richard Schaefer approached me, and he was flanked by (HBO executives) Kerry Davis and Ross Greenburg, and asked me if I would fight Diaz in Houston.

"I was getting ready to fight (Mike) Alvarado and I said, 'Thank you, but no thank you. It's a great opportunity. I would love to fight Diaz in a more neutral situation. I would rather not go to another man's hometown.' And he said, 'What if we get you neutral officials?'

"And I said, 'You know what Richard, it's a great offer, I appreciate the opportunity, but I'm getting ready to fight Alvarado.' And we ended the conversation and everything was fine. I would consider it with neutral officials. Then when Alvarado pulled out (with an injury), I called his bluff. It was only a week or so later."

Ron Rizzo, an attorney working on Malignaggi's behalf for DiBella Entertainment, corroborated Malignaggi's version of the story. In an email to *The Ring*, he wrote, "The terms as originally agreed to on June 8th were main event on HBO B.A.D., Houston, TX site, financial and accommodation terms, and neutral officials."

Schaefer, though in agreement about when, where and under what circumstances he first offered Malignaggi a fight with Diaz, disputes that he promised neutral officials.

"We did talk about the fight at the press conference, but he said he really didn't want to do it because he felt it would basically be an uphill battle," Schaefer told *The Ring*. "He said he was going to go and fight someone else. He had another fight lined up. I said okay, look, at least we tried.

"So Ross Greenburg actually had mentioned that that's the fight, with Diaz, so then I said (to Malignaggi), 'Look, I'm sure you would get fair treatment in Texas,' but I would never and can never go and promise someone neutral judges because the appointment of judges is not up to me, it's not up to any promoter. It's up to the state athletic commission.

"What I did tell Paulie is I will talk to the athletic commission and see what we can do. I will ask them to appoint neutral officials and if at the end of the day they listen to us or not, I cannot promise you, because it's out of my control. You can't promise somebody something that is out of your control. But I told him I will do my best to see if we can agree on neutral officials."

Schaefer said that when he asked the commission—specifically, executive director Bill Kuntz, Cole's superior – for neutral officials, he received an unhelpful response.

"It was, 'Are you implying there is something wrong with our officials?' We said no, we just want to avoid any potential issues, because I don't think it would be good for the sport or for the state of Texas," Schaefer said.

"They were rather clear and direct with us and said, 'The appointment of any officials is up to the state athletic commission. We appreciate your concerns, but we will not take it into consideration because it will look as if our officials are not capable to officiate a bout in Texas, and we cannot allow that perception to be there.' And that was it."

The Texas commission has a reputation for doing things their own way and it would appear the reputation is justified. Although the lack of broad, consistent regulation of the sport across the U.S. means protocol varies from state to state, many commissions are willing to work with promoters when it comes to selecting officials. Greg Sirb, Executive Director of the Pennsylvania State Athletic Commission, told *The Ring* that's part of the job.

"We usually entertain suggestions. There's nothing wrong with that. For example, Paul Spadafora fought many times here for his title. We knew the other guy wouldn't want to see Pittsburgh officials around the ring, so we'd normally get one from Pennsylvania, one from a neutral place, and one from wherever the challenger was from," Sirb said. "You've got different scenarios, but I'm always open-minded and you try to keep it, at least on paper, as neutral as you can."

Sirb recognizes that conflicts exist that are justifiable and that it's better many times to be accommodating, so long as you're not being asked to do something unethical.

"I don't mind if a promoter contacts me or writes me and says, 'Greg, we don't like ref or judge X because we had a bad time with him once.' If it's legitimate, I can see that. I don't want a promoter to come and say, 'I want X.' That's a huge red flag to me. But I'll entertain issues where someone says, 'Hey, we don't want this guy.' I can understand some of this stuff."

That's not the case in Texas. Rizzo, DiBella's attorney, told *The Ring* that on or about June 30th, they were informed by the commission that neutral officials would be "an issue" and they would have to accept at least one Texas judge. Roughly two weeks later, they were given Van Hoy, Kelley Yho, who is from Texas, and Caiz.

The Malignaggi camp was particularly concerned about Van Hoy, who was one of three judges to score the first Rocky Juarez-Chris John fight, also held in Houston, a draw, and about Caiz, whom Malignaggi afterward called a "go-fer for Golden Boy."

Caiz had scored the Erik Morales-Zahir Raheem fight in 2005 closer than had the other judges who gave Raheem the decision win. This made Malignaggi suspicious, as both Caiz and Diaz are of Mexican descent (as is Morales). Other members of the Malignaggi camp felt Caiz had demonstrated a tendency to favor aggressive fighters over stick-and-move boxers like Malignaggi.

According to Rizzo, the Malignaggi camp repeatedly asked the Texas commission to remove Caiz and Van Hoy in the weeks leading up to the fight. They were rebuffed. On August 3, the commission announced that the judges would be Caiz, Van Hoy, and CJ Ross. Ross, a resident of Las Vegas, replaced Yho, who the commission agreed to remove following protests from Malignaggi's camp. Ross was the only judge on a joint list of officials that both promoters had submitted to the commission. The others were Robert Hoyle, Al Bennett, Michael Pernick, Paul Herman, and Glen Feldman.

According to Rizzo, he received a call on August 14th from Dickie Cole, who told him Ross wouldn't be available on the day of the fight and would be replaced by Sutherland. Malignaggi's camp immediately objected and was told the appointments were final, and if Malignaggi didn't want the fight, he could pull out.

In an attempt to clarify the Texas commission's judge-appointment process, for this fight and in general, *The Ring* contacted Mr. Cole. He refused to answer any questions and referred us to Ms. Susan Stanford, Public Information Officer for the TDLR. We asked her why the commission appointed Caiz, who is not a Texas official, when the Malignaggi camp objected to him and he did not appear on the list of judges both promoters accepted.

In an email, Ms. Stanford replied, "Boxing judges in Texas are placed in a rotation and are considered for events on that basis. A judge sanctioned by an organization is also taken into consideration if the event is a title fight.

"Raul Caiz was chosen based on TDLR procedure and his experience as a judge with over 40 title fights in the WBC, WBO, IBF, ... etc."

We also asked why none of the judges had been selected who had been deemed acceptable by both camps. Ms. Stanford replied, "TDLR considers requests from promoters and boxer camps, but it is ultimately the decision of the department to assign the officials." Finally, we asked why Van Hoy was appointed when it was clear the Malignaggi camp objected strenuously to his selection. This was critical in view of Van Hoy's 118-110 score in favor of Diaz, which prompted significant outcry even from those who believed Diaz had rightly been named the winner.

Ms. Stanford replied: "Gale Van Hoy's selection was based on his extensive judging experience in boxing, including over 40 title fights in the United States and other countries."

The Ring spoke with Van Hoy two weeks after the bout and asked him if he'd been aware of Malignaggi's very public prefight statements concerning his appointment. It would not be unreasonable to assume that hearing a fighter predict his own mugging at your hands would impede one's ability to render an impartial verdict.

"Yes, I heard that," Van Hoy said. "(There wasn't) any big deal about it. They all say that. It didn't really impress me because I didn't hear too much about it. It didn't impress me as anything I should be involved in, the little bit I heard. I didn't hear much."

This seems unlikely, given how much noise Malignaggi made about it in the days leading up to the fight. Van Hoy claimed he had no idea going into the fight that the Malignaggi camp had tried to have him removed. "No, I wasn't aware of that. He (Dickie Cole) didn't share that with me." He seemed dumbfounded as to why they didn't want him as a judge.

"I did Malignaggi's fights before. I did Lou DiBella's fights all over America – California, Connecticut, Arkansas, Tennessee, and he's never had a problem with me. I did a Malignaggi fight years ago in

Arkansas. He was in a 10-rounder or eight-rounder or something. But Dickie Cole didn't say nothing to me. I didn't know that."

Van Hoy also seemed incredulous that there was a list of judges that have been submitted by both camps, and that things like that even happen.

"You're talking about things I don't have anything to do with or don't even know about. I didn't know there was a list of judges they wanted. Golden Boy had to approve me or I wouldn't have done the fight, I guess."

That last statement is consistent with information Ms. Stanford at the TDLR supplied in one of her emails, in which she wrote that Ross and Sutherland had been "approved" by Golden Boy. Asked to clarify that statement, and also if DiBella Entertainment had the same "approval" authority, she replied: "TDLR was in contact with Golden Boy Productions (sic) and as stated earlier, the Department makes the final official assignments."

This would seem to contradict Schaefer's assertion that he had next to nothing to do with the selection of the officials.

"When Malignaggi's camp and Lou DiBella called me and said we have to find a resolution here (about the officials) I said 'Lou, you know very well how that goes, you can ask, you can beg, you can make your case, but at the end of the day, you, as a promoter, and us, as a promoter, we have absolutely no say on the appointment of officials," said Schaefer. "There was nothing we could do and it was totally out of our control."

Schaefer also stressed that controversial decisions are part of the sport and that Golden Boy fighters have been on the wrong end as much as on the right end.

"The fact is, sometimes you have fights that go your way, and, talking as a promoter now, sometimes they go against you. When Oscar fought Mayweather, that was a close fight, and when Marquez fought Pacquiao, most media members thought Marquez won.

When Oscar fought Tito Trinidad, I haven't met anyone yet, I mean everyone thinks Oscar won that fight, I could go on and on," Schaefer said. "There's a long list of fights. When Shane Mosley fought Cotto, the opinion was split over who won. The second Bernard Hopkins-Jermain Taylor fight, too. So sometimes you win some and sometimes you lose some, and believe me, Golden Boy has been more often than not on the other side when it came to close fights."

The upshot of all this has been a blow to boxing's reputation, even among the hardcore who expect it half the time. It's also improved Malignaggi's stock. His postfight rant at HBO's Max Kellerman, during which he screamed, "Boxing is full of shit!" had, at press time, been viewed on YouTube more than 53,000 times. In a sense, the loss has helped him.

"He helped himself," said DiBella. "He's created a cause célèbres here. He prognosticated his own screwing, and then it happened. He gave this incredibly passionate speech in the ring that I think most people related to, and most people who got screwed wouldn't take it lightly.

"I think he's a bigger star than he might've been if he won a solid 7-5 decision," DiBella said. "Now Paulie's on the radar screen again as opposed to when he sort of fell off it when he had that bad night against Hatton. Yes, the decision wasn't what he wanted, but you know what? HBO's going to pay a really good license fee to have these guys fight again."

That pleases Anthony Catanzaro, Malignaggi's business advisor. "The fight we want is Malignaggi-Diaz II. That's the fight we're working on. That's the fight the fans want. There was a taste to that night, and it just wasn't right. It was so wrong."

Malignaggi doesn't see how the controversy helped him. He welcomes a rematch but only under more favorable terms.

"It's working out in a positive way, but only because I performed. Had I performed and gotten the decision, I still would have been in a better position regardless. I don't think getting screwed helped me in any way. The performance is what helped me, and the performance merited a victory. My performance spoke for itself, but a 'W' would have been better," he said.

"It was only competitive because of the other things they did to me. It was only competitive because the ring was small. Because I had to make 138 ½ pounds. Can you imagine if the fight was in New York with a 24-foot ring? And give me a judge from New Jersey, a judge from New York, and an Italian judge from Connecticut. And make it 140 pounds instead of 138 ½. Juan doesn't win a half a second of that fight against me. They had all those advantages and still had to rob me to get Diaz a 'W.' That's how much better I am than Juan Diaz."

It would be little consolation to Malignaggi to learn that when we asked Van Hoy if he had watched the fight again since judging it live, he said that he had, with the sound off, and, given the chance, he might have come up with a different score.

"I think I made a mistake—with my brain, not my heart. Rounds nine and 10 could have went either way," he said. "Had I (scored them for Malignaggi), we wouldn't be having this conversation."

That's conceivable. A 116-112 score from Van Hoy would have generated far less heat than did his 118-110 count. But it also would have garnered Malignaggi much less sympathy and support from those outraged at Van Hoy's seeming incompetence, arrogance, or something worse.

As it happened, the sheer absurdity of Van Hoy's score, whatever the cause, was a gift to Malignaggi, whether or not he sees it that way. It sent him back to Brooklyn with a hope not dissimilar to the one he had when he left: a fight with Juan Diaz and a fair shake. Next time, maybe he'll get it.

Epilogue: Four months after their first fight, Malignaggi and Diaz fought in Chicago. Malignaggi won a clear, 12-round decision.

THE BITE FIGHT

IS TYSON FINISHED?

ORIGINALLY PUBLISHED IN *THE RING*, NOVEMBER 1997

AFTER TWO WEEKS of almost suffocating attention, it was over. Just like that, the world moved on. At almost the precise moment at which the Nevada State Athletic Commission announced its ruling to revoke Mike Tyson's license to box, the stare of the industrialized world left the bizarre world of prizefighting and turned its sights on less complex, more familiar subjects.

A final, mad rush was made for an industry source who would pontificate on the significance of the ruling, but that was really the story's last great gasp. Yes, there remained for a day or two the obligatory "do-you-think-the-punishment-was-severe-enough?" angle, and even that was milked, but much of the steam was gone by then. The day after, local evening news telecasts led with stories other than those that involved the latest Tyson sighting, and the tabloid magazine shows saw fit to finally stop reporting the results of those call-in opinion polls that are a staple of a sad genre:

"Should Tyson be banned for life? Should he be tarred and feathered? Deported? Imprisoned? Tell us what you think, America."

Scour the radio as we like, even the all-sports stations, we wouldn't find much more Tyson talk out there.

No, when the last of the non-sporting press gathered up their laptops and left in a bunch from Las Vegas, it was clear that it was over, time to move on to the next headline, to the next topic of the week. The full cast of boxing's misfit characters, brought into the light by the non-boxing media to help illuminate this dark, barbaric world of severed ears and broken hearts for the rest of the world's edification, was free to return to its own kind, where the sights and sounds would be familiar and the lights not so harsh.

So the world has moved on, free to vanquish its next villain or exalt its next hero and it is we who are left—without their able assistance—to ponder what might happen next.

Although to the rest it is old news already, to us there is yet much drama to be played out in the ongoing trial that is Mike Tyson's life, both in and out of the squared circle. If one looks closely, it is clear that there are yet countless details and outcomes to consider and much to be decided.

The story is far from over. In boxing, as in most things, it is while the rest of the world is looking away that the most telling events unfold. Consider, for instance, the language that accompanied the revocation of Tyson's license, and what that language will probably mean in the end. It stated that although his license was officially revoked, Tyson was free to apply for reinstatement after one year and every year thereafter.

In the rest of the world, this caveat would be correctly construed not as a sign of promise, but as a mere requirement of formality; not a thing upon which one might pin one's hopes, but rather a gentlemanly way of breaking things off without coming off unduly harsh. And that's it. A formality. A courtesy extended with the understanding revoked means revoked.

Yet, it is the opinion of almost everyone in this business that the moment the year is up, Tyson's time will have been served, so to speak, and his sentence done. And he will be back in the ring, post haste. Indeed, those who make their livings in Vegas—and even those who don't but know boxing—did not mistake for grandstanding the words of Tyson's attorney (one of an army, one imagines), Oscar Goldman, who, following the ruling, told the Associated Press, "I know these fellas. He'll be approved in a year."

The smart money says Goldman is right, and not because the fix is in or because the commission is somehow subject to the will of unscrupulous Tyson supporters. Rather, it knows, as do the regulators of any major sport, on which side its bread is buttered. What would Michael Jordan have to do to be banned for life from the NBA? Or Ken Griffey Jr. from Major League Baseball? For any number of reasons, some more palatable than others, Tyson is the biggest draw in the sport. *Period.*

It is the largely-held view that for this reason alone, he will be back as quickly as is legally possible, provided he doesn't do something foolish like take his act on the road to Europe, or to some Harlem street comer at 3:00 A.M. (A hired keeper would be a sound investment.) So this gives us what is likely to be a 15-to-17-month window -- because even Don King needs a few months to corral interest in the return, and the bout would then be postponed for the requisite Tyson injury, one imagines -- during which boxing will again find itself without its greatest draw.

And what happens during that period may well determine if Tyson will encounter any difficulty at all in getting back his license, not to mention how he will be received by a once-adoring public once he does return. Assuming the wise guys are right about it being a done deal, the layoff will also figure heavily into what will occur the next time he squares off against another man in the ring -- after all that has happened, and after all that has been said.

See? We told you the story isn't over yet.

The first order of business for those in the Tyson flock will be to institute some damage control measures, since, as the ads will tell you, image is everything. And right now, they don't come any worse than Tyson's.

His fumbling, televised apology to the world notwithstanding, Tyson alienated an entire sport the moment he said to hell with it all and bit down on Evander Holyfield's ear with the kind of malice he used to reserve for overhand rights and, yes, a fairly dependably delivered array of headbutts and elbows.

With the possible exception of the crack management team of Holloway and Horne, there wasn't a single fair-minded Tyson fan left in the building by the time Tyson began swinging at a phalanx of Las Vegas police officers, who had probably thought, like the rest of us, that they were going to see a hell of a fight that night—not be in one. And by the time Tyson, still steaming, got to the runway that would lead back to his locker room, spectators were hurling trash at him from the stands.

Garbage. At *Mike Tyson.*

For a public sports figure, an icon—yes ma'am, even one convicted of rape—it doesn't get much worse. And this whole reprehensible, senseless, exasperating display wasn't played out in front of the usual calloused boxing junkies who would, without thinking twice, fork over $49.95 to watch two burly drunks in an alley getting into it over the last of the Absolut.

This was the richest fight ever. In front of the world. So it would be an understatement to say that in terms of image, there is much work to be done.

Luckily for Tyson, there are few who understand the importance of image better than Mr. King, who himself has some image problems of note these days. Ever-protective of his charge, "Dapper Don" solicited for Tyson shortly after the fight the services of what is known as -- only in America, to be sure -- a professional "image-maker," in this case one who worked with presidents Reagan and Bush. Yes, a one-time adviser to presidents is working for Mike Tyson.

Sound silly? Tyson has made more money in two years than the last 10 presidents combined. There is big, big money at stake. Unless the wounds can be mended, the gravy train ends here. And gravy trains are what this is all about. They're about what *everything* is about, so rarely are they permitted a timely, peaceful death.

"I think his livelihood depends on whether he does and says the right things," said longtime boxing reporter and television commentator Dave Bontempo. "If Tyson goes on a long do-good campaign and it is perceived as sincere and not contrived, people will accept him back. That will pave the way for a return for him, if he makes the right moves."

One suspects of King and the salaried damage-control experts that the right moves are made, and that we will hear about them. If the image-menders do their job, we can expect to read over the course of the next 12 months stories that reveal Tyson the family man, Tyson the philanthropist, Tyson the protector of baby seals, maybe even Tyson the accomplished cellist.

Who knows? We're also sure to hear that he's receiving psychiatric counseling for his violent tendencies. It's all part of the process, you see, the mending.

"Now that he's left such a bad taste in everyone's mouth, he will have to do those types of things," said Bontempo. "At some point, if people believe in him, they'll be able to build his marketability back up. It's all according to how he handles the opportunity."

So the spin doctors will do all they can to wipe the slate clean and, with King's deep pockets, they will have all the needed resources at their ready. But even if Tyson comes out of this looking like Mother Teresa, this is a fighter we're talking about, not a politician. He still has to be able to fight. The best PR team in the world can't help you slip a right hand or dig a hook to the body. If it could, Sugar Ray Leonard would never have lost to Hector Camacho, and George Foreman would be the undisputed king of something other than muffler commercials. In combat, your opponent doesn't care how many turkeys you passed out on Christmas or how many charitable deductions you claimed on your income taxes. Tyson will be nearing 33 the next time he slips on a pair of gloves for pay, and it is certain that the year he spends away from the ring will do little to help him turn back the clock.

There are few things more deadly to a fighter than an extended vacation, and it was clear during the bouts with Holyfield that Tyson was still paying for the time he sat growing rust in an Indiana jail cell.

"That three years in jail did a lot of harm. He wasn't the same when he came out," said Goody Petronelli. Petronelli has been training New England prizefighters for four decades and helped mold Marvelous Marvin Hagler into one of the great middleweights. "He lost a lot of skills, his timing, and some of his speed. He was only about 50 percent of the fighter who went to prison."

Petronelli does not expect the Tyson who emerges a year from now to even remotely resemble the force who once tore through the division, regardless of any efforts that are made to keep him in shape.

"They'll probably have him training to keep his timing and conditioning up, maybe even have him spar, but a fighter has to be busy. You've got to fight the real fights. He's going to be a year older and will have had four years taken out of the prime of his life. He'll never get back to the fighter he was."

It should be noted, though, that we've been lamenting for years— since his 1989 knockout of Frank Bruno, to be precise—Tyson's waning appreciation for the game's subtleties, how he doesn't move his head enough anymore, or punch to the body enough. And still, it is not as though he's been bested by half the division.

Regardless of how humbled he was by Holyfield, we would do well to remember still that Mike Tyson is a puncher, and punchers retain their power long after their other gifts have abandoned them.

Moreover, even with the three years out following the rape conviction, and the quick work that was made of Peter McNeeley, Tyson tore with relative ease through Buster Mathis Jr., Bruno, and Bruce Seldon, each recognizable and highly ranked (if not revered) fighters who simply did not possess the strength or the skill of Holyfield.

One might easily arrive at the conclusion that, if not for Holyfield, Tyson might still he residing at the top of the current heavyweight heap. Pep had his Saddler. Ali had his Norton. Tyson has his Holyfield. Whether that will be the case a year from now is cause for debate.

"He holds his own with the young heavyweights that are out there now," offered Bontempo. "Holyfield's savvy and style are what disarmed him, and the young guys won't have that. On the other hand, they probably won't be intimidated by him the way the older, current crop was."

After a year, though, it may matter little how much Tyson has left when it comes time to re-enter the arena. If the stop is brief enough, the gravy train needs only a little nudge to get started again and, remember, this is boxing. It won't take much. A fight or two against a McNeeley equivalent and people will start to talk again, start to wonder if Tyson can recapture a bit of his old aura, his old power. For no other reason, they'll watch his first fight or two out of curiosity, just to see if maybe he'll snap again.

And before they know it, they'll be hooked.

Before long, the big-money fight will come, maybe a third match with Holyfield, though the odds are against it. If not against Holyfield, it will come against someone else, and there will be those who refuse to watch, purely on principle. The rest of us, though, aren't that virtuous. We'll be watching, even if the rest of the world isn't.

Epilogue: Tyson fought 10 more times after the Holyfield fight, going 5-3 (5) with two no-contests. He retired in 2005 after losing to Kevin McBride.

THE FINAL BELL

(HAPPY AND UNHAPPY ENDINGS)

THE HITMAN WANTS TO
KEEP THE HITS COMING

TOMMY HEARNS'S COMEBACK

ORIGINALLY PUBLISHED AT *HBO.COM* ON March 21, 2003

IF YOU'VE FOLLOWED this business for any time at all, you're accustomed already to the sight and smell of old, broken champions taking bad beatings they've clearly asked for. Like the rest of us, you wonder when they'll learn. You wonder when they'll learn that when it goes it's gone and you can't get it back, that they get old like all of us do, and it's okay, because it has to be.

You wonder when they'll learn that they're too close to it to see it themselves, so they have to listen to us to know when they should go off to wherever it is that old prizefighters go, and do whatever it is that men do whose time for usefulness has passed. After all, it's for their own good. They'll have their memories.

Thomas Hearns turned 44 years old last October. Against the advice of almost everyone, he's in training in Detroit at the old Kronk Gym, which he and Emanuel Steward put on the map 20 years ago, back when Hearns made a hell of a good living fighting and no one told him he shouldn't be doing it, or worse, that he couldn't. Back then, if he caught a right hand sparring, it was because he wasn't paying attention or because, well, it happens sometimes in the ring. If it happens today, it's because he's 44 and deluding himself.

"I'm not a shot fighter," Hearns told me recently. "I'm not shot at all. Ask the guys in the gym if I'm shot. If you get in the ring with me thinking that, you got another thing coming. Thomas Hearns has a lot of fight left in him. I don't want people to think I can't fight anymore. I can do it as well as I want to."

Hearns is looking for a fight that will get him started again. He'd like journeyman light heavyweight Thomas Reid, or maybe former light heavyweight and cruiserweight champion Virgil Hill, who he decisioned and dethroned in June 1991. "Whichever one is available," he said. "Either one, I'm prepared to give it to him." It doesn't matter to him so long as it leads to a shot at one of the belts at either 175 or 190 pounds. He wants to fight for a world title, which would be his eighth. "Nobody's ever fought for eight world titles," he said. "It will be the eighth wonder of the world."

Hearns last fought two years ago. It was a big deal in Detroit—his farewell gift to the city—against cruiserweight workhorse Uriah Grant. In the second round, Hearns twisted his ankle and couldn't continue, and if you were so inclined, you could tell him that ankles wear out on a fighter like anything else, that all the moving parts—as well as some that don't move—break down eventually and we need to find other, less stressful uses for them. You'd be wasting your time. It's clear others have tried.

"I am living my life the way I want to live my life," Hearns said. "This is what makes me happy. I have to retire when I am ready to retire. I can't be dictated to. I appreciate all the people who care about me and love me and don't want me to get hurt but I have to do it."

That's the way fighters are and Hearns has been a fighter for a long time. He first pulled on a pair of gloves at nine and had his first real amateur fight two years later. A long and successful amateur career followed, but it was surprisingly, in retrospect at least, devoid of knockouts for a guy who was arguably the best puncher of his generation.

"Muhammad Ali was my idol," said Hearns. "So I started out

wanting to fight like him. I became a puncher because I knew that in the pros I had to turn my punches over. As an amateur, I knew the goal was to land as many punches as I possibly could to score points. In the pros, you have to get guys out of there. So that's what I started to do."

Few were better at it—maybe four or five guys in history had a better right hand. Hearns was 28-0 with 26 knockouts and impossibly tall and powerful for a 147-pound man when he destroyed the feared Pipino Cuevas in two rounds to win the WBA welterweight title in August 1980. "I felt like I had done it," recalled Hearns. "I had made my manager, my family and myself so happy. Everything just escalated up from there."

You know what followed: three title defenses and then his epic dance with Ray Leonard for the undisputed title at 147 pounds. He says he wanted to box against Leonard rather than punch, to show him that his own abilities were superior to Leonard's. He maintains still that the referee stopped the fight early, although one remembers the way he melted into the ropes in the 14th round, legless, as Leonard, looking fresh and focused still, blasted him.

He wanted to box too against "Marvelous" Marvin Hagler in their magnificent explosion of violence in April 1985 for the middleweight world title. It is better for us, and for posterity, that he didn't. The first round remains perhaps the most furious round in the history of important middleweight prizefights, and among the most exciting at any weight.

"My plan was to box him, to give him a boxing lesson," Hearns said. "I knew I could do that. But just before the fight, when I was in the dressing room, I noticed that my legs felt weak. I said I have to go out there and try to knock him out as fast as I can. I was doing well up until the third round." That was when Hagler landed the two clubbing rights that finished Hearns for the night, delaying his quest for a world title at 160.

"I gave it my best and tried hard to make the public see that I was giving it my best. I broke my right hand in the first round, but I still kept throwing it. The problem was Marvin Hagler was just as determined as I was, so something had to give." Hearns had come close when referee Richard Steele stopped the fight briefly to have the ringside doctor examine a cut over Hagler's eye. "I was praying it was over. When it wasn't, I said, 'Oh my God, we gotta keep going.'"

The conquests and thrills were many: wins over fellow legends Roberto Duran and Wilfred Benitez, titles won on the hides of Juan Roldan, Dennis Andres and Hill, and of course, the rematch with Leonard, which was ruled a draw but which everyone knew Hearns had won outright.

There were hard losses too—namely a pair to Iran Barkley in two brutal bouts. But Hearns wouldn't change much if he were doing it over. "I would do everything exactly the same way, I would put it all right back out there. But this time, I would knock out Ray Leonard. And I would make sure that we fought a third time."

So he's 44 now and training at Kronk, and he's aware enough of himself to know he's different now and that things have to be done differently. "When I was in my 20s, it was more like, I didn't care what happened. I would just get in there and go all out. I didn't care. Now I have a family I love very much. I don't just wing and wing shots. I take my time and set things up. When you're older, you must prepare yourself to the fullest better than when you were 20. But I'm hitting very hard. And even though I'm older now, I want to show the people what great abilities I still have."

Listen to Hearns long enough, or to any fighter who has been where he is now and you find that we've been asking the wrong question. It is not when will they learn, because fighters know themselves better than anyone—in the ring a man learns more about himself than any other place save a battlefield. The question is when will *we* learn?

"I am not going to let anyone change my mind," said Hearns. "This is my life. Please let me live my life the way I want to. I've never been in trouble. I never tell anyone how to live. I live clean and I want to live my life to its fullest ability. Thank you for caring about me and for not wanting to see me get hurt but I'm going to do what I want to do."

Hearns isn't a world-class fighter anymore, he hasn't been in a very long time and probably he'll find that out for himself when he gets in with some young kid who knows what he's doing. He could get hurt - - that's what it takes sometimes for old fighters to face the terrible truth that the long ride is over. They have to experience the pain of it so they can know, finally, that nothing will ever be as good again as it was when they were champions. When they accept that, then they can stop chasing it. They can move on. So let them fight. At the least, we owe them that.

Epilogue: Hearns fought two years after this interview, and once more seven months later, both wins over journeymen, before retiring for good in 2006.

THE FINAL BEATING

BOXING'S NOT SO GENTLE PERSUADER

ORIGINALLY PUBLISHED IN *THE RING*, August 2000

"Once you're a boxer, it's in your blood. You have to get it beaten out of you."

— LLOYD HONEYGHAN

IF EVERYTHING GOES ACCORDING to plan, on July 1, Julio Cesar Chavez, the once-great Mexican warrior, will get another shot at a world title against WBC super lightweight wrecking ball Kostya Tszyu. Don't ask who came up with the plan, because if you don't know the answer to that by now, you haven't been paying attention.

Chavez has always had friends in high places. Even when warring with Don King, which is often, he has the support of compatriot and WBC President Jose Sulaiman. And when he gets back on good terms with King, which is always the case sooner or later, he is assured of a high ranking and the benefit of the doubt. He never used to need that, but he's been shot for four or five years now, and shot fighters with bad backs and a weakness for beer need a break too every now and again, especially if they're living legends.

So when Chavez lost by a mile to journeyman Willy Wise last

October, it might have looked to everyone else like he blew the shot at Tszyu, and that he might get to keep his nose in the front of his face after all. A lot of Chavez supporters were quietly happy about it. Better to be outboxed by a marshmallow like Wise than plowed over by a tank like Tszyu. The ever-diplomatic Jim Gray interrogated Chavez along these lines after the Wise fight, and a dispirited Chavez replied to the effect that one trains differently for a world title fight than one does for a non-title, over-the-weight 10-rounder, and that is true. A dispassionate observer might have reminded him that no amount of pushups or roadwork can restore the powers of youth, a sad reality of which Chavez is no doubt aware but would rather not acknowledge, at least for the time being. You can't blame him.

At any rate, Sulaiman took care of it, deciding that since the Wise fight occurred at 147 rather than 140, Chavez's number-one ranking at junior welter was unaffected, and the Tszyu fight was still on. *With friends like these...*

Of course, Chavez didn't train a lick for Wise, who's a heck of a nice guy with a good story, but not much of a fighter. Even at 37, "The Lion of Culiacan" is better than he showed that night, but not near enough to handle Tszyu, a flawed but dynamite-punching offensive machine. Las Vegas oddsmaker Herb Lambeck calls Tszyu a 100-1 favorite. This is not an even matchup. It's not a competitive matchup, or even a fair one. There is every likelihood that Chavez will get beaten up, perhaps very badly, for as long as it lasts. For some, it will be hard to watch.

Some of the fight game's moralists—there's an oxymoron for you —are lobbying for the bout to be canceled on the grounds that it's a gross mismatch. Put aside for the moment that these same pacifists were nowhere to be seen when Rick Frazier was climbing into the ring to face Roy Jones, or that they utter nary a word of protest when hundreds of other over-matched fighters get their clocks cleaned in clubs and casinos every weekend for a hell of a lot fewer pesos than Chavez will take home.

What these misguided few are forgetting is that fighters, especially great fighters, and Chavez, at his best, was one of the great ones, quite often need to suffer a sound, one-sided beating in order to be convinced that their days as a champion, or even an upper-echelon fighter, are over. The loss to Wise, which Chavez can at least partially attribute to lax training, would never be sufficient to make him consider retirement; there are too many excuses. But a brutal, painful loss to Tszyu, when Chavez is in the best shape he can get himself into, might do it.

Yes, it's ridiculously dangerous for a tired, cranky, old warhorse like Chavez to take on a young, fresh champion when the distinct possibility exists that he will be hurt. But don't think him a madman or even unusual for doing so anyway. Taking that one fight too many is what fighters do. They have to. Even the greatest among them.

It all would have been so perfect if Muhammad Ali had retired for good after whipping Leon Spinks in 1978 and regaining the heavyweight title. He'd beaten everyone there was to beat; between 1976 and '78 he'd squeaked by Ken Norton, survived the right-hand bombs of Earnie Shavers, somehow even survived Jimmy Young when the judges decided they liked an old, slow, soft legend more than a slippery kid who liked to stick his torso outside the ropes whenever the action inside got too intense. He got a couple of easy ones in there, too, playing around with hopelessly ordinary Europeans Richard Dunn and Alfredo Evangelista.

Then came the shocking loss to Spinks in the first match and the inevitable triumph in the return. "This is satisfying," he said then. "They all said I was finished, too old." With the possible exception of "The Thrilla in Manila," there wasn't a better fight on which to end his career. So he did. For two years.

But Ali wasn't convinced that he was done. Plus, he was bored. As much as fighters say they want to go out on top, they can't. They have to be convinced, and Ali's turn, one would have thought, came over 10 horribly one-sided rounds against a young, sharp Larry Holmes, the WBC heavyweight champion. Ali could do nothing but soak up punches all night until Angelo Dundee finally stopped it. Afterward, Ali's terrible weakness was blamed largely on the thyroid hormone pills he had taken throughout training to lose weight. He had an excuse and that's all a fighter needs. Almost a year later, the ordinary but gleefully youthful Trevor Berbick pounded him for 10 rounds in the Bahamas. Ali, at 38, was convinced.

Ali wasn't the only heavyweight from that era who took one fight too many. His rival, Norton, had his ups and downs after losing the WBC heavyweight title to Holmes in '78 in one of the best heavyweight title fights ever. He stopped trial horse Randy Stephens, then was starched in a round by Shavers in '79.

Approaching 37 years old, he drew with journeyman Scott LeDoux and barely decisioned Tex Cobb. That would have been as good a time as any to call it a career. Neither LeDoux nor Cobb were world-class heavyweights, and it was obvious to everyone that Norton's time was up. His legs were gone. He claimed to be 35 but some close to him told reporters he was over 40, and he looked it. He'd retired after the Cobb fight 15 months earlier but there was another big, white heavyweight out there he could make some money against, and, in his mind, handle pretty easily.

Norton met Gerry Cooney in New York in May of '81. Early in the first round, he did all right, slipping Cooney's long jabs and burrowing inside. He even got the big guy against the ropes for a moment, which was probably the last thing he remembered. Showing unusual agility for a giant heavyweight, Cooney spun Norton around and started unloading left hooks. Never one to hold up against a puncher, Norton froze. Cooney's hook landed again and again while Norton drooped, unconscious, on the ropes. Finally, it was stopped, and Norton, upon regaining his senses, needed no further convincing.

You would have thought Cooney would have taken the lessons learned by Norton and applied them in his own career, but he didn't. After losing to Larry Holmes for the title in 1982, Cooney floundered, trained, got injured, trained again, got injured, and even fought every once in a while. He got another shot at the big time when he met the much smaller Michael Spinks in '87, and Spinks tortured him, making him appear clumsy and oafish before stopping him in the fifth round.

That would be the last we'd hear of Cooney for three years, or until he couldn't stand any longer the prospect that he might have been something great if he'd stuck with it. Cooney's hell was one borne of unfulfilled promise, of what could have been, or what should have been. It's the kind of thing that keeps grown men awake at night, and it drove Cooney to call one of his staunchest supporters, Hall of Fame trainer Gil Clancy, to help him get back in shape. And it drove him to accept a fight with George Foreman, who was three years into his own comeback and looking for a name that wasn't too dangerous.

Cooney did well in the first, moving and popping Foreman with some stiff hooks, but in the second, he stood still and Foreman leveled him. Cooney got up and was blasted to the canvas again. *KO 2.* Afterward, he seemed almost giddy with the knowledge, finally, that this was his end, that there would be no more comebacks, no more sleepless nights. He became convinced, and that gave him peace. One could be forgiven for being happy for him. "(The loss) helped me close this chapter of my life and move on to the next one," he said.

Sometimes, one brutal beating isn't enough, especially if you've made successful comebacks a staple of your career. Sugar Ray Leonard retired for the first time in 1982 after discovering he had a detached retina. After a one-fight comeback victory in '84 over Kevin Howard, the former undisputed welterweight and WBA junior middleweight champ retired again and, miraculously, returned three years later to decision Marvelous Marvin Hagler for the middleweight title. After stopping Donny Lalonde, drawing with old rival Thomas Hearns, and dominating Roberto Duran in their rubber match, he retired again, at 33.

But Leonard was restless in retirement and was unconvinced that he had no more greatness left in him. Who could blame him? So in '91 he returned again to face a young, fast Terry Norris, the WBC super welterweight titlist. After Norris pummeled him all over the Madison Square Garden ring, flooring him twice and cruising to an easy decision, Leonard said, "I had to find out for myself. It just wasn't there." He was finally convinced. Or was he?

For the next six years, Leonard stewed and stewed and gradually unconvinced himself again. Finally, in '97, at 40 years of age, he squared off against Hector Camacho, and was knocked out in five rounds. He promptly re-retired, saying afterward, "For sure, my career is definitely over," but shortly revealed that a calf injury hampered his performance, which was all he needed to reopen the door. Three times he signed to fight again but pulled out each time. One hopes he has found elsewhere that which he had been chasing in the ring.

Another Leonard, this one from a different era, also took his career to places it shouldn't have gone, long after what made him special had vanished. But it only took one brutal stoppage loss to convince him that his time was up. Benny Leonard, the outstanding lightweight champion from the 1920s, retired a young (29), wealthy, undefeated champion in 1925. He had it made until Wall Street crashed four years later, and he found himself nearly penniless. Former champions can only do one thing when they're broke, and that's start fighting again. Leonard returned in October '31 and reeled off 18 wins and a draw against opposition that wasn't winning him any respect, but they did get him in position for a big bout against future welterweight champion Jimmy McLarnin.

Leonard probably could have hung around a little while longer against soft touches and then taken his winnings and gone home. He was still among the most popular athletes of the era and was the most beloved Jewish fighter ever. He certainly could have found an easier guy to face than McLarnin, who had established a reputation not only as one of the division's hardest hitters, but as a guy who just couldn't lose to Jewish fighters.

But that was one of the reasons Leonard wanted him, and for a couple of rounds, the old guy did all right in the Madison Square Garden ring. McLarnin's power and aggression were too much, though, and Leonard, pudgy and slower at 36, couldn't hold him off forever. McLarnin got to him in the sixth with a series of power punches, and Leonard crumbled. That was all the convincing this Leonard needed. He never fought again.

Almost 20 years later, an icon even bigger than Leonard suffered the same fate. You couldn't blame Joe Louis for pushing on for as long as he did, and we don't mean for the money he needed to pay off his tax debts. When a fighter is as good at what he does as Louis was, how does he stop? Even after the 25 successful title defenses, after the stint in the Army during World War II, even after the retirement following his knockout win over Jersey Joe Walcott in their rematch, Louis, at 34, was as good as any heavyweight in the world. But when he came back two years later and lost a lopsided decision to Ezzard Charles for the title everyone knew really belonged to the "The Brown Bomber," that should have been the end. Maybe it would have been if he hadn't still been good enough to reel off eight straight wins, including a decision over Jimmy Bivins. Maybe if he'd lost to Bivins, he wouldn't have gotten crushed in his next bout.

The biggest fight available to Louis was against a young kid named Rocky Marciano, and when the two met in Madison Square Garden in October, Louis came in as the 8-5 favorite. He was bigger than Marciano and more polished to be sure, but he was 37 and the steam in his punches was gone. Marciano wore him down with pressure and strength, and by the eighth, the old man was ready to go. Late in the round, a hook floored him, and moments later, a right put him through the ropes and onto his back. It was brutal, and not only because Louis was a hero to millions. It was the kind of physically brutal knockout that was so convincing that Louis never fought again.

Surely, there must have been those at the time, especially those close to Louis, who knew Marciano's capabilities, who hoped to themselves that the fight wouldn't come off. There were plenty who saw Ali with their heads rather than their hearts and knew he stood no chance against Holmes, and the same goes for Leonard against McLarnin. The time comes when those who were great aren't anymore, but the fighter is the only one who doesn't see it. He needs to be convinced, and convincing him isn't an easy business.

Chavez knows he's not the same guy who ran roughshod over three divisions when he was young. But he doesn't know that it's over yet, either. It's Tszyu's job to convince him that it is, the same way it was Marciano's job to convince Louis, McLarnin's to convince Leonard, and so forth. It's not pretty and it's not nice, but it's the way it works. It's the only way it can work.

.   .   .

Epilogue: Tszyu stopped Chavez in six rounds in their meeting in Phoenix, but it wasn't enough to convince Chavez to quit. He fought five more times over the next five years, avenging losses to Wise and a terribly dissipated Frankie Randall. He quit for good after journeyman Grover Wiley stopped him in five rounds in 2005.

LENNOX LEWIS

IT'S NOT HOW MUCH MONEY YOU MAKE, IT'S HOW YOU'RE REMEMBERED"

ORIGINALLY PUBLISHED AT *HBO.COM* ON NOVEMBER 3, 2005

THERE ALWAYS WAS something about Lennox Lewis that we knew was different. Yes, he was a British heavyweight who could fight. He seemed at times a little more refined than we like our heavyweight champs to be, or than we are used to. And yes, he could switch his style radically from one fight to the next, blasting out Frans Botha one night, boxing the stuffing out of David Tua the next. Name another heavyweight champ who was as versatile.

But it was more than that. It always seemed he didn't really need the fight game or its attendant, brutal thrills the way so many prizefighters do. We suspected that all along and sometimes we didn't care for it. But we could see it. So it shouldn't have surprised us that he got out at the perfect time: right after his brutal win over Vitali Klitschko, who defends the world heavyweight title against Hasim Rahman on November 12 on HBO PPV.

Besides Gene Tunney and Rocky Marciano, try to name another heavyweight champ who went out the way Lewis did: wealthy, relatively young, possessed of all his faculties, and satisfied that he had done everything he wanted to—that rarest of things among all men of

234

accomplishment, regardless of the field. And, with a victory over his top challenger, no less.

Lewis was always so different that we knew from the start there would be no embarrassing comebacks, no desperate moments when we'd watch him struggle with some journeyman or other and lament that a few years earlier he'd have owned him. But we weren't the only ones who knew it. Lewis knew it too, right from the beginning.

"When I was growing up, Muhammad Ali was my hero, and I would always hear people say Ali was the greatest but he shouldn't have gone on so long," Lewis told me during a recent phone conversation. "That has always been on my mind. So it was very important to me to retire at the right time, which I did."

Few retirements have been timed better. Indeed, one suspects the difficulty Lewis had on the way to disposing of Klitschko in their June 2003 war, in which several cuts around Klitschko's eyes led to a sixth-round stoppage, had to be a factor in Lewis's decision to retire. One doubts he'd have quit the ring so agreeably had he knocked out Klitschko in a round or two, or had done the same against Kirk Johnson, the opponent he'd originally prepared to fight on that date.

But the savagery of the Klitschko fight does nothing to undermine Lewis's perfectly legitimate belief that he won the fight and square, regardless of Klitschko's caterwauling afterward that the outcome was somehow tainted. In fact, it is Lewis's very comfort with the win that has made retirement so easy.

"With my last fight, with Klitschko, I was satisfied," said Lewis. "If I thought there was a question that he could beat me, I would definitely go back and fight him. But now he's got his own era. With the end of every era, there's a new era and a new star. Klitschko wants it to be him, but he needs to work at it and prove he's the best in the world. It doesn't happen overnight."

Lewis knows about that. It took him a long time to be accepted as the world's best heavyweight, even as he dominated one challenger after another. But he wouldn't have had it any other way.

"I loved the fact that they didn't look at me like I was the best, they were all saying guys like Holyfield, or Tyson. I liked saying, 'I'll prove it so there's no question.' And when you do that there's no question anymore. Until the public sees the fight, they can't make that assessment. But afterward they know it. Like in my first fight with Evander, even though the decision was bad, they all knew who won, so I was happy with it."

Lewis is saddened by Holyfield's refusal to retire in the face of clearly eroded abilities. "It's a sad situation and it's a subject that's very close to me - knowing when to retire unscathed and with all your faculties. It's terrible to have the officials come and pat you on your back and tell you you cannot fight anymore. He's caught up in the drug of the sport. He wants to fight all the time. But there's always a challenger out there.

"Plus, there's the money. If this is how we make money and suddenly you can't do it anymore how are you going to make money? But he has to look at his legacy. It's not how much money you make, it's how you're remembered. Years later, people look at your record and see the fights you lost and they remember that."

Still, there was a time a few months back when rumors flew around the Internet that Lewis was negotiating for a comeback fight with Klitschko. He denies it was ever a possibility, but fighters, even those who are very different, will always have the bug in them after they stop. They're fighters. They can't help but miss it. Can they?

"Only because I'm a competitor and have always been the kind of person who's thinking, 'I can do that better,' or 'I can beat this person,'" Lewis said before he stopped, took a deep breath and corrected himself. "No, I don't miss boxing because I spent enough time in it and accomplished my goal of being the undisputed heavyweight champion. Everything's got a beginning, a middle, and an end, and this is my time to be finished with it. I completed my goals."

So he lives the good life now of a former heavyweight champ. He reads movie scripts, spends time with his 15-month-old son, Landon, and his wife, Violet, and works on his home in Jamaica. "It's great to have the time to do the things I couldn't do when I was boxing because I was always at training camp and doing boxing things," he said.

Though happily retired, Lewis keeps his eye on his old haunts in the heavyweight division and as he's fought both men, he has strong opinions about Klitschko's title defense against Rahman.

"I think it's a good fight. It needs to be fought," he said. "The heavyweight division is in a bit of disarray right now and this is one step toward getting it on the right course. Klitschko has some advantages: he's tall and lanky and he's very awkward to hit. But there are different factors in boxing that need to be considered, like cuts, endurance, nagging injuries you might have and Vitali has had some physical problems that delayed this fight.

"I like Hasim Rahman for his strength, his experience, and his hunger," Lewis said. "He's been waiting and trying to get this fight for a long time because he wants to be heavyweight champion of the world. I don't see Klitschko knocking out Rahman. He's very durable and doesn't waver under the first punch. And he won't give up. Rahman also has a style that's difficult to deal with. It's a good styles matchup. If it ends early, I think Rahman will win. If it goes later, I think Vitali."

One can imagine Lewis watching the fight from ringside, and if he were any other retired champ, we'd expect to see him lost in the action, reflexively slipping a right hand or dropping in a counter hook, just out of habit. That's what fighters do at the fights. But not Lewis. He's always been a bit different. He'll sit back and enjoy it. That's the way he is. And good for him. He's earned the right.

Epilogue: Klitschko and Rahman never did fight one another. Citing repeated injuries, Klitschko retired, then returned three years later to regain a piece of the heavyweight championship.

DEATH IN THE RING

A BOXING WRITER'S
TOUGHEST ASSIGNMENT

ORIGINALLY PUBLISHED IN *THE RING*, DECEMBER 2001

BY ALL ACCOUNTS, Beethavean Scottland was a good guy. After he died, people said he was a decent man, a family man. As fighters go, he wasn't that special. He was tough all right, the sort of guy who could take it probably a little better than he could give it. His toughness was what he was proudest of. You could see it in the way he fought, how he'd take a shot or two or three flush and just stare at the other guy. He liked to show it off.

Lots of fighters are like that, when tough is all they've got, more or less, but Scottland showed it too much against George "Khalid" Jones in June. Right or wrong, no one around him convinced him that sometimes it's not so good to be tough, that sometimes too much tough will get you into deep trouble. They let him be as tough as he wanted, and after he went down in the 10th round, he didn't get up. He died a few days later in Bellevue Hospital in New York, and I thought it was ironic and a little sad that a hell of a lot of fight writers, myself included, knew his name then, but didn't when he was alive. But that's the way it is: A fighter dies, he gets press. Someone has to cover it and fight writers have to eat, too.

Guys in the fight press watch fighters get killed in the ring. Beaten to death, if you want to be damned honest about it. In a sense, we participate in it. All of the industry does, anyone who makes money in the business. We write about it -- as well as we can, really, because why should the writing suffer?

We go at it with a great understated flourish (we hope), with dark prose so the tone is flat and respectful and reads like a soft obituary almost. We eulogize the guy if we knew him at all, talk him up, share a revealing anecdote -- but not too revealing -- and maybe appeal to fans to send his kids a few bucks because you know the guy was broke.

Maybe in a fit of melancholy we'll question right there on the page why this dirty business is legal at all and what's wrong with us all for watching it. Maybe it's just for the sake of the piece that we do it, maybe it isn't, but it's done now, we put a period at the end, give it a last read, and off it goes. Next?

At least that's how it works for me. I can get reasonably close for a while, in a literary sense, to a fighter who has been killed in the ring. I can write the piece. But I prefer not to. It does him no good if I get very close, and it certainly doesn't help me. Better, more courageous writers than I, and there are many, have gotten right up next to Benny Paret and Willie Classen and Jimmy Garcia, crawled up right beside them on the slab and gotten their stories, gotten so close they could hear the whispered secrets, and they made the reader know the fighter – *forced* them to know the fighter in life and in death.

Not for me, thanks. That's too close, especially if the guy left kids behind. No, let the other guys do the death operas. They'll line up for them. Sportswriters, fight guys included, get bored writing just about sports -- it's all so trivial. But throw a good death into the mix, especially in the melodrama that is pro boxing, and you have the makings of a Pulitzer. It'll be the best they've ever written.

It's not that I fear that if I get close to the story of a killed fighter that somehow I'll find the business too repugnant to cover any longer. It is true, I think, that there's a certain desensitization that one needs to undergo in order to get involved to a great degree in this game, a sort of screen one must erect that sifts through and separates what is acceptable violence -- one fighter striking another in the face -- and unacceptable violence, the kind that might make us look away at the moment of impact or attempt to intercede, if we can: a fight in the street between laymen, for example, that is wholly one-sided and instigated by the more menacing of the two and that you can see promises to end badly. All punches to the face are not equal.

To many outside the game, the two scenarios are equally abhorrent. To the fight fan, only the latter is, and even that's not a given. Our "screen" allows for the former, relishes it even. We learn to distinguish between the two, even if fundamentally there is no significant difference.

So it's not that subconsciously I'm repulsed by the violence and keep its worst results at arms' length lest I'm forced to reconsider vocations. I don't apologize a lick for the fight game, nor for my involvement in it, ancillary or not. Why should I? Guys who cover auto racing have no qualms I've ever heard after they watch and cover drivers getting burned to a fine crisp inside their racing suits. I don't know anyone who quit the high school football beat because of all the 17-year-old kids who drop dead in the middle of August scrimmages. They accept, I suppose, that it's going to happen sometimes. That's what we all should do.

I know, the fight game is held to a different standard, probably for no better reason than we can see the fighter's eyes right up until the last second there's a light in them. In these other high-risk arenas, a helmet covers their face, and even if it didn't, the activity precludes a close-up. You can't get close enough to the athlete's eyes to see inside of him. Not so in the ring. Boxing is very viewer-friendly. That's one of its allures. No uniform. No helmet. Close-ups galore: before the first bell, getting referee's instructions, between rounds, taking a punch. Slow motion was made for the fight game.

If a fighter took a few stitches over the eye or in the middle of his forehead after he fell off of his bike when he was nine, you can see the scar. (He'll probably tell you the story if you ask him.) If he misses his mother who died when he was 11, you know her name because you can see it tattooed on his arm, or across his back, or maybe stitched into his trunks. If you believe every man has a soul, you can see that in the ring, too. Watch Johnny Tapia sometime, and you can see what is in his heart and his gut, for better or worse. He doesn't have a choice. It's all laid out for you.

There can be no pretense when so much of a man is laid open like that, and when there is so much life in him, moving, pivoting, punching, ducking, sweating. And then, when he is tougher than he should be and all that life suddenly stops, it's like his battery just ran out, and you realize it didn't just run out for no good reason. It was pounded on and pummeled and stepped on until it went crooked and bent and shorted out.

But know this: If not for the purity of purpose, you wouldn't be watching. What makes it compelling is the same thing that makes it terrible. You can't have one without the other. You can try to minimize the risk, but after a certain point, you're watering down the spirits. There must be risk. Without risk and danger there is no compelling reason to watch—or to do.

The first fighter I saw get killed in the ring was Classen. I watched Wilford Scypion pound the life out of him on the 11:00 news. I was a kid. I had read about Paret, of course, had seen that famous still of Emile Griffith pounding him into the bare metal ring post. (How could there be no padding around the ring posts?) There were others I'd read about -- Ernie Schaaf, Sam Baroudi. But they were before my time. Scypion looked to me like probably the evilest person on earth, he seemed to so enjoy torturing poor Classen, but how could he know what would happen? Or maybe he knew and didn't care, and we couldn't blame him if he didn't. That's why we watch.

Classen, a hard-luck fighter who never was going to be a champion, a lot like Scottland, took a hard beating, and then just completely swallowed four or five rattling head shots before finally collapsing and falling through the ropes onto his back. His face looked suddenly flat and blank. Then the clip ended, Warner Wolf said something about an investigation, and it was over.

Three years later, Deuk Koo Kim had that same strange, blank look when Ray Mancini killed him in Las Vegas. Watched that one from beginning to end, but I didn't really get it, not fully, when they strapped Kim down and hurriedly carried him off. It was television. It was real, but it wasn't. Not like professional wrestling unreal, but not quite like *real-life* real. Classen and Kim were dead in the way the German soldiers were dead in the old black and white World War II movies my dad watched on TV -- something called *dead*, whatever that really was. Gone for good or something. I was a kid with a fuzzy understanding of dead, made more distant because it was on TV.

A couple years ago, Paul Vaden poked Stephan Johnson with a harmless-looking left jab in the 10th round of their fight in Atlantic City. Johnson had taken and given better punches than that all night and was giving Vaden a good tussle. But after taking this almost apologetic jab, he stumbled slowly backward, then slid down the ropes and fell onto his left side. He lay there a long while. I watched from the press section on the other side of the ring, diagonal from him, as his life ran out. A bunch of people crowded around and huddled over him, and then a bright yellow stretcher was forced through the ropes. They hoisted him onto it.

Right outside the ring there was a young woman, hysterical, an older woman next to her trying to calm her and not succeeding. I presumed the younger one was Johnson's wife, and I tried to imagine what it was like to be her at that moment. I got just a taste, then stopped, looked away from her and soaked in the Atlantic City Convention Center.

A Def Leppard song from the 1980s roared from the public address system, oblivious to poor Johnson's state, and in every direction and every corner of the arena, people lied in whispers and drank soda and beer and gossiped loudly and hollered because it was fun and giggled and pointed at one another, and smoked Camels and ate hot dogs and argued money and minutia and loved and hated. They lived.

Later, after the main event (Michael Grant KO 10 Andrew Golota), a gaggle of fight writers weaved their way over to the conference room that would host the post-fight press conference. Along the way, a guy asked if anyone had heard any news on Johnson. A veteran, who has watched a lot of fighters die in the ring, didn't look up but said softly: "Not good." Nobody said anything for a few beats -- a moment of silence? Then someone made a joke about Golota quitting and wasn't it predictable for that nut job. The group loosened up and slid comfortably into fight talk: How Grant would do against Lennox Lewis, how Golota could have finished him if he only had the heart of a real fighter. Johnson died a week-and-a-half-later.

Unlike pro football and baseball players, fighters generally don't get their asses kissed from the time they're little kids on up. To the contrary, most of them grow up hard, and here's a news flash, they're usually not happy, secure guys because happy, secure people rarely take up and then stick with a hobby as dangerous and desperate and unforgiving as prize fighting. What this hard life and this hard game give them is humility, maybe a little pride, but not too much. They've been to places inside themselves that we'll never risk, asked and answered questions we would never dare. But most of them are too naïve and beaten down to realize that it makes them better than the rest of us, so they remain humble.

All of this makes many of them, I think, good men, even if they never will be great fighters. But they die sometimes doing that which made them what they were, and if we're lucky, we get to know them a little bit before it happens. That's why fight writers stay with it: the fighters.

That's why I do, even when the life runs out of one of them right in front of me. It's harder now than when Classen and Kim were just images on a screen. I am older and, in the business, peripherally. I know some fighters and know that they have lives and families and good reasons to live, just as I do. Perhaps that's why I prefer to keep the death tales at a reasonable distance: If these strong, hard men can die so suddenly, what chance do I have?

I accept death as part of the game. I don't have a choice. None of us does, least of all the fighters. All we can do is hope someone is there to tell them when they've been tough long enough.

WINTER IN MANILA

MANNY PACQUIAO'S END OF DAYS

ORIGINALLY PUBLISHED IN *RINGSIDE SEAT*, SPRING 2018

HE IS STILL the king of everything in the Philippines, and try as you might you won't find anyone on the archipelago willing to say Manny Pacquiao isn't all that he once was. Even at 39 years old, even coming off a bloody loss to an earnest but ordinary pug in Jeff Horn, even without Freddie Roach and Bob Arum and others we have associated with his success, in Cebu and Davao and Manila and yes, in the slums of Eastern Samar and Apayao, Pacquiao remains forever the brilliant terror he was over the first decade of the new millennium.

This is the way the Filipinos honor their boxing gods, from Flash Elorde to Pancho Villa, from Little Dado to Small Montana. These are no small figures and when their fistic decay could no longer be denied or hidden, they passed from fighting heroes to legends. Although to many Pacquiao is the best of all of them, it is the path he too will take because it is the path all of the great ones take, in the Philippines and elsewhere. There are no U-turns.

This is the case whether or not Pacquiao beats Lucas Matthysse on July 15, supposedly in Kuala Lumpur, the national capital of Malaysia, which was chosen by Pacquiao, it is said, largely for its location beyond the reach of the IRS, to whom he is said to owe millions (another shared circumstance of the greats). The "Thrilla in Manila" and "Rumble in the Jungle" notwithstanding, we have come to view with skepticism big fights that typically would occur in America coming off in countries whose names and economies make Westerners uneasy.

Though at this writing the bout is a mere eight weeks away, doubt remains that it will come off. As Arum told a group of reporters in March, "The Malaysia part is up in the air. I don't know these Malaysian people. If they put up the money, it'll happen, happily. But do I know whether the money will be put up? No, I don't. It's as simple as that. It's exactly like usual. The only difference is the action has now moved from the Mideast to Asia. It used to be the Mideast. How many stories were there about Abu Dhabi, about Dubai, about Saudi Arabia?"

As recently as May 19, a Philippine news source reported that a television station in Argentina, Matthysse's home country, announced that the fight was going to be postponed over, what else but "financial disagreements" among the fight's backers. This so rankled Pacquiao that he gathered the local press at the Elorde Boxing Gym in Manila to dispute the report, claiming that certain parties were out to "sabotage" the event. While it's true that the Philippine press cover all of Pacquiao's various comings and goings with a kind of wild-eyed hysteria, including, perhaps, this one, the fact remains it would surprise no one if the fight fell through, just as did Pacquiao's planned rematch with Horn.

So this is how the end days arrive for one of the great prizefighters of modern times -- not with a single surprising loss that convinces him to walk away suddenly, like Kostya Tszyu did after losing inexplicably to Ricky Hatton; not with a too-hard victory, such as the one over Vitali Klitschko that convinced Lennox Lewis it was time; and not with the revelation that he, Pacquiao, was pushed to his very limits by one as ordinary as Horn (even if you think Pacquiao deserved the decision); but with a bout of questionable certainty in the Far East against a similarly past-his-prime puncher goaded out of what seemed a well-timed retirement with, as always, the promise of unlikely riches.

And make no mistake—Pacquiao is in the homestretch. Like the many before him and the many who will come after, he has ignored the signs of decay that were evident over the last several years—not necessarily in the losses to Floyd Mayweather and Juan Manuel Marquez, though they didn't help, but in the absence of ferocity and precision in wins over Timothy Bradley and Brandon Rios.

The cracks were visible too in victory over Jessie Vargas and Chris Algieri, cracks that were manifest in, among other things, a strange contentment with going the distance that never was visible in his butchering of Hatton or Miguel Cotto or Oscar De La Hoya, which showed us Pacquiao at his most vicious and most efficient. The loss to Horn, disputed as it was, represented the latest stage in what has been a kind of gradual and wholly natural defanging of a once-lethal predator.

Pacquiao responded to the loss the way fighters do: not by acknowledging the inevitability of his dulling, but by blaming those around him and closing ranks. Gone is Roach, who generally is credited with helping to transform Pacquiao from a crude, left-hand puncher into a fighter skilled and varied enough in the exploitation of his talents to fight to a standstill (the last bout notwithstanding) the great Marquez, one of the best and most cerebral technicians of his time. That Roach learned of the end of his 16-year tenure as Pacquiao's head coach by news release rather than from the fighter himself is par for the course in an industry where confrontation is limited mostly to the ring and courtrooms. He handled it well, saying, "Manny and I had a great run -- longer than most marriages and certainly a rarity for boxing. I wouldn't trade any of it."

Still, it had to sting that his duties, at least for the Matthysse fight, will be handled not by another high-profile trainer, but by Pacquiao's lifelong friend and assistant trainer Restituto "Buboy" Fernandez, who will be assisted, ably one assumes, by another Pacquiao chum, Raides "Nonoy" Neri, known primarily as the camp cook. For the record, the purported reasons for Roach's dismissal involve his failure to lobby the referee hard enough to penalize Horn for head-butts and because he had the temerity to suggest to the press after the Horn fight what everyone else was thinking: that Pacquiao should fight the rematch and then retire.

Gone for this fight too is Arum, who, after a long and rocky relationship with Pacquiao, is relegated to handling the TV deals for the Matthysse card while Pacquiao's promotional company, "MP Promotions" – what else? – does the heavy lifting. The final straw for Pacquiao with respect to his association with Arum for this fight was likely Top Rank's attempt to match him in April against woefully shopworn Mike Alvarado underneath (!) Horn against Terence Crawford. To Pacquiao, this was an "insult," according to his media manager in the Philippine Senate, Aquiles Zonio. It is interesting to note that while Roach and, to a lesser degree, Arum, have been cast aside, Michael Koncz, Pacquiao's longtime advisor, remains.

Incongruous among all this talk of Pacquiao's degradation is the likelihood that he will beat Matthysse; at this writing, he remains a slight betting favorite. It does not aid Matthysse's cause that he happened upon this opportunity by virtue of a dubious but title-winning knockout of an undefeated and curiously highly-ranked Thai who had never before fought outside his homeland.

Nevertheless, Tewa Kiram was boxing well enough when a pair of well-timed jabs brought his evening to an end, much to the delight of Golden Boy Promotions, who were hoping for precisely this eventuality, as even a degraded Pacquiao rises high the tide – in this case to a reported $15-million. And Matthysse is a good soldier, following perfectly the script supplied him by his promoters.

"It's a great opportunity for me to fight Manny Pacquiao. It's a dream come true. It's an honor because he's a legendary fighter," Matthysse said in April. "It's the first time defending my world title, which was very difficult for me to attain. I'll die for the title if I have to. I'm going to defend this title to the death." These are strong words indeed to attach to a belt so vulnerable to the whimsy of a criminal alphabet body, but that's never stopped a fighter before from sacrificing himself for the wealth he hopes it will bring him.

It's worth noting that for reasons that may or may not solely encompass its attractiveness from an aesthetic point of view, the promoters involved have wanted this bout for a significant period of time. Matthysse had merely to get by Viktor Postal in October 2015, and it would have happened then. He did not. This time around he had an easier opponent in Kiram, but the same reward.

It is to Pacquiao's benefit that the bout is taking place in the summer, as the Philippine senate is in recess. Senator Pacquiao's duties as a politician were long a sticking point for Roach and others whose job it was to ensure Pacquiao's fitness and readiness for battle. "You can't be an elite fighter and be a senator at the same time. It's too much," Roach said after the Horn fight. By timing his comeback the way he has, Pacquiao seems to have conceded the point and given himself the best chance he could to recapture what made him what he was. But there are things that mere training cannot restore and no amount of determination or denial will make it otherwise. Nature will prevail.

There is a proverb among the Philippine people: "Mahirap gisingin ang nagtutulog-tulugan." Translated from Tagalog, the language of the Philippines, it is roughly: "It is hard to wake up someone who is pretending to be asleep." Or, it is hard to convince one of something he does not want to see. This is a hard one for fighters to learn. They all learn it anyway, sooner or later. Pacquiao will too.

Epilogue: Pacquiao stopped Matthysse, then beat Adrien Broner and Keith Thurman in 2019. After two years of inactivity he lost to Yordenis Ugas in 2021 and retired. In 2025 Pacquiao returned to the ring and drew against Mario Barrios in a welterweight world title fight.

HE'S SPILLED HIS LAST DROP

NOW IT'S TIME FOR GATTI TO SAY GOODBYE

ORIGINALLY PUBLISHED IN *THE RING*, NOVEMBER 2007

GATTI!

Gatti!

Gatti!

You couldn't tell it was over from the way they still chanted his name, even near the end, when all was clearly lost. If you closed your eyes, it could have been the Wilson Rodriguez fight in The Garden again, or Gabriel Ruelas right here in Atlantic City, or either of the wars with Ivan Robinson. But it wasn't. Those were years ago, so many years and punches ago and pints of blood and broken hands and swollen eyes ago. It was now, and Alfonso Gomez was punching him all over the ring, so easily it would almost have been comical if it weren't so painful to watch and almost certainly permanently damaging.

Gomez hit their man with about every punch with which one can hit another, and you got the sense watching it that if someone invented a new punch and whispered it into Gomez's ear between rounds he'd have started landing that one too. That's how easy it was. But every once in a while, when their man wound up a hook or right hand and cracked it home, like he'd always done before, it gave them hope and they chanted again:

Gatti!

Gatti!

Gatti!

So you wouldn't have known it from the chant, but you had to think some portion of the 9,438 fans who drove out to the Atlantic City boardwalk (or went "down the shore," in Jersey parlance) must have been realists. Some had to know, or suspected at least, that it would be the last time they would make the drive to their beloved Boardwalk Hall for an Arturo Gatti fight. It would be the last time one of their buddies at a July softball game would ask, "What are you doing next weekend?" and the reply would be: "We'll be down the shore; Gatti's fighting." Not "Arturo Gatti" and a long explanation of who that is. Just "Gatti."

It already was a done deal that so long as he beat Gomez, Gatti would fight Julio Cesar Chavez's kid, and after that, who knew what could happen? It's ironic that it was Chavez's old man who brought back the farewell tour, and if *he* was able to make a few bucks doing it, why couldn't Gatti, for just a couple fights?

You could just see it: Gatti beats Gomez, because, well, let's be serious, Gomez is a guy from *The Contender* TV show. Certainly Gatti had enough left to qualify as a step-up for a guy who'd recently been a little lucky to get a draw with Jesse Feliciano, right? We mean, how shot could he be? So Gatti would beat Gomez, then slap around Chavez's kid because he wasn't his old man, never could be, and Gatti couldn't lose to some snot nose like him. No way.

That was the optimists' view, and you could make a case for it: Big deal that Gatti had lost, resoundingly, to Floyd Mayweather and then Carlos Baldomir (sandwiching a win over Thomas Damgaard). Where was the shame in that? Zab Judah had done the exact same thing (except for the win over Damgaard, and in reverse order), and no one was telling Judah he was shot. So to the optimist, there still was the chance that Gatti would be around for a little while longer and maybe even had one more "Fight of the Year" left in him.

In case you haven't noticed, optimists are disappointed a lot of the time. It comes with the territory. They were again when Gatti, the wonderful, bloody dream of a prizefighter he had been for the better part of a decade, found he no longer could wade through punches to batter a man who just seconds earlier had appeared his master -- even a lower rung one like Gomez. If it wasn't a surprise to the pessimists among us, it was to his trainer, Micky Ward, who, in better days, famously engaged Gatti in a bloody trilogy that ranks among the best in the game's history.

"There was no indication before the fight, in the gym, that anything was wrong," Ward told *The Ring*. "He had the legs, his speed was still there. He looked great in the gym. But when he got up in the ring, he just didn't have it. He wasn't right from the start. That's what happens sometimes, it just all catches up to you one night, and I guess that was the night for him. All those wars just caught up to him. It was just time."

Ward caught criticism in some corners, perhaps deservedly, for not stopping the bout as Gatti reeled around the ring in the seventh round, getting battered. But Ward was a blood-and-guts fighter too, as stubborn and resilient in the ring as Gatti. Small wonder he couldn't convince himself to pull the plug. Guys like him and Gatti and a few others live by an entirely different code, and don't bother trying to understand it. You can't.

"I thought about it," he said. "A couple of times, I was close. But every time I thought about it, he'd land a wicked left hook, and I'd think, 'He still has a puncher's chance.' You don't want anybody to get hurt bad, but I thought, if it was me in there, I wouldn't have wanted my corner to stop it. I wouldn't have wanted that."

Neither, apparently, did referee Randy Neumann, who stood by slack-jawed as Gatti took a tremendous hammering throughout, but particularly in the seventh. Oblivious to both the damage Gatti was absorbing and to the cries of a few bleeding hearts in press row who pleaded with him to stop it, Neumann even started to count over Gatti after a final right hand bent his upper body backward over the top rope and then dumped him on the canvas. A week after the fight,

New Jersey boxing commissioner Larry Hazzard had no regrets about overruling Neumann, as he did when he leapt into the ring to stop it himself at the 2:12 mark.

"I'm not in the habit of criticizing referees, referees that I appoint myself," he told *The Ring*. "In that seventh round, Gatti had taken, by my count, 20 unanswered punches and gave great credence to the expression 'beaten from pillar to post.' When he took that final right hand and went to the canvas, that fight should have been stopped right then and there. He had not landed a telling punch for six rounds. One more punch might have been the end of Arturo Gatti, and I was not going to let that happen. Randy Neumann and I were not on the same page mentally."

It was over just like that for Gatti, and don't get the wrong idea: There's nothing special or unusual about a 35-year-old pug getting his head handed to him by a younger, stronger, more skilled fighter. That's been going on for as long as guys have been putting on gloves and giving one another brain damage. It's part of the game and a necessary one at that. Besides that, no one should be crying for Gatti. He made a hell of a lot of money in this business ($1.7 million for Gomez alone) and experienced things in his life, in the ring and out, that those smartass suits with their capped teeth and smooth eyebrows and pinkie rings could only dream about.

Has he accepted a big mortgage for those moments and for the big paychecks that came with them? Damn right he has. We don't know how painful the payments on that mortgage will be to make or whether they'll come due in 10 years or 30 or in five. They'll come due eventually; they always do, for fighters and for us. And whenever they come, only Gatti will be able to say whether or not the price he paid for what he got was fair. Only he will know if he got a good deal, if he made the right choices.

It's important, too, that we not confuse Gatti's in-ring persona with his real one either, the way many confused those of Diego Corrales in the days and weeks after his death. Gatti, 40-9 (31), is no angel outside the ring, and, to be clear, never was a great fighter in it. Even the Atlantic City regulars, if they're honest and know what they're talking about, will tell you that. Maybe in a different era, when a lot of guys could fight like Floyd Mayweather or Oscar De La Hoya and also had to weigh in on the day of the fight, maybe he wouldn't have done as well as he did.

But it never was about how good Gatti was in the ring. It was about how resilient he was, how he didn't give up, how he could turn it around in a microsecond, and, most of all, how much of himself he was willing to mortgage for the win. Ward, slow-footed and unimaginative in the ring, made Gatti look like a damn talented fighter in their second and third fights, and lesser guys sometimes made him look like more than he was. He never was great. But it didn't matter. That's not what it was about.

Gatti said afterward that he's retiring for good, blamed it on the odd happenstance that he's too big for junior welterweight and too small for welter. That means that he might be the only fighter in history who would need, in order to continue fighting successfully, his own weight class somewhere between 141 and 146 pounds. It's nonsense, of course, and even if he believes it now, the day will come when he will see it for what it is. That day always comes.

Should Gatti decide at some point to come back, as fighters so often do, he would not find the road welcoming. "Arturo Gatti would be hard-pressed to box in New Jersey again," Hazzard said. "He has a right to engage all of the legal processes at his disposal. I couldn't just say 'He can never fight here again.' But the feeling is we concur with his retirement and we would not like to see him fight again anywhere. I've seen enough to know that the Gatti era is over."

All of us have. We have all awakened, regrettably, from the wonderful, bloody dream that was Arturo Gatti.

Epilogue: Arturo Gatti retired after the Gomez fight and died in a hotel in July 2009 in Ipojuca, Pernambuco, Brazil, while vacationing with his wife and their 10-year-old son. Authorities initially charged Gatti's wife, Amanda Rodrigues, with murder but later reclassified the death as a suicide, saying Gatti hanged himself. He was 37 years old.

EVANDER HOLYFIELD

HIS HEART WON'T ACCEPT WHAT
HIS BODY ALREADY KNOWS

ORIGINALLY PUBLISHED IN *KO*, AUGUST 2001

Guys in the fight media love to tell fighters when they should walk away. A guy hits 35 or 36, loses a step or two, maybe gets stopped two or three times, and all of a sudden every pencil-neck with a word processor is on his back, hounding him, criticizing him, almost demanding that he get out.

They don't tell the fighter what he's supposed to do with the next 30 years of his life, or how he's supposed to pay the mortgage or put his kids through college. They don't tell the guy, who's been in the gym since he was 11, how he's supposed to learn a new trade and completely reinvent his life. All they know is he's not what he used to be—as if *they* are—and since he can't do the things he did when he was 24, he shouldn't do them at all. The best they can do is hope he saved his money, if he made any.

Don't be too hard on the guys in the press. Most of them love fighters. If they could, they'd be fighters themselves. They tell old, worn-out fighters to quit because, like everyone else, they have heroes in their lives and it's no fun to watch your hero get beaten up. It's no fun for the hero either, but there's a distinct sadness to witnessing a fighter, especially one who was once great, get abused by a guy who has no right abusing him. Ask the guys who went to the Bahamas to watch Trevor Berbick pound Muhammad Ali. It's true that the humbling of heroes is an integral part of this business. That doesn't make it any less difficult to watch when it comes around.

Evander Holyfield is a hero to a lot of fight guys. Forget all the kids out of wedlock and all the marriages, and forget the religious rhetoric if it bugs you. Forget that he uses that bald head for a lot more than thinking when he's in the ring, and forget that he's made as much money in his career as probably any fighter, ever, because we really don't like our heroes to be filthy rich if we can help it. You can even forget Evan Fields.

You can forget all of it because Holyfield is an all-time great. He earned the status little by little over a 17-year professional career and three reigns as a heavyweight champion – four if you count the title he won over John Ruiz in their first match, which, frankly, was beneath him and did little to enhance his legacy.

You can quibble that Holyfield struggled with a lot of guys he shouldn't have struggled with as a heavyweight champion, or that he was inconsistent, or that he frequently fought down to the level of his competition. "The Real Deal" is a legend and will be viewed even more so in that way in the years to come.

He is also a terribly shot fighter and we would prefer if he not fight any longer.

History tells us fighters age in sections, piece by piece. First the legs go, then the reflexes and speed. If the guy had a good punch in his prime, eventually that leaves him too. At the end, when nothing is left, he can't even take one on the chin anymore. It doesn't matter if he could take it all night as a kid. When he's done, an average shot, the kind that would have charged him up when he was fighting six-rounders, does him in.

That's usually what convinces guys their days in the ring are over. If an old pro can stay with some young lion, not beat him, but stay with him and not embarrass himself or get hurt, he can bullshit himself into thinking he was just a lucky shot or two away from another big score. So long as he doesn't get busted up or bounced around, the judges were bought or he just needs a new trainer or he was injured and didn't tell anyone. He can still fool himself. But if he gets hurt, if he gets banged around and dropped, if he has to grab his man around the waist and tackle him to keep from getting brained, then that's usually enough to do the trick – especially if the guy doing the hitting is no big puncher.

The right hand that Ruiz used to belt Holyfield to the canvas in their rematch in March probably isn't the best right hand that Ruiz, who is no great hitter, has ever thrown. Certainly it wasn't the hardest shot Holyfield has ever taken. He's swapped leather with much better punchers: George Foreman, Lennox Lewis, Riddick Bowe, Ray Mercer, Michael Moorer, even Bert Cooper. Bowe stopped him once in three tries and Cooper came damned close for a minute or two, but none of the rest ever noticeably hurt him, including Lewis, who put in 24 rounds with him.

Yet Ruiz's right cross was enough to send Holyfield sprawling to the canvas, those familiar, disproportionately thin legs giving way under him as he bounced off the bottom rope, his face twisting into an unsettling and wholly unfamiliar grimace. He never saw the punch, he told us afterward, and we know by now, because we've been told a thousand times, that those are the ones that get you. But he got up, barely, and tackled Ruiz and wrapped him up as best he could manage with no legs, and held on for as long as it took for referee Joe Cortez to wriggle between the two of them, which was a long time. And he lasted. It was the most hurt we've ever seen him, worse even than when Bowe stopped him in 1995.

To those who love Holyfield and are honest with themselves, the knockdown, along with the subsequent decision loss, seemed almost like a good thing at the time. It was convincing. Sure, Holyfield, 37-5-1 (25), would see it now too, he had to, at 38 and with a lot of hard miles logged, he was done and he could go quietly and proudly and with a little dignity. Sure, he'd lost the title but who cared? It was worthless, everyone knows it and besides, he'd proved all he had to years ago. What a sendoff he'd get, and how we'd miss him, and wouldn't it be great to look back on him and remember what a warrior he'd been? It was a good loss to go out on, if there is such a thing. Just be happy it was against a plodder like Ruiz, 37-4 (27) and not some young gun who could really crack, like David Tua or Wladimir Klitschko.

He'd have to see it now. He'd accept it the way eventually they all had, and in a few years he'd be in the International Boxing Hall of Fame, and since he would quit now and avoid all those messy beatings he'd have gotten fighting into his 40s, he'd still have enough left later on to look back on his career and remember how great he used to be. Sure, it would have been better had he quit after either of his waltzes with Lewis, or even after the first Ruiz fight, which, frankly, should have convinced him, even though it lacked the requisite knockdown. But he had that broken eardrum, or whatever, the first time. There weren't any excuses this time, though—he'd said so before the fight. So this would be it. The end of the Holyfield era.

"My goal is still to be the undisputed heavyweight champion of the world. I just have to get back in line." He spoke the words clear and firm moments after the decision came, and not 10 feet from where Ruiz, apparently having shed for the moment his "Quiet Man" persona, yelled, screamed, and danced an awkward jig that looked not unlike his battle maneuverings. The words saddened anyone for whom Holyfield has been a hero—even those who accepted his greatness only recently, and grudgingly at that.

We hoped that this loss, to this opponent, this way, with the knockdown and the bruises that shadowed his face, would have been enough. It wasn't. A day later Don King was pitching Ruiz-Holyfield III in China. He might beat Ruiz in China, but what of it? It would be life and death again against a guy who has beaten no other top heavyweight, a guy who was flattened by Tua and put in serious trouble against a thoroughly washed Tony Tucker. Ruiz is determined and feisty and has average skills and power. That's all. And that was good enough to beat Holyfield— convincingly.

He doesn't care.

"I never thought I'd be a five-time heavyweight champion," Holyfield said at the postfight presser. "I guess now I'll have to be."

Even heroes wear out. Holyfield wore out years ago. Many would tell you his last good showing was his 1997 knockout of Moorer, and that wasn't a walk in the park either, at least early on. But then he started landing right hands and Moorer, who as of late has not needed extra convincing to sit down when caught cleanly, succumbed to Holyfield's will. Others will argue that Holyfield has been shot for longer than that, that Bowe ruined him for good when he stopped him in '95. Count the number of subpar outings after that night, and you'll come up with Bobby Czyz, Vaughn Bean, the two Lewis fights and the two against Ruiz. On the plus side were the two wins over Tyson—whom Holyfield owns outright and you can speculate as to why that is—and the Moorer fight.

Fighters fight. Great ones, like Holyfield, do it successfully for the better part of their adult lives. How silly it is for us to think they should be able to just stop doing it one day just because they get beaten up, and because a bunch of sportswriters tell them they're shot. To a guy like Holyfield, who has overcome odds and popular opinion so many times, it's just another hurdle to overcome, like when everyone said he was too small to become the heavyweight champion, or that he was too old to whip Tyson. A lot of fight guys were worried Tyson might kill him. So winning a title again, in Holyfield's mind, is a perfectly reasonable possibility.

No one can defy time and the odds forever. If Ali couldn't do it, if Louis couldn't do it, if Sugar Ray Robinson couldn't do it, Holyfield can't do it. Time runs out eventually. "I had a bad night," he told the assembled press after the Ruiz fight.

That's a 38-year-old fighter in denial, a fighter whose every success has been built on self-confidence and belief in himself. He can't turn it off now and he can't admit that a bad night is the only kind he'll have anymore, that the good nights, against good opponents anyway, are long gone and best not chased after. You can't turn it off after using it as fuel for so long, and now, in his mind, it must be louder than ever, his belief must be stronger than it ever had to be before. Deep down, he has to know. But the same will that led to his success keeps him in the ring. That's what keeps all the great ones there. Your heart doesn't know when your body is shot.

But Holyfield is shot, and not a little. He couldn't do anything useful against Ruiz, and it doesn't matter a bit if Ruiz was faking, as Holyfield claimed, the effects of the low blow Holyfield landed in the 10th that cost the old guy a point. (He complained too that Ruiz wasn't penalized for retaliating.) And finally, from the guy who refused to admit that Lewis beat him fair and square in the first match in Madison Square Garden in 1999, came this gem: "All three judges got it wrong. I won the fight." Denial is a wonderful thing if it doesn't carry with it the likely possibility of imminent dementia and a host of other symptoms of brain damage. The possibility is real. Holyfield has been through more wars than many fighters with twice as many fights. And his defense isn't likely to get any better.

We could be all wrong about this, of course. It wasn't that long ago that Alex Stewart beat Foreman's face into a swollen, bloody boil, and we couldn't get on Foreman fast enough to retire. A couple of fights later, he flattened Moorer and didn't we all feel silly? Anything's possible. That's why we would never say Holyfield shouldn't be *allowed* to fight. He's a grown man and knows well the risks he takes. He has every right to take them. But we'd hate for him to keep chasing something he caught long ago at the risk of losing all that he's won.

Roberto Duran is still fighting. Hector Camacho, too. Simon Brown may still be at it, and don't be surprised if you hear that Julio Cesar Chavez is back in training. If not for a recent spate of new legal troubles, Bowe probably would have fought by now. It is easy, considering the depth of Holyfield's denial, to envision him three or four years from now getting pummeled by prospects, still convinced that he can do what he did so well for all these years. How painful it would be to see him that way, still fighting because he feels like he hasn't done enough. He has. And now he should walk away, proudly. Like a hero.

Epilogue: Holyfield fought on for 10 more years after the loss to Ruiz, going 7-5-1 with one no-contest (including a victory over Ruiz) in his last 14 fights. His final professional boxing match was a stoppage win over Brian Nielsen in Copenhagen in May 2011.

WHO IS RESPONSIBLE
FOR DONALD CURRY?

ORIGINALLY PUBLISHED IN *RINGSIDE SEAT*, FALL 2021

LAST MONTH, a person claiming to be the son of 1980s welterweight champion and junior middleweight titlist Donald Curry took to *Twitter* to share unfortunate news about Curry and "spread awareness" of his condition toward finding help for retired athletes suffering with CTE and mental illness.

According to the thread, which is found under Curry's Twitter handle, @LoneStarCobraTX, Curry, who was inducted into the International Boxing Hall of Fame in 2019, has been in and out of jail, exhibits deficits in cognition and memory, has poor balance and motor skills and is hostile in his personal relationships. All of these are indeed symptoms commonly associated with CTE or other brain damage that we see in former prizefighters and to a lesser degree in other athletes who experience long-term head trauma.

We see this too much in boxing. Or, more to the point, we don't see it enough. We see what causes it—the punishment, obviously—but when the fighter inevitably drops out of view we forget him and move on to the next young warrior, leaving the memories where they are. The fighters are frozen in time as young men. We move on. By the time we see them again they are like Curry—broken, jumbled, at odds with their existence.

A summary of Curry's career is in order: He won around 400 amateur fights and lost four. He won the 1977 National Junior Olympics, the AAU National Championship in 1978 and '79, the National Golden Gloves championship in 1980 and would have been favored to medal at the 1980 Olympic Games if not for the U.S boycott. As a pro he won the IBF and WBA welterweight titles, then stopped Milt McCrory to unify. He was 25-0 (19) and considered the next Sugar Ray Leonard when Lloyd Honeyghan upset him in 1986. He won a junior middleweight title in 1988 then lost it and several subsequent title fights before retiring for good in 1997.

The news of Curry's condition stung Generation-Xers who grew up watching his rise and sudden fall. At his peak he was a heck of a prizefighter. It's always hell watching life expose your heroes not just as human, but as frail and as vulnerable as we are. The news wrought too the usual amount of well-intentioned hand-wringing that accompanies any such announcement, most of it along the lines of "boxing has to do a better job" and "we are all complicit" and the like.

Donald Curry did what he did best in front of tens of thousands of fans in packed arenas and to the delight and wonderment of millions watching on television. He saw the world, fighting in Las Vegas and Italy and Monaco and England and France, not to mention the countries he competed in as an amateur. He made millions of dollars, bought houses and luxury cars and had scores of beautiful women throwing themselves at him. As a successful, well-known athlete in the United States of America in the 1980s he was wined and dined by men wearing three-piece suits and pinkie rings to whom he'd have been invisible driving a cab or tending bar or answering phones.

Donald Curry was a kind of royalty and was treated as such. How many men do you know who lived like a king even for a year, a month, a week? How many men can say that for a while they were among the best in the world at what they did? How many men get to hear thousands chanting their name for their ability to knock another man unconscious? Most men go through their whole lives never creating anything as perfect as the hook Curry landed that knocked McCrory stiff. Surely this is a kind of paradise, and such a rare thing that it has to come with a cost. It would be unfair otherwise.

The bill has come due now and Curry is paying it. He's not the first and won't be the last. For decades on decades the working classes have sacrificed their bodies and minds on the altar of economic success -- in factories, in mills, on farms, while building skyscrapers and underground tunnels and in prize rings. Was it worth it to them?

Was it worth it to Curry? We don't know and shouldn't presume to. Only Curry knows. But we would do well to remember what Muhammad Ali, in the throes of Parkinson's syndrome, said when he was asked if he would do it all over again. He said that of course he would, that if he'd never boxed he would have been a sign painter like his old man and never gotten out of Louisville.

The larger question, though, beyond what cost a man is willing to pay to be a god for a short while, is: Who should care for him when the bill comes due? It is fashionable for those on the periphery of the sport to blame boxing for not having the infrastructure to support its stars when they are no longer useful, but boxing, particularly in the United States, is merely following the economic model of its benefactor.

That is to say, old, used up, broken-down prizefighters, like everyone else who has become unproductive, should pull themselves up by their boot straps lest they end up homeless, deranged and/or in prison. In a country so in love with the myth of rugged individualism, why should we expect anything else?

Boxing and Donald Curry had a deal.

They both got what they wanted. It is not boxing's responsibility to take care of Donald Curry. It is the responsibility of the country of which Curry is a citizen to care for him, as it is for all who live here.

Curry should have easy access to the best medical care the country can offer, which is quite good indeed, and the best support that can be had, not because he used to be a star, but because he is a human being and because we can easily afford it, for him and everyone who needs it. We need merely to look around the world to other civilized countries to see how easily it can be had.

If your hope is that boxing, out of the goodness of its heart, implements some kind of pension and health plans along the lines of what exists in the NFL or major league baseball, forget it. It will never happen. And you feeling guilty for watching fights and thereby "contributing" to stories like Curry's is nonsensical.

Abandoning the sport for moral reasons just hurts the fighters. If you want to help Curry and the others who will come after him, you must demand that our political leaders do what can and should be done with the American healthcare system but haven't yet for lack of political will and for greed. Anything else is subterfuge.

THE HISTORY

WHY WE LOVE DURAN AS HE HEADS INTO THE HALL OF FAME

BAD MEMORIES ARE LEFT BEHIND

ORIGINALLY PUBLISHED IN *THE RING*, APRIL 2007

ROBERTO DURAN WILL BE FORMALLY INDUCTED into the international Boxing Hall of Fame in June, and assuming he attends, his induction will receive the loudest cheers and longest ovations of any heard all weekend—even if those who understand no Spanish will have not the foggiest idea what he's saying in the speech that follows.

The reception will easily surpass in volume and sentiment the output that greets the speeches of fellow inductees Ricardo Lopez and Pernell Whitaker, both of whom probably equal Duran in ring skills and dominance, fall far short of him in numbers of sins committed against the fight game, and yet are far less beloved.

Indeed, the ambivalence held by many fans toward Lopez, a brilliant, tiny oddball of a Mexican star who eschewed the fighters' diet of whores, alcohol, and gambling in favor of cerebral pursuits involving poetry and philosophers, and Whitaker, always an abrasive, surly little bastard in spite of, or maybe because of his ring brilliance, will only serve to amplify the difference: Lopez and Whitaker will receive polite, measured, appreciative applause. They deserve at least as much.

Duran's ovation will rock the tiny hamlet of Canastota, New York to its quaint little core. (And will feature the same unanimity, one would imagine, as that comprising the cacophony of jeers we hope will hound at every turn fellow inductee Jose Sulaiman. But that's another story.)

Yet neither Lopez nor Whitaker ever said "No mas" in the middle of the biggest fight of his career, stunning an entire sporting culture, for the echoes of Duran's submission against Ray Leonard, his bitterest rival, carried far beyond boxing's jagged borders. It introduced "No mas" to the American lexicon. It wasn't as though we could justify Duran's enormous emotional failure in New Orleans in November 1980 the way we could Jake LaMotta throwing his fight against Billy Fox; it was the only way LaMotta could get a title shot. Fighters quit all the time in the ring, but we forgive it on the spot if the right circumstances exist. Duran's capitulation was far worse than Max Baer quitting against Joe Louis, for example; Louis had all but brained him moments before. Duran was merely being outboxed and taunted. His failure of will, of ego and constitution, made everything he had accomplished up to that point look like the cheap work of a common bully.

Yet we have forgiven Duran, all of us have, and we have a love for him that, as compared to his contemporaries and those who came a full generation after he was in steep incline, like Lopez and Whitaker, can be difficult to justify. It cannot be explained by his prowess in the ring alone, for certain fighters such as Lopez and Whitaker did about as much and are as accomplished. Indeed, Duran wasn't even the most successful fighter of his era.

You can argue that his era really was the 1970s, and it's true during that period, when he was at his terrible best, you could flip a coin to decide who was the best fighter in the world, he or the great Carlos Monzon. But we would do well to recall that Duran made the choice to fight at welterweight and beyond, and ultimately fighters only can be judged on whom they whipped and who whipped them in return. Leonard, Marvin Hagler, Thomas Hearns, Wilfred Benitez, and a few others all beat Duran. Hearns nearly killed him.

It is readily conceded, though, that Duran was a brilliant fighter—in his prime and well after.

"There wasn't anything Duran couldn't do in the ring," Hall of Fame trainer and manager Gil Clancy told me in December, shortly after the announcement came that Duran would be inducted. It was against Clancy's fighter, Ken Buchanan, that Duran won the WBA lightweight title in 1972.

"Anything you wanted him to do he could do: turn around and box southpaw, go after a guy, it didn't matter. And he was a hell of puncher. Anything and everything, he could do it all."

What Clancy recalls is true, but it doesn't explain Duran's enduring popularity. Perfectly brilliant, inoffensive fighters have been forgotten by the dozens over the years, their brilliant corpses anonymously and peacefully clogging up cemeteries and mausoleums the way their ring exploits once filled up seats in arenas and fight clubs. Brilliance in the prize ring appeals strongly only to those so deeply invested in the business that they have little influence elsewhere, so their voices and numbers are small. Duran is loved by all.

It never was as though Duran courted this affection from the masses. In his prime, his post-fight comments usually centered on how badly he wanted to hurt his opponent and regardless of how successful he'd been in the regard, it never seemed enough afterward. He always gave the impression he'd be willing to take on a few fans on the way back to the locker room if any would have him.

He didn't engage in baby-kissing exhibitions, or in flashing infectious smiles full of straight, even, blinding teeth. To the contrary, he went frequently, though quite naturally, to great lengths to be the antithesis to Leonard's all-American pretty boy image. One could make the argument that that was mere marketing, that he was cast as the villain as a means to increase the gate for the Leonard fights. But Leonard was nowhere to be found when Duran spoke, famously now, of putting poor Ray Lampkin in the hospital as though it was a failure, and that if he'd only been in better shape, Lampkin would have been in the morgue.

This was no Ricardo Mayorga press conference trash talk. Duran was one nasty son-of-a-bitch in the ring and around it too -- but in a charming way. When asked once how he would do in a street fight against Muhammad Ali, Duran sneered: "I beat the shit out of him."

There has been too, especially later in his career when he became less threatening, a kind of lovable-scamp persona that Duran adopted, probably quite by accident. It's the same vibe given off by the actor Jack Nicholson. In many ways, Duran is a kind of a Nicholson for the fight game, the lovable ne'er-do-well (once dangerous but not anymore) who, when we see him, compels us to smile broadly, point and say his name out loud, like he's an old dear acquaintance. And he is, even if we've never met him.

Today, Nicholson can waddle around on the sets of horrid films, a bloated memory of what he used to be, and still we love and revere him for what he was back then and also for the presence he retains. Duran, later on, could lose to Hector Camacho and Vinny Pazienza, and we still loved him. He could make us know the names Kirkland Lange and Pat Lawlor and cringe at them and we could get mad at him for not showing up in shape and losing to bums and for fighting on too long.

But we never could stay mad at him. Hell, most of us couldn't care less that his first world title was won on a foul. In the end, we could hold none of it against him. He's Duran. No matter how far he fell— and it was far against Leonard and a few other times too—Duran was forgiven. Why is that?

"It wasn't like he was some nothing fighter with no personality that no one cared about," said Don Fraser, who promoted all the biggest fights on the West Coast throughout the '70s. "He was a very colorful and charismatic guy. Even though he learned some of it, he never would speak much English, but he related to the fans anyway. He was that kind of fighter."

Still, Duran would have disappeared from our collective consciousness had his comeback after the embarrassment against Leonard gone nowhere. Instead it was after his lowest point that

Duran enjoyed some of his greatest moments. He had to fight, and fight well, to get the stink of New Orleans off him. And he did.

"When he fought Davey Moore and really beat the hell out of him that put him back in favor with the fans," said Fraser. "He had the Davey Moore fight, he was in it the whole way against Hagler, and then he beat Iran Barkley. And they were always good fights with Duran. He was a real exciting fighter who always made for good fights. He entertained his fans."

In the ring, Duran was boxing's improv man, bouncing about, feinting, going in and out, always looking for the angle, his wild black hair glistening and bouncing around in all directions. He would improvise mid-combination, start an attack two steps away as a righty and then be a southpaw when he was on you, digging a right hook under your heart. It's a cliché already to say he was underrated as a technician.

Is the secret to Duran's enduring appeal a matter of simple timing? His linking today's older fans to the last great "Golden Age" of the 1980s? Or is it because he bridges the gap from that generation to an older one, and was so good that even the old-timers who grew up with Ike Williams and Beau Jack respect him? Is that it? Can it simply be that he's what we call today a throwback?

No. It's more.

Maybe it's the stories they still tell about Duran, about him knocking out a horse (whether it's true is immaterial), or the one about his impression of his pet lion at the moment of owner-induced ecstasy. Maybe we like it that he got under Leonard's skin the way he did (it was about time someone did), or the way he intimidated even Hagler in their fight. Maybe, in some way too, it was seeing how intimidated and impotent he appeared against Hearns, when, in a terrible styles match-up that he seemed to recognize for just that the moment they were in the ring together, Duran committed the unforgivable novice's sin of sitting right out at the end of Hearns' punches.

You never can overestimate the power of redemption, either. The wins over Moore and Barkley gave us all a reason to celebrate and that's all most of us want. We all want to believe we too can come back the way Duran did if we should lose our way, as he did against Leonard. He quit without really quitting in their third fight, but his important work was already done.

Today, Duran is a burgeoning promoter and he bounds into the ring at his fighters' bouts, happily fat and gregarious, injuries from a car wreck having ended his fighting days, finally, five years ago. He looks happy with the love he gets from fight people, happier and more at peace than he did when he was fighting, and that's surprising and a little sad. It always seemed to those watching that he was born to fight, but maybe when you do something long enough you get it out of your system, eventually.

Duran was like beautiful, terrible music in the ring and maybe that explains a lot. But you don't need us to tell you why you forgave him for quitting against Leonard, or why you love him today. There's no mystery. It's no more involved than this: *He is Duran.*

THE DAY I WON THE TITLE

10 CHAMPIONS RECALL THE DAY
THAT CHANGED THEIR LIVES

ORIGINALLY PUBLISHED IN *THE RING*, MARCH 1998

FOR A PROFESSIONAL FIGHTER, there is no greater accomplishment than winning a world title. It represents the culmination of everything he has worked toward in a life dedicated to his art. It speaks to his talent, of course, but even more to his sacrifice, his pain, and his dedication. It is recognition. It is why, even in this age of split titles and multiple governing bodies, you see grown men leap and sob for joy at the right to slap a gaudy plastic belt around their waist, if for no other reason than the fact that it bears the word "champion." Indeed, despite the best efforts of our friends over at WBB, WBF, IBC, et al, it remains still only the rarest of men (and women) who can turn the sweat of a thousand days and nights of anonymous, painful toil in dark, grimy gyms into fame, respect, and riches.

There are parallels in other professions, of course. The writer who pens a Pulitzer Prize-winning essay, for example or the film director who crafts an Oscar winner, has much in common with the pug who, through his own despair and sacrifice, eventually wills himself to the summit. It is true, the fighter's craft is less esoteric and the tools cruder, but the accomplishment yields rewards just as grand. For the right to glimpse such rewards, men have been wounded and vilified, robbed blind, and, sometimes, killed. Those who survive, who become world champions, enjoy moments, however fleeting, and gained at great cost, that the rest of us will never know.

In this feature, *The Ring* talks with 10 world champions and asks them to share their recollections from the day they won their first world title. Their revelations reveal anger, pathos, pride, humility, and, in some cases, humor. Each has his own story to tell. Their memories are their own.

HAROLD JOHNSON won the world light heavyweight title with a 15-round decision over Doug Jones on May 12, 1962 in Philadelphia

For most fighters the joy and gratification one usually associates with a title fight can only be experienced through winning. After all, in retrospect, to say a fighter challenged for the title is a gentle way of saying he didn't win it. But for Harold Johnson winning the light heavyweight championship was almost anti-climactic. The real accomplishment was getting an opportunity at all

"I was just so happy to be getting a shot," he said. "People were congratulating me for even getting the chance -- my family, my trainers, everyone. That's because I had a hard, hard time getting fights against light heavyweights. I had to fight a lot of heavyweights, guys who have weighed me by 30 pounds. It was so hard for me to get fights that one day I finally told my trainer that I had to go see a doctor. He asked me for what? I said, 'To see if I have some kind of disease or something.' Some days I'd look in the mirror and think to myself: *What makes you so tough that nobody wants to fight you?*

Finally getting the shot, though, had the effect one might expect. "I was kind of nervous about it," Johnson recalled, tension creeping into his voice at the recollection of an event that took place 35 years prior. "I was nervous. I couldn't wait to get it over with. It was the first time I ever really wanted anything." Humble words from a guy who had beaten, among others, Ezzard Charles, Arturo Godoy, Nino Valdes, and Archie Moore.

"It was a tough, tough fight. He took a really good punch. When you're a good puncher—and I had been knocking down heavyweights —and you hit a guy with your best punches and he doesn't even blink you start thinking *Can I even hurt this guy?* He was one of the toughest guys I ever ran across but I was faster and landed the more meaningful punches."

As soon as he won the title Johnson kept a promise that he had made to his mother years before. "When I was just a kid I would tell her that someday I would be a success and I'd buy her a new car. She'd say that I was just talking. My mother never wanted me to be a fighter. She always was scared for me, afraid that I was going to get hurt but she changed a little after I started bringing home some money. She was no softy though. Sometimes she'd box me around better than Jersey Joe Walcott did (Walcott stopped Johnson in three rounds in 1949.) But nothing was more important to me than making money to give to my mother. So right after I won the title, I bought her a brand new car like I always said I would. I was so happy that I was able to do it that it brought tears to my eyes and hers too. It meant as much to me to see my mother smile as I did to win the title. I had made my mother proud of me."

CARLOS ORTIZ won the lightweight championship of the world with a 15-round unanimous decision over Joe "Old Bones" Brown on April 21, 1962 in Las Vegas.

As a one-time junior welterweight champion who had long stalked the lightweight belt, Ortiz hardly required extra motivation going into a fight against Brown. In Ortiz's eyes Brown had ducked him for years. Extra incentive came, nevertheless, when a series of events leading up to the weigh-in made the challenger hungrier than ever.

"I got up early the morning of the fight and I figured I was going to be okay as far as my weight went, because when I had gone to bed the night before, my weight was perfect. But while I was sleeping I must've been dreaming that I was eating or drinking water or something because when I woke up and weighed myself I was over the limit by a pound-and-a-half."

As any dedicated challenger of his time would, Ortiz donned a plastic sweatsuit, slipped out of the hotel and headed out to the Las Vegas desert to run. "The whole time I was running I just couldn't figure out how this had happened," he said. "After running for about 30 minutes I was very tired I got back to the hotel and weighed myself again and I was still a half-pound over." Ortiz went back out into the heat again, walked for a while, then returned to his room soaked in sweat, figuring he had done all it would take to get him sufficiently under the 135-pound limit.

"We went to the weigh-in, I got on the scale and I was 6 ounces over." Ortiz was relieved, figuring six ounces was no big deal; it wasn't even half a pound, after all. Surely he'd be allowed to conserve his remaining energy for the fight itself. The champion's handler's however, had other ideas. "Brown's camp told me I had to take the six ounces off," Ortiz remembered, still incredulous at the thought. "I got so pissed off but I put my sweat suit back on and went for another walk in the desert. I came back soaking wet. The whole time I was thinking, *He's going to be sorry for this!*

Brown did ultimately pay for the behavior of his handlers but not because Ortiz battered him from pillar to post in a dehydrated craze. "The fight was a stinker," Ortiz said. "Brown had a very good counter right hand and I used to press a lot, so they figured I would go in there and slug it out and he would be able to counter me. But I started out with a jab. From the first time I hit him with a jab he was confused. And it went like that all night."

Midway through the fight, and with the crowd voicing its disapproval over the lack of action, Ortiz returned to his corner and said, "This is silly. It's too easy!" His corner told him to forget about the crowd and stick to the game plan. He did and won 14 rounds. It was that easy. Much easier than, say, a 30-minute run in the desert.

VITO ANTUOFERMO won the middleweight world title with a

15-round split-decision over Hugo Corro on June 30, 1979 in Monte Carlo, Monaco.

As any experience observer of the fight game will tell you, looks are frequently deceiving. Guys who are musclebound and look like granite are often the most fragile. Conversely, the frailest looking fighters are often the toughest. Sometimes, though, a fighter's appearance tells more about him than he would probably prefer. Ask Antuofermo.

"Corro had never lost a fight and I had seen him on television when he beat Rodrigo Valdes twice and Ronnie Harris," Antuofermo said. "He made Harris, who was a good fighter, look bad. I thought he was really good and I was concerned. He was very clever." That concern turned to something else when he finally met Corro in person a short time before the fight.

"I couldn't believe it. Here was a guy who had 48 or 49 fights and his nose didn't look like it had ever been broken, like it was never even touched. There were no marks and scars around his eyebrows. He looked like a girl, like someone who had never been hit. That's what I knew I was going to walk right through him."

Antuofermo did indeed walk through Corro that night, but that's not how everyone saw it. At least, not until the fight was just about over. "It went 15 rounds and I couldn't get a good shot in. If anyone landed a punch the whole fight it was me because he was just looking to survive," Antuofermo said, sounding as though he wouldn't mind an opportunity to get a good one in now 18 years after the fact. "But afterward Alex Wallau told me that during the entire fight Howard Cosell was talking like he had Corro winning and saying that Corro was ahead on the scorecards."

According to Antuofermo, Wallau sneaked a peek at the actual scores after the 14th round saw that Antuofermo led on two of the three judges' cards and told Cosell. "Suddenly Cosell changed his tune and had me ahead."

Antuofermo didn't sleep that night, instead enjoying a party thrown for him by his promoter, a celebration he called the biggest he had ever seen. The next day he and his camp drove to Milan so he could visit with family. One the way they saw something out of a nightmare. "We were on the highway and we're about to go under an overpass. I looked up and saw a car they had driven right off the bridge. It was literally flying through the air. It was about to fly right into one of those big cement columns that hold the bridges. Then I saw it hit. The crew kept driving." Later Antuofermo was presented with a medal of honor in Rome.

Even with the victory the celebration and the medal Antuofermo felt something was missing. In his next fight he found out what it was. "Winning the title was good but it didn't mean as much as when I fought Marvin Hagler (a 15-round draw on November 30, 1979). That was the night I felt like I was fighting for the title."

TERRY NORRIS knocked out the feared John "The Beast" Mugabi in the first round to win a junior middleweight world title on March 31, 1990 in Tampa, Florida.

According to the teachings of the legendary Cus D'amato and other wise, old boxing sages, fear can be a prizefighter's best friend or his worst enemy. At its worst it paralyzes a fighter, rendering him helpless against an opponent's attack. At its best at heightens his awareness to such a level that he performs better than he could otherwise.

Like most fighters, Norris knew fear. Going into his fight with Mugabi, he had more reason than most to be nervous. Thought to be perhaps just past his prime, Mugabi still inspired fear in his opponents. Regardless of any erosion of his skills, he remained a terrifying puncher who demanded respect in the ring.

"Everyone was afraid of him. I remember thinking, *I'm going to fight 'The Beast,'* Norris said, emphasizing the nickname Mugabi carried with him into the ring like an extra weapon. If that wasn't enough, Norris had the memory of his first title shot (a knockout loss to Julian Jackson) still ringing in his head. "I was wondering, *What if I get caught with a good shot the way I was against Julian Jackson, and get knocked out?*"

As it turned out, Norris's nerves helped him. "I've noticed since then that I fight better when I go in a little nervous. If I feel a little scared before I go in, a little jittery, like the day I won the title, then I know I'm going to fight my best." Indeed, it was Mugabi who suffered the stunning knockout that day. "I figured he would be set and ready to go. But he made a couple of mistakes and I caught him," Norris said. After the first hard punch landed, causing Mugabi to wilt, Norris had a revelation: *"I remember thinking, 'This is going to be easier than I thought!'"*

It wasn't as easy or fun as what the new champion did later that evening. "After I won the fight, my wife and I went home and made my son. That was the most important thing about that day." Terry Jr., now seven years old, is probably too young to understand yet his connection to the day his famous father won his first world title. Maybe someday Norris will let him in on the secret.

CARMEN BASILIO knocked out Tony DeMarco in the 12th round of a thriller on June 10, 1955 in Syracuse, New York to win the welterweight championship of the world.

Followers of most any sport are familiar with the term "game face." It is used to describe the anxious, belligerent state of mind most athletes exhibit in the final days before competing, especially in a major event. For the normally docile Carmen Basilio, an upstate New York onion farmer when he wasn't bashing heads in the ring, the term took on new meaning before his fight with DeMarco.

"Before the fight, my two managers—I had a pair of managers I couldn't stand —kept coming around, and were always asking me to do stuff I didn't want to do," Basilio remembered, without elaborating on specifics. "Now, I was always a little mean on the day of a fight, a little on edge, and even more so before a big fight. My one manager, Joe Netro, came around on the day of the fight, bugging me about something. I just start screaming at him, really let him have it. That was it. They wouldn't come around me again before the fight. They knew I'd scream at them."

Considering the DeMarco's reputation as a fierce left-hook artist, Basilio could be forgiven for his outburst. "I was a little nervous going to the fight. I knew DeMarco was a great puncher, because he had just knocked out Johnny Saxton in the 14th around. So I knew he was dangerous and that I had to be real careful. But I was in great shape and it was the best fight of my life."

As for his managers, things didn't get much easier down the road. "I was that way, especially before a big fight," Basilio recalled with a chuckle. "And they were all big fights to me."

JAKE LAMOTTA won the world middleweight title by stopping Marcel Cerdan in 10 rounds on June 16, 1949 in Detroit, Michigan.

It's been said often that good things come to those who wait. Another school of thought holds the better things come to those who hustle.

"I was the uncrowned champion for five years before I finally got a title shot, and even then I had to pay $20,000 under the table to get it," LaMotta said, still full of resentment, but not anger, at the memory. "I was on my way out already." That he viewed himself as being used up didn't take away from his confidence, however, nor from his determination to win the championship. He had waited too long.

"The day of the fight, I said to my brother, 'Joey I'm going to be the world champion by the time the day is over. I think I could lick Joe Louis tonight.' I was just so naturally high that I could've licked five champions at night. I just had so much will power and determination. I was obsessed by it."

That the opponent was Cerdan, whom LaMotta calls "probably the greatest champion to ever come out of Europe," mattered little. "I had to be the champ that night. That night, no punches bothered me." He added with some bravado, "Well, punches never really bothered me, but especially not that night. I just kept pushing and pushing and giving everything that I had."

With all that pushing, something had to go and, eventually, it was Cerdan. "When the fight was stopped, I kissed everyone in my corner twice and touched the ground, and said, 'This is my town. Detroit is my town.' I was in another world. I was so happy. I had achieved my goal, something I had prayed for all my life." The euphoria, as you may have guessed, didn't last long. "Then, about two days later, I said to myself: *Where do I go from here?*"

BOB FOSTER anesthetized the great Dick Tiger in the fourth round on May 24, 1968 in New York to win the light heavyweight world title.

Some fighters fight for the love of it. Some because they know of nothing else to do. Others, perhaps many more than we would prefer to think, do it almost solely for the money it will bring them. We shouldn't think any less of those who are inspired only by the promise of endless riches. A king's ransom, indeed. It is called *prize*fighting, after all.

"What do I remember about the day I won the title?" Bob Foster said. "That I didn't make enough money to pay for a cab to get my mother back to the hotel." Foster is joking. Sort of. The bitterness is still there.

"The light heavyweight division has always been a bad division for making money," he lamented, thus explaining all those unsuccessful forays into the land of the heavyweights. "And no one really wanted to fight me. I didn't make any money at all off the Tiger fight. I had to give Tiger $100,000 to take the fight, even though I had been the number-one contender on and off for several years."

Essentially, Foster was paid training expenses for the fight, which was his ticket to making the kind of purses that many—including himself—thought he had long deserved. As it was, his title shot came at the fairly advanced age of 29.

At 38, maybe Tiger knew he couldn't win and this was his chance to make a few bucks of his own before being put out to pasture. Certainly, the oddsmakers thought so, making Foster at 12 to 5 favorite. And just as surely, the challenger thought so as well. "I knew I was going to become the champion. I knew as soon as I saw Tiger that there was no way in God's creation that this guy was going to beat me. I wasn't even worried about the fight at all."

It wasn't that Foster was one of those fighters who had no fear— even with that paralyzing power. He freely admits that "at other times

I would get nervous like any other fighter would. But not for Tiger. Once I sized him up, I knew there was no way he was going to be me. He was just too small."

RAY MANCINI won a lightweight world title with a sensational first-round knockout of Arturo Frias on May 8, 1982 in Las Vegas.

Strange as it sounds, for Mancini, the fight was the easy part. It was the time leading up to the fight that proved most harrowing.

"About two weeks before the fight, we were at training camp in Tucson, Arizona, and two detectives showed up saying they needed to speak with me," Mancini said. Intrigued, he listened to the officers tell him that they had received a call from a maid who was employed at the hotel where Mancini and his camp were staying. According to the maid, two men—one armed with a rifle, the other with a shotgun—came in asking where Mancini's room was. The maid pleaded ignorance. After taking a quick look around, the two gunman left, returning to the car with several other rifle-toting passengers awaiting their return.

"The police asked maid what she thought might have happened if they found me. She said she thought they were going to kill me." Undeterred, Mancini did his roadwork the next morning—with the two detectors in tow. "To this day we don't know what that was all about," he said. "At the time, I wasn't nervous about it because I was so focused on the fight. But to think about it now, it's pretty scary."

Mancini and his camp proceeded to Las Vegas, and things progressed without incident until just before the final press conference when David Wolfe, Mancini's rather eccentric manager, became annoyed with some aspect of the promotion.

"Something ticked him off and he told the promoters and everyone that we weren't going to the final press conference. I said 'Dave, bullshit! Are you crazy? This is my fight and I'm going.' We didn't speak to one another again until after the fight. Now, at the same time, Frias had gotten a nick on his nose in training, and they didn't want anyone to know about it. So he didn't go to the press conference, but his manager, Norm Kaplan, did. So there we were; I was a fighter with no manager and he was a manager with no fighter."

It did not start well for Mancini. "He hit me with a hook and then jumped on me. There was a point for several seconds when I was just trying to survive the round. Then I fired back and dropped him." For Mancini, a fighter who relied as much on his adrenaline as he did his left hook, that was all the pushing needed. "At that point, I was Hercules. There was such a rush of euphoria. And when I won, it was the single greatest moment of my professional life."

DWIGHT MUHAMMAD QAWI bludgeoned and stopped Matthew Saad Muhammad in 10 one-sided rounds to win a light heavyweight world championship on December 19, 1981 in Atlantic City, New Jersey.

It was all about staying power. If you were one of Saad Muhammad's title challengers, you would have zeroed in on that porous defense and the tender facial skin and figured, "All I have to do is jump on this guy, empty my guns, and maybe go home early." Take a shot. Why not? Even if you knew also of his granite chain, heavy hands and legendary recuperative powers, it seemed as reasonable a strategy as any other. Qawi had a different view.

"I knew the most important thing would be my conditioning because he would always keep coming back. So I put it in my head that I could go 30 rounds if I had to."

Always in shape but hardly a Spartan, Qawi went the extra mile in anticipation of Saad Muhammad's doggedness. "I had just beaten James Scott and stayed in the gym a lot. I even went away for three weeks prior to the fight to prepare and tighten up. My game plan was that I had to have a lot of stamina. As the fight approached, I visualized myself winning the title."

The plan proved to be the right one, as Qawi started fast and never relented. When Saad Muhammad try to surge, Qawi wouldn't let him. "He was a sharp puncher but he couldn't wear me down." As dominant as Qawi's performance was, the fight was not without its scary moments. "He hit me once in the middle rounds, and all of a sudden I saw the floor where the ceiling was supposed to be. But I came back because of my conditioning. That was the key."

After he won, the key was coming back down. "I was on a natural high. It was like, *I have arrived*. It was a euphoria that lasted for a while. It was overwhelming, emotionally. And then I thought, *"Let me get back down to earth."*

No sooner had the thought entered his mind that he received just the kind of help he had been seeking. "One guy, a friend of mine, had just bought a brand new Cadillac. The day after I won the title he said, 'Hey champ, why don't you take her for a ride?' So I did, and on the way back I stopped to get gas. As I was backing into the gas station, I ran right into one of those big steel poles they have. That brought me right back down to earth. That calmed me right down."

CURTIS COKES won a 15-round decision over Manuel Gonzalez on August 24, 1966 in New Orleans, Louisiana to claim a world welterweight title.

Though some fighters are known for their creativity when it comes to skirting the curfews mandated by their trainers, others are just as good, if a little less creative, at enforcing them. For Cokes, the training camp intended to prepare him for his first world title shot was no place for play—even if it was located in one of the nation's biggest party towns.

"We were training in New Orleans, and some of my sparring partners were going out at night drinking and partying," Cokes recalled. "One of them, Willie Warren, would climb out of the window every night and sneak out to go partying. Finally, one morning I got tired of it. The next time he came into the gym, I gave him a good shellacking in the ring and told him, 'If you're gonna stay out all night, you can't spar with me.' After that, he didn't go out again."

Warren must have shaped up in time to give Cokes the work he needed, because the fight itself went exactly as planned. "I felt all along like I would win the fight. I had beaten Gonzalez three times before. He was my first opponent as a pro. Since we had fought already, it was nothing new to me. It was just like working out in the gym."

The outcome was extra sweet for Cokes, who was angered by the Gonzalez camp's prefight demand that he shave off the beard he typically wore when fighting. "I always wore a beard. They tried to unnerve me before the fight by telling me I had to shave it off. I guess they thought I would refuse or something, but I was there to fight. I shaved it off and said, 'Let's go.'"

To the victor go the spoils. For Cokes, the spoils were of a four-wheeled variety. "I had promised my wife before the fight that if I lost, I would buy her a new Mustang. If I lost, that would be all I could afford. But I also told her that if I won, I'd buy her a brand new Oldsmobile Toronado. So the whole drive back to Dallas she kept pointing out every Toronado we passed, or even cars that looked like a Toronado. She kept bugging me, asking when we were going to get her Toronado." Rest assured Mrs. Cokes got her Toronado.

WHERE GENIUS GOES TO DIE

PERNELL WHITAKER'S BITTER FRUIT

ORIGINALLY PUBLISHED AT *HBO.COM* ON APRIL 21, 2006

OLD GRUDGES DIE HARD. And the years have not mellowed Pernell Whitaker.

We're used to fighters softening a bit once they're away from the drama and desperation of the prize ring. Hated rivals become blood brothers, linked by their shared trips to hell and back. Champions break bread with their challengers, share war stories, lament the softness of the generations that follow.

Retirement changes fighters, generally. Some of them go crazy from it and can't stay out of trouble. But many more are civilized by it over time, provided they fought long and well and had little left at the end. They mellow. They're still fighters; they still have it in them to want to fight, and that eats away at them. But eventually, advancing age brings a kind of resigned stillness that would have seemed impossible during their fighting days.

Whitaker, who retired with a record of 40-4-1 (17), one no-contest, after losing by knockout to journeyman Carlos Bojorquez in April 2001, still carries a chip on his shoulder the size of all Virginia. He had it when he was one of the two or three best fighters in the world, a period which lasted for roughly a decade. He had it when, inevitably, he started to decline. He has it now.

Ask him about Oscar De La Hoya, who fights May 6 on HBO PPV against Ricardo Mayorga and you get an answer that seems unlikely. "I haven't followed his career," Whitaker told me recently. "I know he's a promoter now, or whatever. But other than that, I have no knowledge of him. I haven't seen him fight in a long time."

This from a guy who knows enough about today's game to say about Floyd Mayweather, "He's good. He's got good skills, good mechanics. I respect him and I don't take anything away from him. But he ain't no Pernell Whitaker."

De La Hoya is the most popular fighter of his generation. His fights have earned him and his associates untold millions in revenue. More than any non-heavyweight since Ray Leonard, he transcended the fairly narrow confines of the fight game and broke into the mainstream. And Whitaker disavows knowing any recent detail about his career.

You wonder how that could be. Then you remember that the decision De La Hoya won over him in Las Vegas in April 1997 was fairly unpopular, insulting even, to Whitaker and his camp, and the process of selective memory makes sense. Whitaker confesses no particular enmity toward De La Hoya, but often the best way to insult a man is to deny knowledge of his existence -- or at least of his success.

He gives just slightly more credit to Felix Trinidad, who decisioned him soundly in February 1999 in Madison Square Garden. At least he acknowledges him. "I fought six rounds with a broken jaw, and if not for that he wouldn't have gotten out of there (on his feet)," Whitaker said. "He did it with an elbow. I see that as a victory for me because I went six rounds with a broken jaw."

A good way to describe Whitaker, then and now, is surly. But no one said prizefighters had to be charming. You don't get extra points in the ring for congeniality. One's got nothing to do with the other. Besides that, geniuses more than anybody are under no obligation to make nice. And clearly Whitaker qualifies as a genius of the ring.

You can start with the gold medal he won in the 1984 Olympics, which Whitaker recalls as the proudest moment of his career. Even with his long reign as the lightweight champion and the alphabet titles he subsequently won at junior welterweight, welter and junior middle, it is his Olympic accomplishment that stands out.

"Anybody can win a world title," he says, and you realize more clearly than ever how easy it was for him in the ring. "But not everyone can win a gold medal. That (opportunity) only comes around once every four years. And as a fighter, you only get one shot. That was the best."

What followed was the building of a certain hall-of-fame career that included victories over some of the best lightweights in the world: Greg Haugen, the great Azumah Nelson moving up, Freddie Pendleton, Anthony Jones, Harold Brazier, Jorge Paez. Soon after, Whitaker jumped to 140 and, after taking a belt from Rafael Pineda, jumped up again and took Buddy McGirt's welterweight crown. That set up a superfight between him and the 88-0 Julio Cesar Chavez.

It was, for anyone who saw it, a complete victory for Whitaker against the man regarded generally as the best fighter on the planet. That the judges scored it a draw was an abomination, but it wasn't the first time it had happened to Whitaker. His March 1988 decision loss to Jose Luis Ramirez in France in his first title fight was at least as bad.

Some fighters go a whole career without getting robbed at a high level the way Whitaker was twice -- three times if you count the De La Hoya fight, which Whitaker does. Why did it happen to him?

"I don't know," he said. "Maybe I was just too good. I don't think I ever walked into a ring where I was favored to win. The odds were always against me. I always made it look easy and they couldn't take it. The fans know. They understand. You could always hear them grumbling and booing in the crowd."

To Whitaker, the fans were the ultimate arbiters. "Controversy sells," he said. "I always let the fans make the decision. If the fans felt I won, they voiced their opinion. If I didn't get the decision but the fans thought I won, I was content with it."

Today he's content enough training fighters. He's working with pro junior welterweight Dorin Spivey, who, like Whitaker, lives in Virginia. "He just came up to me one day and asked if I would help him out. We started talking. I knew he'd been around for a while. He asked for help. I knew he was a pretty good kid, so I agreed. I'm just getting my foot in the door."

Athletes of Whitaker's caliber rarely make great trainers. Ted Williams was a terrible batting coach. The great featherweight Willie Pep, to whom Whitaker was often compared, wasn't a great corner guy. Geniuses are never able to suffer gladly the lesser talents of the mediocre. They don't understand how it doesn't come as naturally to everyone as it did to them. Whitaker doesn't anticipate any great challenges, however.

"It's weird to be on the other side looking in," he said. "But I had good trainers. I called Ronnie Shields. He said I just have to be patient. No one's going to be Pernell Whitaker. They all want to be but they can't be. Everyone's got their own natural abilities. I don't want to teach anyone the sport. I just want to refine and improve guys.

"All I can do is tell a guy what it takes for him to win and be successful. I like teaching the science of the sport. Give him the way to win and give him a champion's mentality and teach him to pay attention to his corner. Let the trainer watch the tapes, give you the game plan, and if it doesn't work out, then the trainer takes full responsibility."

Whitaker says he doesn't miss being in the ring but that the fans miss seeing him in there. "I've done it all. There's nothing else to do. I'm content. But there are no eye-opening fighters out there anymore. There are no Pernell Whitakers out there today."

There have been problems in retirement. Whitaker has been jailed several times for charges relating to drug possession and driving offenses. (Many will recall his October 1997 decision win over Andrei Pestriaev in Connecticut that was changed to a no-contest when postfight tests revealed the presence of cocaine in Whitaker's bloodstream.). In 2003, he received a 27-month prison sentence for violating probation on a prior cocaine conviction. About these events and others, he says only, "The judge did what he felt like he had to do and I did my time and just dealt with it. I'm out now and life is good."

Whitaker makes it clear that he is not the stereotypical penniless former fighter. Despite rumors that he has blown through the millions he earned as perhaps his era's best fighter (and clearly an all-time great), he says: "I'm doing excellent financially. I've got more than most. I'm stable. I don't need for anything. Anything I want I can buy. I don't want for anything. Make sure you write that." It was not a request.

Whitaker said he doesn't regret anything in his career. No bad choices, no mistakes. "I regret nothing whatsoever. My career was one to remember. I wouldn't change a thing. Nothing."

How could it be otherwise?

Epilogue: Whitaker was killed on July 14, 2019, at about 10:00 PM when he was struck by a vehicle while crossing at the intersection of Northampton Boulevard and Baker Road in Virginia Beach. The cause of death was multiple blunt force trauma. Whitaker was 55.

TWO SECONDS TO PARADISE

MELDRICK TAYLOR'S RECKONING

ORIGINALLY PUBLISHED AT *HBO.COM* ON APRIL 12, 2003

IT DOESN'T SOUND right to say it, but some prizefighters are pacifists. They make their living in the ring, and probably they're not too happy about it, but they do it because they're good at it and can make a few bucks so what the hell. They take care not to do much damage while they're in there and they don't risk much either. They want to get in, do their thing, hope no one gets hurt and then get out and pay some bills.

There are those too, thankfully, who are on the other side—who fight because it's what they love to do. They need that hard contact: gloves cracking against jawbone, skulls banging together, blood in the eyes, the thrill of the pain and the exhilaration at the brutal end. If they didn't need money to live they'd be just as happy fighting for nothing.

It is one of nature's better jokes that neither temperament is bound to an appropriately corresponding set of talents. Roy Jones, for example, has the weaponry to have stopped every professional fighter he's ever faced and a good number he hasn't. But as far as fighters go, he's a pacifist. So he lets guys hang around. That's him.

You can say Meldrick Taylor was the opposite of Jones even if it gives the wrong impression. But he was. He had fast hands and good wheels, too. He could box and move and barely get hit when he was in the mood to do it that way. He wasn't a big hitter. He never was. But he fought a lot of the time like he was. He loved the rumble. He loved the action. That's what got him going.

"I didn't like to box all the time," Taylor said recently. He's 36 now and only semi-retired from the ring. More on that later. "It was too boring. I wanted to get in there and mix it up. Maybe I was too brave for my own good."

It was said often throughout Taylor's career, and particularly in the latter stages, that he had too much Philadelphia in him. You know, too much of the stuff that's been floating around in the gyms there for the past hundred years or that runs through the water and makes Philadelphia fighters too often braver and tougher and more in love with the fight than they should be.

"That might be a fair assessment," said Taylor, who more or less ended his career with a record of 38-8-1 (20). The thing is, he never really had a choice. He was all fighter, right from the start. He grew up in North Philadelphia, hoping to emulate older brother Myron, a heck of an amateur who grew into a pretty decent professional featherweight himself.

He first put on gloves at eight years old. He proved a prodigy, winning his first national title at 15. Two years later he found himself in Los Angeles on the 1984 US Olympic team with future world champions Pernell Whitaker, Evander Holyfield and Mark Breland. In the finals, Taylor whipped Nigerian Peter Konyegwachie for the featherweight gold. He was 17 years old.

"Winning the gold medal was phenomenal," Taylor said. "I had dreamed about it for so long and then finally made it a reality. I worked so hard for it then when it happened it was surreal." Taylor signed with the Duvas and turned pro later the same year, eventually bulking all the way up to 140.

He won 12 straight and his strengths were obvious: he had impossibly fast hands, and he was mobile and skilled. But he fought angry. Sometimes he fought like he had a bigger punch than he did and it got him hit when it wasn't necessary. But his chin was sturdy enough and anyway that was the way he liked to do it and you couldn't tell him otherwise.

In August 1986 Taylor drew with 1976 Olympic gold medal winner and lightweight title challenger Howard Davis Jr. It didn't slow him down. Eight fights later he challenged Buddy McGirt for the IBF junior welterweight title. McGirt, known today as one of the game's best young trainers, was 38-1-1 (33) and making his second defense of the belt. He was a superb craftsman in the ring and had twice the number of fights Taylor did. It didn't bother Taylor.

"I had to win it because he was considered a big puncher," Taylor said. "I was the underdog. He didn't respect me. He said he would knock me out. In the first round he tried. I was in a corner and he hit me with his best punch. After that I took over with my speed. He was a very good puncher and he was very game. He kept trying the whole fight but I out-speeded him." Taylor stopped McGirt in the 12th round.

Taylor defended twice and took a couple non-title bouts before engaging the most important fight of his career against living legend Julio Cesar Chavez. By this time Taylor had convinced many that he was among the best fighters in the world. But Chavez already was a three-division champion, owner of a 68-0 (55) record, and the consensus best fighter pound-for-pound on the planet. More than the undisputed junior welterweight title was at stake.

"It was inevitable that we would fight," said Taylor. "He was considered the best fighter in the world and that's what I wanted to be. In order to be the best you have to beat the best. I would fight anybody. I've never backed down from anyone. I didn't feel a lot of pressure. He had much more experience than I did. And I still got a lot of respect and acclaim even though I lost."

On St. Patrick's Day 1990, Taylor and Chavez took one another to places few fighters have gone. For 11 and 3/4 rounds they struggled against defeat and against one another. Taylor was faster and more active. Chavez was more accurate and heavier-handed; by the end

Taylor's face was swollen and bloody. It was a magnificent display of brutality and will and going into the final round Taylor led on two cards. He needed just to stay away and the fight was his.

He couldn't do it. It wasn't in him to. He fought the way he had all night, more or less right in Chavez' range and with about 15 seconds left Chavez landed a short right that hurt Taylor and another sent him down. He rose and turned to trainer Lou Duva, who was on the ring apron, shouting. Two ticks remained on the clock -- not enough time for Chavez even to cross the ring. Referee Richard Steele stopped it.

Today Taylor is philosophical about the loss. "I don't feel bitter at all about it. It was for a reason. Everything happens for a reason. I was never meant to beat Chavez." It was The Ring magazine's Fight of the Year and later its Fight of the Decade, too. But in the eyes of many Taylor paid a heavy price. A lot of guys will tell you he was never the same. He disputes it and makes a reasonable argument, asking how he was able, then, to go up in weight and win another world title (the WBA welterweight title from Aaron Davis). "The Chavez fight didn't ruin me," he said. "One fight doesn't ruin you."

That may be, but things went downhill from there. Taylor made two unimpressive defenses of the welterweight title before junior middleweight champion Terry Norris massacred him in four rounds in a fight Taylor knew he shouldn't have taken because of the size difference. But after winning a nationally televised bout, Norris had called Taylor out. "I couldn't back down," he said. Afterward he dropped back down to defend his title and was brutally stopped in eight rounds and dethroned by hard-punching Crisanto Espana.

Taylor's last big fight was the rematch with Chavez. It happened in 1994, about four years too late. Taylor blames dueling television networks for delaying what would have been a wonderful rematch, and blames himself for losing to Chavez again. "I was using my speed early, then I decided to go punch-for-punch," he said. "We rocked one another in the sixth round but I fought the wrong fight." Chavez stopped him in the eighth.

Since then Taylor has fought sporadically and without good results: wins over a couple of journeymen, losses to several. Almost universally within the business there is a sentiment that he shouldn't be fighting, and not just because those who have seen him in action insist his skills have seriously eroded. His words tend to melt into one another. One hopes to squint oneself into understanding him better. He has the thick tongue and jumbled diction we've come to recognize as the result of a brain damaged from too many punches.

But Taylor remains true to himself: Obstinate. Stubborn. Proud.

"It's bogus. A lot of fighters can still fight (when they get older): George Foreman, Larry Holmes, Ray Leonard. Why is there a double standard for me? I went to Mexico and beat the shit out of that guy over there (respected journeyman Kirino Garcia, who won a decision over Taylor in February 1999). Get the tape. I won 10 out of 12 rounds but it was in his backyard so they gave it to him.

"I beat the hell out of that guy in Denmark, too (Hasan Al, who decisioned Taylor in August '98). But it was in his hometown in Denmark so they gave it to him. I busted him up and beat him up. If I'm so washed up how am I beating these guys? Why aren't these guys knocking me out? I'm losing decisions in their backyards."

Taylor last fought in July 2002, dropping a decision to prospect Wayne Martell. He says he still can beat any top-10 welterweight in the world if they give him the chance but he refuses to sell his soul "to make other guys money that want to use my name. If I don't get any TV fights I'm not fighting, because if the fights aren't on TV I'm not going to make any money. I'm not going to waste my time."

So he is semi-retired now but busy. He just finished writing his autobiography, "Two Seconds to Glory." He is a minister, has been for eight years at the Israel Church of God & Jesus Christ in Philadelphia. "We have schools and teach in all the inner cities of America." He has a website too—meldricktaylor.com—where you can get T-shirts and videos of some of his old fights, or even hire him as a personal fitness trainer or nutritional consultant.

He denies having regrets. "What should I regret? I did a lot of things most people never get to do. I was a two-time world champion. I fought in one of the greatest fights ever. All things happen for a reason. This is the way things go in life." He paused an inserted an afterthought: "Maybe I would have fought smarter and not played to the crowd so much. Hector Camacho said he never cared that the crowd booed him, as long as he won the fight. Maybe I should have been more like that."

Perhaps. But he couldn't be more like that. It wasn't in him. Fighters, like the rest of us, can only be every day who they are—pacifist or warrior—and there is no higher calling than that. With Taylor, there was no mistaking which it was.

ACKNOWLEDGMENTS

There are surely dozens, maybe hundreds of people, who, knowingly or otherwise, directly or indirectly helped this project come to fruition. I'm guaranteed to forget many of them in this space, and a few of them should consider themselves lucky for the omission. But by and large I've been the fortunate beneficiary of the benevolence and generosity of a few good souls who opened doors for me at the exact time that I began knocking. My work for *The Ring* and *KO* and their sister magazines, which comprises much of this work, would not have been possible without Nigel Collins, Steve Farhood, Eric Raskin and Stu Saks.

Likewise, the work herewith from *Ringside Seat* magazine would not exist if not for the vision and talent of Michael Kronenberg, who founded the magazine and then, in an act of great faith, asked me to take the reins as editor-in-chief. It is not hyperbole to say that running *Ringside Seat* was the best gig I've ever had and the culmination of a lifelong affair with boxing. Michael was also instrumental in helping me acquire the rights to many of the pieces included here, a favor of no small import for which I will be forever grateful.

My thanks, as always, to my wife Kim, to Glenn Dowd, my dearest and oldest friend, to Danny Thomas, who was exactly the coach and friend I needed, to my sister, Mary Dettloff-Reilly, and to Michael Dolan for taking on this project. Lastly, my deepest gratitude to the fighters and to the writers who came before me.

ADDITIONAL BOOKS
BY WILLIAM DETTLOFF

BOX LIKE THE PROS (co-written with Joe Frazier)

EZZARD CHARLES
A Boxing Life

MATTHEW SAAD MUHAMMAD
Boxing's Miracle Man

ABOUT THE AUTHOR

William Dettloff grew up in the Parlin section of Old Bridge, New Jersey and boxed as an amateur in the 1980s. He started writing for *The Ring* and its sister magazines, *KO* and *World Boxing*, in 1995. He was the senior writer there for 15 years. He also wrote about boxing for *HBO* and *ESPN* during that time, and later co-hosted a popular boxing podcast.

In 2017 Dettloff was named editor-in-chief of *Ringside Seat* magazine, which *The London Times* called "a thoughtful boxing magazine for the discriminating fight fan." In 2025 Dettloff was inducted into the New Jersey Boxing Hall of Fame.

Dettloff has been married to the former Kim Minetta since 1990 and has three adult children: Kayla, Angelina, and Billy. They all live in the Lehigh Valley in Pennsylvania.

www.ingramcontent.com/pod-product-compliance
Lightning Source LLC
Chambersburg PA
CBHW030402130626
46549CB00004B/1598